...ies.
...pire
...eatest
...enith
...uickly

1054

The Christian Church splits into the Orthodox Eastern Church and Catholic Western Church, beginning a schism that continues to this day.

1066

The Normans, led by Duke William of Normandy, defeat King Harold II at the Battle of Hastings and take control of England.

c.1060

In the canyons around Colorado's Mesa Verde, peoples related to the Anasazi begin to build settlements similar to those of Chaco Canyon.

1050

from 1050

The Hausa people take control of trade in Central Africa, creating wealthy and powerful city-states.

1061

Yusuf Ibn Tashufin and his Almoravids subjugate the Berber tribes of southern Morocco, bringing all the Sanhadja Berbers under his control. Two years later, he founds the city of Marrakesh.

1040

...rmies under
...Tugril Beg,
...oss Iran on
...conquering
...em.

1055

The Seljuks conquer Baghdad and oust the Buwayhids to become the dominant power in the Middle East.

1068

At the behest of Emperor Shenzong, Wang Anshi reforms the Chinese state system in an attempt to curb corruption and to combat poverty among the broad masses of the people.

from c.1050

The Polynesian settlers on Rapa nui, or Easter Island, begin erecting their extraordinary monumental statues, known as maoi.

EUROPE

1071

The Seljuk victory at Manzikert in Armenia begins the decline of the Byzantine Empire.

1077

Germany's King Henry IV travels to Canossa, Italy, and begs forgiveness of Pope Gregory VII in an attempt to end the conflict between them.

109

El Cid, hero Spanish Reco dies in Valenc

AMERICA

1070

AFRICA

1094

Caliph Al-Mustansir of Egypt dies after a reign of almost six decades. With his death, the Fatimid dynasty goes into decline.

ASIA

1072

The Seljuk ruler Alp Arslan dies, leaving his son, Malik Shah, to inherit a gigantic empire stretching from Afghanistan to Egypt.

1099

The Crusaders conquer Jerusalem after a fierce and bloody battle.

OCEANIA

c.1100
Armoured knights begin to dominate the battlefields of Europe. In France, the medieval culture of knighthood develops, while music and literature embrace the art of courtly love.

1112
Roger II succeeds his father as king of Norman Sicily and southern Italy.

1122
The Concordat of Worms ends the long-running power struggle between the German Holy Roman Emperor and the Pope.

1139
Alfonso I founds the state of Portugal.

1154
Norman rule comes to an end in England with the death of King Stephen of Blois.

c.1100
The flourishing settlement of Cahokia in the Mississippi Valley becomes the largest city of pre-Columbian North America.

c.1100
After many setbacks and battles with native tribes, the Vikings abandon their attempts to establish settlements in North America.

1130
The Anasazi culture collapses after recurring periods of drought.

c.1150
The Chimú become the most powerful ruling culture in South America before the coming of the Incas, opening up large parts of Peru with a well-organised system of roads and canals.

1100

1130

1107
Ibn Tumert returns to Morocco from Mecca and the Middle East, and begins to preach against the decadence of the Almoravids and their ignorance of true Muslim culture.

from 1113
The accession of King Alaungsithu launches the heyday of Burma's Buddhist empire.

1145
The Hausa city of Kano is a thriving hub of trade in Africa.

1147
Ibn Tumert's Muslim reform movement pushes out the Almoravid dynasty and establishes the Almohads in power in North Africa.

1148
The Crusaders' ill-judged siege of Damascus comes to an ignominious end and the Christian armies retreat home to Europe.

from 1150
Japan slides into civil war with the collapse of the Fujiwara dynasty. The Minamoto clan eventually emerge the victors and the era of the Shoguns begins.

912

Abd Ar-Rahman III becomes Caliph of Cordoba, taking the Iberian Peninsula firmly into Arab control.

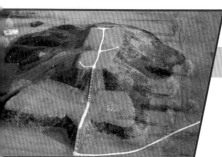

955

Otto I, the Great, defeats the Huns at the Battle of the Lechfeld. He is crowned German Emperor in 962.

980

Vladimir I becomes Grand Duke of Kiev. The kingdom of the Kievan Rus will experience its greatest expansion under his rule.

987

Hugo Capet is elected king of the Western Franks, heralding the birth of France.

1000

Stephan I is crowned king of the Hungarians. He unites and Christianises the Hun peoples, who now settle in the new European state of Hungary.

1025

Emperor Bas The Byzantine has reached extent, but of its pow passes.

c.950

The Chimú create a kingdom along the coast of Peru. Their capital, Chan-Chan, grows to be the largest pre-Spanish city in South America.

987

With his followers, the god-king Quetzalcoatl Ce Acatl leaves the Toltec homeland. They conquer the Maya territory on the Yucatan Peninsula and build the city of Chichén Itzá.

c.1000

The Anasazi build their astonishing pueblo complexes in Chaco Canyon in the arid southwest of North America.

c.1000

Leif Eiriksson sets out from the Viking settlement in Greenland and sails west to America.

950

1000

969

The Fatimids replace the Abbasids in Egypt.

c.1000

A Berber tribe, who will become known as the Almoravids, found the oasis town of Timbuktu on the river Niger. The town soon grows to be the most important trading centre in the western Sahel.

1003

An era of religious intolerance begins in Egypt under Al-Hakim, the radical Fatimid Caliph of Cairo. Both Christians and Jews are discriminated against.

960

Emperor Taizu, first ruler of the Song dynasty, embarks on the renewal of the Chinese Empire.

918

Wang Kon proclaims himself King of Koguryo and thus founds the Korean kingdom.

c.1000

The *Genji monogatari*, better known in the West as 'The Tale of Genji', first appears in Japan. Written by a woman, Murasaki Shikibu, it is later acclaimed as the world's first novel.

fro

The Sel their le sweep horse all befo

c.1000

A group of Polynesian seafarers arrive in New Zealand in the last great wave of Pacific colonisation.

THE EARLY
MIDDLE AGES

907–1154

PUBLISHED BY THE READER'S DIGEST ASSOCIATION LIMITED
LONDON • NEW YORK • SYDNEY • MONTREAL

The Great Mosque of Córdoba Vistas of columns and arches recede in all directions in what is undoubtedly one of the wonders of the medieval world. Begun by Abd Ar-Rahman I in 785, it was substantially added to in the 9th and 10th centuries by caliphs Abd Ar-Rahman II and Al-Hakam II and by vizier Al-Mansur. The great size and magnificence of the building reflected the importance of Córdoba itself, then the largest and most cultured city in Europe.

EUROPE 4

ASIA 64

A WORLD OF WARRIORS 114

AFRICA 122

AMERICA 148

OCEANIA 178

EUROPE

1. Ottonians and Salians establish an empire — 6

2. The Capetians and the birth of France — 13

3. The Moors in Spain — 20

4. The rise of the kings of Denmark — 28

5. Towards a united Hungary — 33

6. Byzantium – a great Mediterranean power — 36

7. The kingdom of Kiev – origins of Russia — 42

8. Cluny – fount of monastic reform — 46

9. The Norman kingdom in Italy — 50

10. The Normans conquer England — 54

11. Pope and King in conflict — 60

Ottonians and Salians establish an empire

The foundations of what would become the Holy Roman Empire were laid by the Ottonians and Salians, who took on the role of royal protectors of western Christendom.

Louis 'the Child' was just six years old when he ascended the throne of the East Frankish kingdom in 900. The great days of Charlemagne's Carolingian Empire were already gone, and Louis would be the last Carolingian king of the eastern Franks. In fact, he never truly reigned: his kingdom was afflicted by attacks from the Magyars and racked by internal power-struggles and dissent. Louis died in 911 at just 18, and though he had a successor in Charles III, king of the West Frankish kingdom, the Carolingians had lost their dominant position. East of the Rhine, powerful lords were now minded to go their own way. At Forchheim, in Franconia, the dukes of what we would now think of as the 'German' Franks met with lords of the Saxons, Bavarians and Swabians to find a ruler more to their liking. The election of Conrad I marked a moment of severance: though ethnically Frankish, he was not closely related to the Carolingians, and under his successors a specifically 'German' empire would arise.

Otto triumphant
King Otto I's victory over the Magyars at Lechfeld in 955 was the decisive step towards his attaining the imperial crown. The momentous encounter is shown here in a 15th-century book illustration.

Conrad himself did not live to see such a realm. His electors, the tribal dukes, had won their own power and prestige the hard way in defensive wars against the Magyars, Normans and Saracens, and were not about to bow meekly before any king. Conrad spent the eight years of his reign wrangling with the dukes at every turn, but on his deathbed he showed himself both magnanimous and far-sighted when he delegated power to his strongest opponent among them, Henry of Saxony.

Ottonian success in Germany

King Henry I turned out to be a resourceful and pragmatic ruler, as he founded what would become known as the Ottonian dynasty, at the heart of an important central European empire. He acknowledged the political realities that prevailed in his kingdom. Respecting the rights of the tribal dukes and princes over their own territories, he confined himself to protecting the wider realm from external threats. He fortified his royal authority on the battlefield, with victories over Magyars and Slavs. By the time he died, at his palace in Memleben in 935, his kingdom had won recognition and respect from all its neighbours.

Henry's son and successor, Otto, accordingly inherited a throne enhanced with the weight of authority, and was in a position to weld the endlessly squabbling tribal dukedoms into a single political entity. From the day of his coronation, in

The emperor and his queen
Enthroned in stone together in the Chapel of the Holy Sepulchre in Magdeburg Cathedral are Emperor Otto I and his English first wife, Editha of Wessex, who died in 946.

What made a king want to be emperor?

Rulers strove so hard to attain the title of Holy Roman Emperor not for any tangible increase in power that it represented, but for the divine aura that was attached to it. The Emperor seemed to represent the secular sword of the papacy, the guardian of the faith around which European identity was constructed. To him fell responsibility for protecting Christendom from pagan invaders, for promoting missionary zeal, and for defending the authority of the Pope and the Church against all enemies. This placed the Emperor in a protective role with respect to the Church, whose internal problems inevitably reflected back on the Emperor – hence the incessant imperial interference in Church affairs.

The modern West has prided itself on scrupulous separation of Church and State, but this would have made little sense in medieval Europe. There, the Emperor and the Pope, both enjoying divine approval, were intended to lead Christendom jointly. However, the high level of cooperation created by the Ottonians was lost as successive popes manoeuvred to increase their own power at the expense of the imperial monarchy, leading in time to a fatal struggle for supremacy.

Emblem of power
The *Reichsapfel*, the 'royal apple' or orb, was a key symbol of the Emperor's royal insignia, representing his authority to rule over all the world.

Aachen on August 7, 936, Otto I – 'Otto the Great' – showed his intention of taking the kingdom into a new era. Though a Saxon himself and proud of it, he acknowleged the power of Charlemagne in the splendid ceremony at which he had himself crowned. As reported in an account written by Widukind of Corvey, the archbishop of Mainz called out to the people assembled in the basilica of Aachen, 'Here I give you the man, chosen by God and designated as successor by Henry I, and now selected by all the princes – King Otto!'

Then Otto received the coronation insignia – sword, cloak, sceptre and rod – and took his seat on Charlemagne's throne. During the banquet that followed, the dukes acted as his servants: the head of Lorraine as chamberlain, the Frankish leader as high steward, the Swabian as cup-bearer and the Bavarian as marshal.

Otto consolidates power

At the age of 24, Otto was more than a match for the most ambitious aristocrat. His father, Henry I, may have been content to be first among equals, but Otto was resolved to build royal power and right from the start he insisted upon his authority as King. Conflict was inevitable: for years he had to fight rebellious vassals, who found common cause with his own disgruntled brothers, Thankmar and Henry. However, Otto was also a master of diplomacy and the principle of divide-and-rule. By ensuring any vacant estates went to loyal members of his own faction, he drove a wedge between the tribal principalities.

At the same time, he bestowed new powers and wealth on the Church, making it an effective counterweight to the nobility. Churchmen received government appointments, and valuable lands and estates were conferred on abbots and bishops in exchange for providing taxes, fulfilling government duties and supplying manpower for military service. The resulting *Reichskirchensystem* (the 'State-Church system') became the most reliable pillar of Otto's internal politics. A prototype of the new *Reichsbischof* or royal bishop was his younger brother, Brun, who served as both Archbishop of Cologne and Prince of Lorraine.

Thus consolidated within, the kingdom presented a more formidable face to the outside world. In the East, Otto established huge marches – militarised border regions – to hold the Slavic tribes at a safe distance, while in the West he pursued a policy of matrimonial diplomacy. He married off both his sisters – Gerberga to the western Frankish king, Louis IV, and Hadwig to his arch-rival, Hugo of Franconia. Otto took seriously his role as protector of Burgundy, appreciating that this, too, would help to ensure the security of his German realm.

An imperial crown

Otto's greatest triumph, however, came in 955 when the Hungarian Magyars were defeated at the Battle of Lechfeld, outside Augsburg. In an unprecedented show of solidarity, the Germanic tribes came together under Otto's banner to win an historic victory over their longstanding pagan enemy. Otto's policy of uniting the kingdom had plainly proved itself in Germany's hour of need. He is said to have been proclaimed imperator, 'Emperor', by his soldiers while still on the battlefield. By his victory Otto had established his position as protector of western Christendom, but he did not have the imperial crown – yet.

The imperial crown could be endowed only by the Pope himself in Rome, and it had long been in Otto's sights. Just as Charlemagne had done before him, Otto had crossed the Alps, in 951, to assert his right to rule in Italy. His imperial claims had been rebuffed that time, but his journey was not entirely in vain, since he married the young widow of King Lothar II of Italy, Adelheid of Burgundy, and with her came the kingdom of Lombardy, in northern Italy. Now, his hand immeasurably strengthened by his victory over the Magyars, Otto travelled south once more, and this time, the crown would be his.

Held in St Peter's Basilica in Rome, on February 2, 962, amidst the utmost pomp and splendour, his imperial coronation was the climax of Otto I's life. Rome's ancient world empire might be no more than a memory, but the city still radiated glory and majesty and all the religious aura that went with its status as the seat of the papacy. Dressed in heavy ceremonial robes, Otto bent his knee to receive the golden crown from the hands of Pope John XII. The Pope dipped his fingers in holy oil and anointed the king's forehead. With the cheers of the Romans ringing in his ears, Otto felt his destiny as Charlemagne's successor had been fulfilled.

Working with the Pope brought even more prestige for Otto, and it also allowed him to realise some far-reaching policies and plans – such as the foundation of the archbishopric of Magdeburg as a 'missionising' base for the Slavic East. By Christianising the Slavs and incorporating their Church into his *Reichskirchensystem*, he hoped to pacify what had been a decidedly restless frontier and extend Saxon authority as far as the river Oder.

As his power grew, so too did the glamour surrounding Otto's court, which he established at his favourite royal estate of Magdeburg. He had spent his early years here with Editha, his English first wife. Now, Magdeburg flowered as a 'third Rome'. (The 'second' was, of course, Constantinople, capital of the Byzantine Empire and true inheritor of the imperial lineage of Rome.) Otto encouraged this flowering, himself laying the foundation stone of a splendid cathedral which he

Majestic monument
A counterpoise to St Peter's in Rome, the huge cathedral at Speyer in Germany, here seen from the rear, defiantly proclaimed the power of the Holy Roman Empire. It provided a place of interment for the Salian emperors, successors to the Ottonians.

A powerful weapon
The Holy Lance was counted among the royal treasures from King Henry I's time onward. It was reputed to contain a sacred relic – a nail from the Cross of Christ.

NORTH SEA

BALTIC SEA

Hamburg
Saxony
Magdeburg
POLAND
Aachen
Rhine
Mainz
Worms
Speyer
Franconia BOHEMIA
Danube
Swabia
Bavaria
Salzburg
Kingdom of
Burgundy
Carinthia
FRANCE
Lyon
Rhone
Milan
Po
Canossa
Arles
HUNGARY

MEDITERRANEAN
SEA

Papal
States
Rome

▨ Ottonian Empire

● Main towns and cities

meant that on his death, in 973, he left a difficult legacy for his son, Otto II, and soon thereafter his grandson, Otto III.

Collapsing ambitions

Otto II was only 18 years old when he ascended the imperial throne, with his highly educated Byzantine-born wife, Theophanu, at his side. From the start he found he had to fight hard to assert his authority at home, but this did not prevent him from pursuing an ambitious Italian policy. His aim was nothing less than a renewal of the ancient Roman Empire, but he could not prevail against the Saracens in southern Italy.

This failure in its turn undermined Otto II's position within Germany: the Danes and Slavs rose up in 983 and Otto the Great's carefully built imperial edifice came crashing down. German authority east of the Elbe collapsed and the bishoprics of Brandenburg and Havelberg were swept away; Hamburg was sacked and even the imperial seat at Magdeburg was threatened. That same year, as his dominions disintegrated around him, Emperor Otto II died in Italy.

His three-year-old son, Otto III, had already been chosen as successor, under the guardianship of his mother, Theophanu, and his grandmother, Adelheid of Burgundy. In 994, aged 15, Otto became ruler in his own right and took up his father's project of creating a new Christian Roman Empire. Realistically, such a scheme could only be brought about in conjunction with the papacy, which meant that more pliable popes would be required. So Otto III broke with the tradition of selecting only Romans for this role and, in 996, made his

designated as his burial place, furnishing it with precious marble columns and holy relics from Italy. One effect of this boosting of Magdeburg was to shift the centre of gravity of the Germanic state further eastward.

Otto's connection with the papacy did much to exalt his status, but it also brought problems. Shortly after his coronation as Emperor, he had made a contract guaranteeing the existence of the *Reichskirchensystem* in exchange for an oath of loyalty by the Pope and a say in the selection of the Pope's successor to St Peter's throne. This embroiled Otto in the often labyrinthine politics of the Italian nobility and

Imperial founders
This illustration from the fontispiece of the Golden Gospel, kept in Speyer Cathedral, depicts Henry III paying homage to the Virgin Mary. Henry (on the left) is offering his Golden Gospel to Mary; his second wife, Agnes of Poitou, is on the right and the four cardinal virtues are depicted around the border.

cousin, Brun, the first German Holy Father. Having given himself the title of Gregory V, Brun obligingly crowned Otto III as Emperor. With the support of Gregory and his successors, Otto III set about realising his dream of a federation of Christian states under imperial rule and the extension of Christendom into Poland and Hungary.

On a pilgrimage to Poland in 1000, Otto III made Gnesen an archbishopric and appointed his friend Boleslaw, a Polish duke, as *patricius*, or imperial deputy. The next year he did the same in Hungary. His ambition and aplomb astonished his peers, who called the youthful emperor *Mirabilia Mundi* – 'wonder of the world'. Otto had his critics too, however, and over time they became increasingly vocal, claiming he was neglecting his own homeland 'because his yearning to stay in Italy was so great'. All his high-flying plans crashed down to earth in 1002, when he died – only 22 and childless.

EVERDAY LIFE

Famine and failed harvests

In the 11th-century, rural existence was characterised by backbreaking toil in all weathers, attended by constant want and frequent hunger. Europe was ravaged repeatedly by famines caused by population increases, failed harvests and natural disasters. The Great Famine of 1032–3 afflicted the entire continent. A contemporary chronicler, Raoul Glaber, records an apocalyptic scene:

'Due to continuous rainfall, the ground was so soggy and full of decay that for three consecutive years it was not possible to plough a furrow that would have allowed the sowing of seed. After using quadrupeds and birds as food, people now suffering from the dreadful torment of hunger began to consume any kind of meat, even from cadavers and other revolting sources. The terrible hunger pangs even led people to eat human flesh.'

In the middle of the 11th century new land began to be brought into production through clearing woodland, building dykes and draining marshes. Slowly, arable farming methods improved and displaced much of the cattle farming which had predominated. By the high Middle Ages, the supply of food was much more regular.

By hard work and prayer
The 9th century manuscript illustration shows peasants sowing seed and offering up a sheaf of wheat for a good harvest.

Return to realism

Otto's cousin and successor, Henry II, was careful to restrict himself to what was politically realistic – resurrection of the German Frankish kingdom and the rebuilding of royal power at home. Though crowned Emperor in Rome in 1014, Henry saw his religious and imperial authority primarily as tools to be used in the reconstruction of the *Reichskirchensystem* in Germany itself.

To achieve his aims, Henry was high-handed in his interference in Church matters; he took the chair at synods and picked his own pet bishops. Even more than Otto the Great had done, he endowed bishoprics and abbeys with lands and economic privileges, including the rights to grant markets, mint coinage and raise tolls. Henry saw as his crowning achievement the foundation of the bishopric of Bamberg in Bavaria in 1007, established in the face of fierce resistance. 'Here, heavy silverware can be seen gleaming beside mountains of gold, and precious stones shine upon shimmering silks,' wrote an awestruck Abbot Gerhard von Seeon of this 'Frankish Rome'.

The Salian succession

Yet even this pious foundation could not prevent the Ottonian extinction: in 1024 Henry II died childless. Conrad II, a great-grandson of Otto I, took over, inaugurating a new dynasty – the Salians.

The second-last Salian
The Salian Emperor Henry IV, depicted in a gold and enamel image to be seen at the shrine of Charlemagne. In Henry's time, conflict between emperor and papacy escalated still further.

The Frankish Salians inherited an inestimable prize: a kingdom that was internally stable and outwardly secure. They would reign over it for the next century, until 1125. The addition of Burgundy – left to Conrad by another childless king, Rudolf – consolidated their hold still further. Power to rule over the church was also further augmented by Conrad and under his successor, Henry III, imperial power attained its peak.

Henry ruled over the three kingdoms of Burgundy, Germany and Italy, wielding autocratic power over aristocracy and Church. A genuinely religious man, Henry III was in sympathy with a growing movement outraged at a perceived slackness and immorality among the clergy. Like his predecessors, however, he was happy to exercise control over the Church as an instrument of government, interfering in ecclesiastical affairs more than any ruler had before.

Power over the Church

The Synod of Sutri in 1046 saw Henry's control over Church affairs at their triumphant height. It followed a period in which ecclesiastical infighting had descended into downright farce. In 1044, the opposition in Rome had deposed Pope Benedict IX and put Sylvester III in his place. Just seven weeks later Benedict was returned to power, but within weeks he was gone again – voluntarily, this time, bribed to step down in favour of a new candidate. Henry III, unsurprisingly, saw this as completely unacceptable. He travelled to Italy in 1046 and organised a council of bishops at Pavia. Here, he issued a formal proclamation forbidding the sale of high positions, which left none of the current claimants for the papacy with a legitimate claim to power. At the Synod of Sutri, on December 20, 1046, Henry deposed all three and had Gregory VI, who had the largest following, arrested and taken to Cologne. Henry then installed his own Bishop of Bamberg as Pope Clement II; he in turn promptly crowned Henry as Emperor. After Clement II's death, Henry III installed a further three Germans as pope, all of them close confidantes.

Recurring problems in the kingdom

Henry's interfering ways were resented, however, and the problems rumbled on into the reign of Henry IV, who followed his father onto the throne at the age of barely six in 1056. Taking advantage of the boy king's weakness, the most powerful men in the kingdom seized aspects of royal power for themselves. Archbishop Anno of Cologne had Henry kidnapped, so that he could rule as guardian: the very authority of the monarchy was in doubt.

Once he gained his majority, Henry IV tried to reverse this trend. He promoted and supported a new class of modestly born ministry officials, establishing them as 'administrative civil servants' in an attempt to marginalise the aristocratic magnates. The powerful princes were angered and there was an uprising in Saxony. Henry was forced to submit to his vassals and although his rule survived it was fatally compromised. Ongoing conflict between Emperor and Church was exploited by the princes to further undermine imperial power – even to the proclamation of rival kings, and in 1105 he was deposed by his own son, Henry V.

In 1111 Henry V was crowned Emperor by the Pope in Rome. A decade later he reached agreement with the Church in the Concordat of Worms, signed in 1122. But the Salian dynasty was doomed. In 1125, Henry V died childless, the last of the Salian emperors.

The Capetians and the birth of France

Towards the end of the 10th century, Hugo Capet inaugurated a royal dynasty which was to determine the destiny of France for 800 years.

When, in 911, the nobles of the eastern Frankish kingdom came to choose a king from among their own ranks to succeed Louis 'the Child', Charles III had been ruling the western Franks for 18 years. As a Carolingian and descendant of Charlemagne – and tempted by the power-vacuum prevailing since the death of his kinsman, Louis – Charles 'the Simple' invaded the eastern kingdom. Instead of renewing the Carolingian Empire, however, his invasion failed and became its final end.

Holy mountain
Capetian France was famous for its piety. Many monasteries were founded at this time, including Mont St Michel, just off the coast of Normandy. It was said to have been built on the orders of the archangel Michael.

Capetian founding father
The seal of Hugo Capet, who in 987 gave his name to a new French royal dynasty. In his right hand he is holding the *main de Justice* (see page 18). The Capetians ruled – including collateral lines and with some interruptions – until 1848.

Judgment day
Fear was an essential element in medieval religious belief. This 11th-century illustration shows the fifth angel of the Apocalypse dragging a sinner off to Hell.

The Treaty of Verdun, signed in 843, had already pointed to a parting of the ways for the Frankish kingdoms: this east-west partition was confirmed as a result of Charles's ill-judged venture. The two countries we know as France and Germany were now irrevocably embarked upon separate courses. Moreover, the failure of his campaign weakened Charles domestically, allowing local lords and princes to chip away at his kingly power. The struggle reached its climax on June 22, 922, when the nobility toppled Charles and crowned Robert of Neustria in his place.

Robert I did not reign for long. Charles fought back and his usurper was killed at the Battle of Soissons the following year – but Charles was defeated and imprisoned. Within a few hours of Robert's death, his brother-in-law Rudolf declared himself his successor, though the power of the 'Robertines' was to be challenged constantly over the coming decades. At last, on July 3, 987, the French princes put an end to all the wrangling by crowning Hugo Capet as King of France.

The succession principle

Hugo Capet was the Count of Paris and an extremely pious man – even his name has a religious origin. It is believed to have derived from a holy relic, the *cappa* ('cape' or 'cloak') of Saint Martin, whose shrine stood in the Monastery of Saint Martin at Tours, on lands which had belonged to Hugo's family for generations. The bulk of his estates lay around Paris, in the Ile-de-France,

which gave its name to the whole country. Through shrewd diplomacy and matrimonial alliances, the Capetians would succeed in enlarging their possessions – but first the new ruler had to secure his crown. And Hugo had a bold and brilliant idea: to replace the time-honoured principle of royal election with a law of succession. From now on, he declared, the King's eldest son would be co-ruler at his side, and take his place on the throne on his father's passing.

Hugo's son Robert II, who reigned from 996 to 1031, arranged his own succession in the same manner. In stark contrast to the kings of the Ottonians and Salians to the east, who had a habit of dying without issue, the Capetians ruled with 'wonderful fertility' for a further 200 years, after which the collateral lines of the Valois and Bourbons would endure until the French Revolution.

Church relations

The remarkable resilience of the Capetians was based to a large extent upon their close connections and cooperation with the Church. They ruled 20 bishoprics, including the most influential ones, Rheims and Chartres. Close friends, such as Abbot Suger of Saint-Denis or the great St Bernard of Clairvaux, became important advisors to the Capetian kings. The royal house always took pains to keep leading prelates on their side.

The second Capetian king, Robert II, was renowned for his honour and piety – according to some, he was even reputed to have worked miracles. The chronicler Helgaud records that one day, at his palace in Paris, Robert was handed water to wash his hands. Seeing a blind man standing nearby, the King sprinkled some of the water upon him and immediately the blind man recovered his sight, to the astonishment of onlookers. As a monk from the loyal Benedictine monastery at Fleury, Helgaud clearly wished to underline the divine majesty and virtue of a king he hoped to see accepted as God's representative on Earth.

In fact, for all his much-vaunted piety, Robert 'the Pious' had his more worldly concerns. In 996 he seized control of the Duchy of Burgundy by marrying his cousin, Bertha of Burgundy. When the desired male heir did not materialise, he put Bertha aside and married another. This sort of ruthlessness in marriage was by no means unusual among medieval kings, and in Robert's case brought no more than a rebuke from the Pope.

Generally, however, the Capetians were careful to nurture their good relations with the Church, maintaining close cooperation with the Pope himself. It was Robert II's great-grandson, Louis VI ('the Fat'), who introduced the policy of sending priests from France to Rome for further education. In return, the Pope allowed reforms in French monasteries. It was not by chance that new communities, such as the Cistercian order, were founded in France.

Spreading the word

Monastic schools contributed to both the spiritual and cultural life of the country, and wandering monks carried Christ's message among the rural poor. One such was Bernard of Clairvaux, who travelled widely through the south of France in the 12th century, winning new adherents and support for the Second Crusade. Among the most urgent concerns for medieval

Medieval world view
Only three continents were known in Europe at the time of the Capetians: Asia, Africa and Europe itself. This 11th-century map shows the world in the form of a disc, with Jerusalem and the Holy Land at the centre.

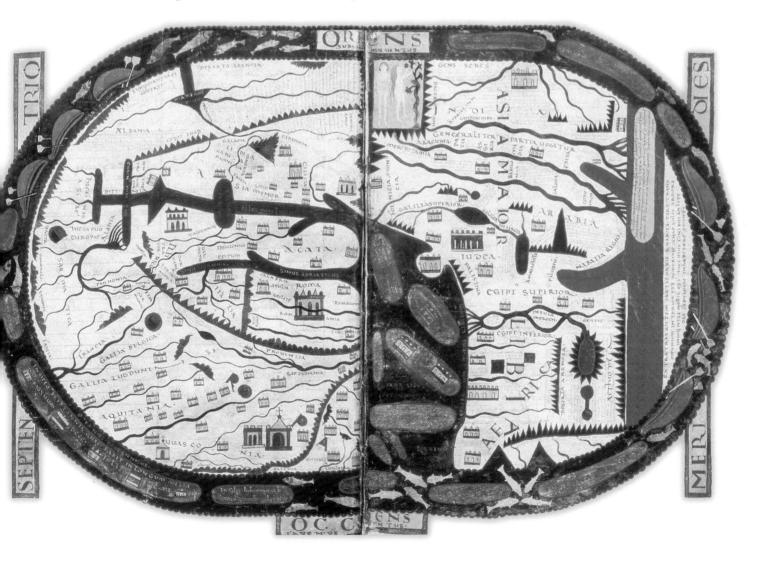

people was the need they felt to gain an understanding of how God had ordained their universe, but they were concerned too for their destiny after death.

The final destiny of human souls was to be decided at the Last Judgment, when God would assign them either to

monks, both through their missionary preaching and in the theological texts they wrote and copied so lovingly.

The writing chambers (*scriptoria*) of the monks were hives of industry in the 12th century, and in secular society, too, literacy was becoming more widespread. Young ladies, though allowed to learn to read, were generally dissuaded from writing. But education was spreading amongst the wives of merchants, who learned to read, write and calculate in order to do the book-keeping for their husbands, despite being excluded from church and cathedral schools. In these, the forerunners of universities, the masters introduced their students to all areas of knowledge. Famous cathedral schools evolved in Chartres, Reims and Paris, where one could learn all there was to know about medicine, mathematics, theology, astrology, geography and the arts.

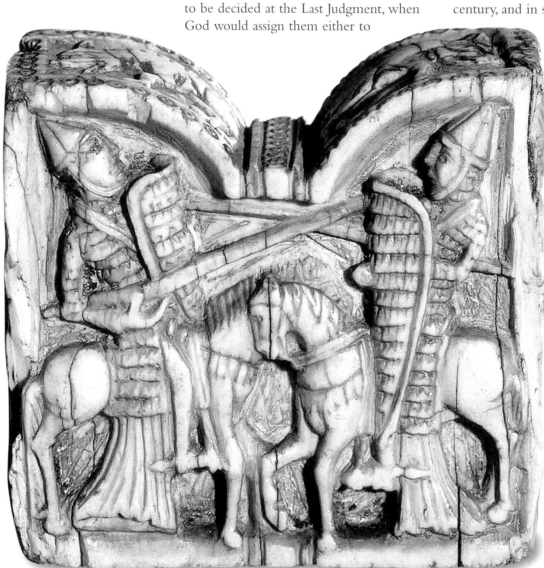

Sporting spectacle
Exquisitely carved in ivory on a 12th-century chess piece, two knights are engaged in a joust. In an actual tournament, after trying to unhorse one another with lances they would have dismounted and continued the fight on foot with swords.

Heaven or to Hell. Angels of Heaven and the demonic servants of Satan were believed to wrestle over every soul.

An active fear of Hell was important in the medieval mentality. It was thought one could influence one's fate by praying and making penance. A truly terrible end awaited those unfortunate enough not to have been baptised: they would burn for ever in a kind of ante-chamber to Hell. Such was the message spread by the

Saint-Denis and Louis VI, 'the Fat'

The Capetians' most important monastery was Saint-Denis in Paris. Hugo Capet, the dynastic patriarch, was buried in the chapel there and it became the burial place of France's kings. Here, too, were kept the royal crown and the *oriflamme*, a purple banner that started out as the emblem of the monastery and was adopted by the Capetians as their royal standard. At the outset of every new military campaign, it was ceremoniously brought forth from the chapel by a band of the king's most trusted knights. The most famous head of Saint-Denis was Abbot Suger, close confidant of Louis VI. His account of Louis's life has become an important historical source. It tells in particular how the King extended the possessions of the French crown and made Paris the royal seat and capital city.

When Louis ascended the throne in 1108, the population of Paris was no more than 3000; by his death in 1137 it had more than doubled. Louis brought in merchants and money-changers to stimulate the economy, and he improved the city's bridges and roads. Not only did Louis play a crucial part in building the country we now call France, but his reign also saw an impressive cultural flowering with major advances in architecture, the sciences and education. But there was little sense of France as a centralised state, and society would lack a system of law for a long time to come. In the *contés*, or counties, it was the nobles who looked after law and order.

The knightly ideal

It was in Louis's reign that a separate class of knights began establishing itself, having received official sanction with the knighting of Prince Louis himself in 1098. The highest-born young men of France flocked to follow his example, and many went on to fight in the Crusades. The spirit of chivalry was advertised far and wide, and soon the forms of French courtly life were becoming standard all over Europe. The homage rendered by the knight to his lady; the tournament; the ideals of knightly learning; and the custom of being dubbed a knight – all were French conventions enthusiastically copied elsewhere. France led the way in the arts of gracious living, from fashion to food and wine, and the rules of etiquette.

Literature – poetry and prose – became increasingly fashionable in courtly society. Wandering minstrels had long recounted stories, some fictional but others true, and in doing so, of course, they were disseminating news. Less obviously, they helped to register changing attitudes and shifts in sensibility. Now they spread the growing vogue for 'courtly love'. Deliciously melancholy tales were told of gallant knights in hopeless thrall to noble ladies, who could not requite their passion because they themselves were married.

Such tales were sung by troubadors – 'inventors of songs' – who declaimed their verses in a sing-song manner.

BACKGROUND

Developing musical notation

In the 7th century, Isidor of Seville complained that musical notes could not be written down. In fact, the art of writing down music had been invented long before – the ancient Egyptians had used a system of musical notation almost 3500 years previously – but such knowledge had long been forgotten. Until as late as the 10th century, melodies could only be passed on orally and memorised.

At around this time, however, a new form of musical notation was developing. It had its origins in the accent symbols of Jewish chanting and the neums of Latin church songs. Neums are the dots, lines and hooks that were inscribed above the text in plainsong. Though such markings gave no indication as to precise rhythm or pitch, they offered the singer a reminder of the overall melodic shape.

In the 11th century, Guido of Arezzo introduced lines to fix the level of the notes in a song. He distributed the neums onto four different-coloured lines, which he then arranged in a sequence of thirds. Later, this evolved into symbols for notes with individual values. These symbols, written down according to a system known as 'mensural notation', are the precursors of those we have today. Notation varied from place to place and would continue to change – at different times notes were shaped like nails, squares or horseshoes – but the outlines of written music had been established.

Words and music
This beautifully illustrated sheet of music comes from a book of liturgical songs. It was painted on vellum in the 13th century and the illuminated 'A' shows St Gregory.

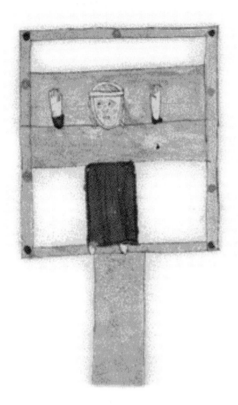

Rough justice
In France in the Middle Ages there was no universal established code of law. People were tried instead according to traditionally accepted usage, and this varied from place to place. This French illustration made around the end of the 13th century shows a woman in the stocks – a very common form of punishment.

A universal method of writing music was soon required to record these poems. Though the knight of poetic tradition was generally portrayed pining away in hopeless love, his warlike role was not forgotten. The famous heroic epic, the *Song of Roland*, was written in France around 1100.

Sporting activities were popular, too, but a distinction was made between knightly skills and sports which were open to one and all. Along with handball and archery, games of dice were the most popular of these. (Chess was reserved for noble circles.) Later, card games were added to the list. The Church disapproved of gaming, yet it took advantage of it by heavily taxing games of chance.

Standardising law and order

Until the 12th century, French life was governed not by laws as such but by *coutumes* or customs, a bewildering range of highly localised, orally transmitted conventions of uncertain origin. With no clear or consistent code to regulate conduct, disputes were inevitable and quarrels quickly flared to violence: armed 'feuds' were semi-formalised as a way of resolving differences in the Middle Ages.

This anarchy was banished by the Capetians, who brought in a universal system of French laws for the first time. The duty to establish and uphold the law was central to the ideals of the Capetian monarchy, and was a key component of the coronation oath from Hugo Capet on. The tradition would long outlive the Capetians: as late as the 19th century, France's ruler was the only sovereign in Europe to carry not a sword but the *main de Justice* (the hand of Law) with the sceptre at state functions.

In any case, the Capetians cleared away the tangled thickets of local traditions and replaced them with a single codex modelled on that of ancient Rome. And with law came order: old-fashioned feuding was rendered obsolete once men came to feel they could find redress for wrongs by legal means.

Urban freedom

As the authority of the Capetians grew, one castle after another was brought into their sphere of influence, and something like a centralised state started to form. Louis VI chipped away at the power of the aristocratic landowners by awarding new rights and privileges to the towns, which then became magnets, drawing peasants from the surrounding countryside. Those bound to their lords by feudal ties could find freedom here: any man who spent a year and a day in a town, keeping its laws and paying its taxes, automatically won his liberty. He was then in a position to take advantage of all the rights of the citizen: a free choice of residence, the purchase and sale of property, and (for men) a voice in electing the town council. Jews were generally excluded from these rights, as were journeymen (as yet unqualified tradesmen), maidservants and unskilled labourers. High municipal office was open only to the patricians, a group drawn from the nobility and the mercantile and landowning elite.

Life in the growing towns could have its drawbacks, however, especially in the fastest-growing metropolis – the burgeoning Capetian capital of Paris. With so many crammed together in close quarters, conditions could be smelly, unpleasant and even dangerous, with disease a constant threat. In part, this was because some of the fundamentals of civilised city-living had been lost: drainage and sewerage systems as developed by the Romans, for example, were long forgotten. Parisians were requested to keep the Seine clean and not to foul the streets and wells in the town, but these standards were almost impossible to enforce.

Moreover, many town citizens found it hard to shed the habits of their rural backgrounds. It was common practice to keep domestic animals, as they would have done in the country, and these could be both a nuisance and a health-hazard – at times in dramatically unexpected ways. Louis VI's eldest son fell victim to an accident right outside the royal palace when a pig ran across the street in front of him, startling his horse which suddenly reared. The prince was thrown, landed badly and died of his injuries.

Noble nuns

Life for women – be they peasant girls or princesses – was severely restricted in the Middle Ages. In general, the important positions in society were all held by men. Declared adults at between 12 to 14 years of age, boys acquired the rights to carry weapons, rule or wed. Women, on the other hand, remained the property of their fathers until the day that they were handed to their husbands. Then their great obligation was to provide healthy – preferably male – offspring. That a woman might aspire to anything more was not considered. Ladies who had no husbands accordingly had no recognisable role in

society, and they generally ended up going into convents. Such houses were often founded by queens and princesses for women of their own class, many of whom appear to have found fulfilment there. Louis VI's wife, Queen Adelheid, endowed a convent, the Montmartre, after the tragic death of her son, presumably hoping to secure the easy passage of his soul to paradise. But it became a sort of spiritual home for her as well, and when she felt her own end approaching in 1154, she found a haven there and died attended by her nuns.

Hugo Capet had clawed his way to pre-eminence through a group of jostling, squabbling princelings and lords. By the time of Louis VI's death, the crown had been secured for the Capetians. The country of France as we know it did not yet exist, but Paris was established as the capital of a royal state whose extent and influence was inexorably growing.

Religious wealth
Unmarried ladies who lived out their lives in convents often bestowed what would have been their bridal dowries on the religious houses that received them. This is how France's monastery of Notre-Dame Aubazine came to have this sacristy cupboard.

The Moors in Spain

In the 10th century, under Arab rulers, much of Iberia enjoyed a golden age. To the north, however, Christian kings were resolving to reconquer al-Andalus and expel the Moors from the peninsula altogether.

When Abd Ar Rahman III accepted the title of Emir in 912, he knew he was taking charge of a stable and prosperous Arab kingdom in Iberia. His predecessors had achieved much since 755, when Abd Ar Rahman I had landed at Almunecar, east of Málaga. The last surviving member of the famous line of Umayyad caliphs, Abd Ar Rahman I had arrived a fugitive in an alien environment, but he had stayed to establish a new and vibrant Islamic realm. Cleverly exploiting internal conflicts, he had carved out a kingdom for himself in what the Arabs called al-Andalus, rising inevitably to the position of Emir. Later, in 844, a very different set of adventurers, the Vikings, had attempted to seize Seville, but Abd Ar Rahman II had successfully seen them off. As the 10th century began, therefore, everything seemed set fair for the future of Islamic Spain.

An Islamic utopia?

The kingdom of al-Andalus is now seen as a model of a peaceful, prosperous multiracial society, a goal still largely eluding the democracies of the 21st century. No doubt the picture is to some extent idealised, but the apparent ease with which very different groups of people lived and worked together was remarkable. First there were the Arabs themselves, whose ancestors had entered the country at the time of Abd Ar Rahman I's invasion, and who were distinct from the later arrivals, the North African 'Syrians' and Berbers. Then there were the much larger numbers of indigenous peoples, most of whom had converted to Islam, though those who chose to remain Christian were accepted. Members of this group were afterwards referred to as 'Mozarabs' – from the Arabic *mustaribun*, 'Arabised ones' – for they adopted the ways, if not the religion, of the invaders. Known as *dhimmi*, non-believers in Islamic society were compelled to pay special taxes and were excluded from certain positions, but other than that they were treated tolerantly. Jews in al-Andalus certainly found far better treatment than their brethren in Christian Europe, where persecution and pogroms were a regular part of life.

The concept of the 'Golden Age' of al-Andalus is not unrealistic. The Arabs were scientifically advanced, they had revolutionised the agricultural economy with ingenious irrigation systems, they created stunning buildings and ornamental gardens, and they encouraged scholarship and learning. The capital of Córdoba, with its magnificent Great Mosque and library, reflected the wealth and sophistication of a society which Christendom could only regard with awe.

Córdoba – city of splendour

The capital was divided into 21 quarters in all; two formed the old town, which was accessible through seven gateways, with the remaining quarters spread out beyond to the west and east. The Emir's Palace and Great Mosque stood in the centre. Little is known about the Palace, the Alcázar, but the Mosque is one of the most sublime buildings ever built. It was founded in the late 8th century by Abd Ar Rahman I and was much added to thereafter. Eventually it comprised 19 architectural subdivisions, with 665 soaring columns, gilded capitals and extravagant mosaics that took the breath away. This was a very special place of prayer and a fitting religious centre for the western Islamic world.

Hero of the Reconquista
The knight Rodrigo Díaz de Vivar became the Spanish national hero 'El Cid', famed for his heroic battles against the Moors. This miniature shows him beheading a vanquished enemy.

Emblem of Córdoba
Córdoba's Great Mosque and Cathedral as it looks today. Following the Christian victory over the Moors a cathedral was constructed in the very heart of the mosque, creating a powerful visual symbol of Christian dominance.

Woven details

A motif from the cloak of the last Moorish king of Seville. Although depictions of animals and people were prohibited in Islamic art, the Moors in Spain often took a more relaxed attitude than their fellow Muslims further east.

A new caliph

Contemporary Arabic sources say Abd Ar Rahman III was an intelligent, courageous polymath. Blue eyes and reddish hair betrayed his European origins on his mother's side. His piety was widely recognised, and so, too, was his tolerance, which went too far for some Islamic scholars. In addition to the Islamic lands under his rule, he also enjoyed sovereignty over the still-Christian marginal areas of Spain: Asturias-León, Castille, Navarra and Barcelona. His position was challenged only once, when he was unexpectedly beaten in a battle against a Christian alliance, an occasion on which he almost lost his life. In 929, after 17 years as emir, Abd Ar Rahman III accepted the title of Caliph, acknowledging his place in the

Umayyad dynasty and as an independent ruler within the Islamic world.

And a new city

In 936 he set about the construction of a residential city some 5km (3 miles) from Córdoba. Medinat al Zahra, the City of Zahra, was named for his favourite wife. It was a gigantic project conceived on a lavish scale, which occupied 10,000 workers and 20,000 beasts of burden for many years. Marble basins were brought from as far away as Byzantium and Syria, and more than 4000 marble columns were shipped in from North Africa. The gargantuan costs involved were funded by the income from taxes and trade that was pouring in.

The stupendous wealth of al-Andalus was founded in its flourishing agriculture. Olive oil and wine were traditional products, but under Moorish rule many new crops were introduced. These included date palms, oranges, lemons, rice and sugar cane. Mulberry trees were also planted – their leaves provided food for the silkworm caterpillars also introduced by the Arabs for silk production. Other profitable craft-industries included the manufacture of textiles, leather and metalware, such as the famous steel sword-blades made in Toledo. The high quality of such goods ensured that trade was a reliable source of income.

Among other goods, al-Andalus exported saffron, sugar, cotton and olive oil through the ports on the south coast to destinations as far afield as Alexandria, Byzantium and Baghdad. This intensive traffic left linguistic traces in numerous nautical terms – words like 'admiral', 'arsenal' and 'corvette' originate in Arabic.

Abd Ar Rahman III moved the state mint and seat of government to the new city of Medinat Al Zahrat as early as 947,

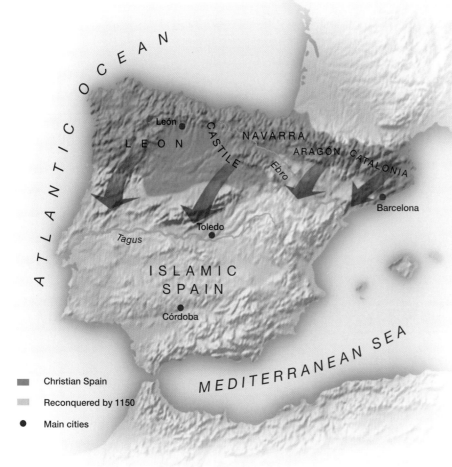

ATLANTIC OCEAN

León
LEÓN
CASTILE
NAVARRA
ARAGÓN
CATALONIA
Ebro
Barcelona
Toledo
Tagus
ISLAMIC SPAIN
Córdoba

MEDITERRANEAN SEA

- Christian Spain
- Reconquered by 1150
- ● Main cities

but building went on after his death in 961. His son and successor, Al Hakam II, had supervised building work from the start and lived to see it finished. The result was as splendid in its way as Córdoba: the city occupied three terraces, laid out as steps and separated by surrounding walls. On the top terrace was the Caliph's residence, with government offices and dwellings of the court officials a step down, while the ordinary people and soldiers lived on the lowest terrace. Here, too, were public facilities such as the mosque, baths and various markets and pleasure gardens.

The huge demand for water – the houses were equipped with water closets – was met by great cisterns filled by channels and aqueducts bringing supplies from high up in the Sierra. The water was collected in a tower, then ran via a marble basin and lead pipes into the town. Fish swam about in countless artificial pools: it was claimed a daily ration of 12,000 loaves of bread was required to feed them. The city's human inhabitants had to be fed, too, and the palace alone is said to have consumed 7000kg, or 7 tonnes, of meat daily – a credible figure given than the Caliph's 'Slavic Guard' alone numbered 3750 men. This troop included not only Slavs, but also Franks, Lombards and Christians from the north of Spain, all captured or kidnapped in early boyhood and sold as slaves.

Soon, the world was beating a path to the Caliph's door, not only the numerous legations from Berber princes, but diplomats representing Emperor Otto I (the Great) and the Emperor of Byzantium. They were left in no doubt that they were the guests of a great ruler. The pomp and circumstance of their reception – and the psychological acuity with which all was arranged – are clear from a report by a Christian ambassador

from northern Spain. To impress his visitors, the Caliph had the whole path from Córdoba to his residence covered with mats. Ranks of warriors held up swords to form a 'roof' of blades across the road. Reaching the outer walls of the royal residence, the overawed visitors found that their way inside was lined with sumptuous

fabrics. At intervals they met splendidly dressed dignitaries, to each of whom in turn they made obeisance, believing it to be the Caliph, only to be told, 'Lift your head. This is just one of his slaves.' At last they came to an inner courtyard covered with sand, where a solitary figure sat upon the ground. His head was bent in humility and he wore the simplest clothing. A fire burned before him; beside it lay a sword and a copy of the Koran. Only now, open-mouthed in amazement, were the ambassadors at last told: 'Pay your respects to the ruler of al-Andalus.'

Although Al Hakam II's reign was short (961–976), he made a name for himself as an architect and was remembered, above all, as a friend of the sciences, a scholar and bibliophile. Sadly, his great residence

Precious handiwork
This richly adorned gilded silver casket once belonged to Caliph Hisham II (966–1013), who succeeded his father Al Hakam II in 976. It displays abstract decorative elements typical of Islamic art.

at Medinat al Zahra did not last much longer. It was destroyed by rebellious Berber troops in the 11th century.

Al Mansur

Al Hakam's son, Hisham II, was only 10 years old at the time of his accession and his inexperience was exploited by an unscrupulous court official. Mohammad Ibn Abi Amir managed to gain the position of Hajib, a kind of chamberlain or vizier. Known by his honorary title Al Mansur, 'the Victorious One', he is recorded in Christian sources as 'Almansor', and before long he was the real ruler of al-Andalus.

Guardian of the well
This bronze lion with an articulated tail was once the cover for a well in an Ummayid palace. The water would have flowed from the lion's mouth. The background image is of an Emir of Cordoba, with his followers.

From 981 onward, Al Mansur was effectively a dictator. His reign changed the cultural character of the kingdom. Bidding for the support of conservative religious scholars, he clamped down on all departures from orthodoxy, publicly burning priceless volumes from Al Hakam II's great library. Al Mansur stopped short of naming himself Caliph, but Hisham II's power was only nominal, running to little beyond his name on the kingdom's coins. Al Mansur also reformed the army, dissolving the old, tribally based units with their traditional loyalties, and recruiting Christians and Berbers as mercenaries. Thus equipped, he led several military campaigns against the Christian kingdoms of northern Spain.

In 988, Al Mansur's warriors stormed the heavily fortified town of León. Nine years later, in 997, they sacked Santiago de Compostela, one of the most important pilgrimage sites in Christendom. The victorious army returned to Córdoba with rich booty. Among the spoils were the doors and bells from the church at Santiago de Compostela, which Christian prisoners were forced to drag through the capital. Just five years later, however, Al Mansur died unexpectedly in the course of a military campaign. Christians saw his death as divine judgment. A century later, Alfonso VI of Castile would return some of the humiliation when he used the site of Al Mansur's grave as the platform for his throne to receive a delegation from the Moorish ruler of Zaragoza. In al-Andalus, the more immediate consequence of Al Mansur's death was instability. His sons were unable to establish a firm hold on power, and in 1009 their puppet caliph, Hisham II, was forced to abdicate. In 1031 the Caliphate of Córdoba was abolished altogether.

El Cid and the reconquest

The period that followed is known as the Taifa period, from the Arabic *muluk al taiwaf* – 'little kings'. Arab culture continued to flourish in Spain, literature and the arts continued to thrive, agriculture and commerce kept the economy buoyant. Politically, however, al-Andalus was dying, disintegrating into a host of disunited kingdoms. Looking on from their northern strongholds, the Christian kings sensed that their time was coming and they set about preparing to reclaim Spain in a struggle that became known as the Reconquista.

The wars that followed were far from a plain fight between forces of Christianity and of Islam. Opportunistic rulers – Christian and Muslim – pursued shifting alliances as they sparred and manoeuvred over constantly changing fronts, often waging war against others of their own faith. And far from being some defining 'clash of civilisations', the conflict brought the two cultures closer than they had ever been before, each adopting ideas, artistic influences and customs from the other.

Among the many rulers involved in the fighting, a few stand out – in particular, Alfonso VI, 'the Brave', King of Castile and León. Alfonso was the king whose reign was most closely connected with the life of Rodrigo Díaz de Vivar, better known to posterity by his nickname of 'El Cid'. Born in 1043, this Spanish nobleman started out serving Alfonso VI's brother, King Sancho II of Castile, and was outraged by his murder in 1072. With most to gain from the assassination, Alfonso was widely suspected of having hired the killer, and legend has it that Sancho's supporters required the new king swear publicly to his innocence before he ascended the throne. Three times Rodrigo repeated the formula: 'If you are lying, then may God kill you by the hand of a treacherous vassal in the same way as Vellido Adolfo killed your brother.' Only then did he swear his oath of allegiance to the new King, an oath which he would keep faithfully until his death.

So fluid were the alliances of the time, however, that loyalty to Alfonso could take many forms, and Rodrigo sometimes found himself fighting on the Moorish side in local conflicts. It was then, it is assumed, that he was given the Arab honorific Sayyid, or 'Lord', the title which, in Castilian, became 'El Cid'.

The Almoravids

While the fortunes of both sides ebbed and flowed, one thing was now becoming clear: Alfonso VI was slowly but surely making headway against the Moors. In 1085, he captured Toledo, a major psychological blow to his Muslim enemies who, in panic, looked to North Africa for support. They

EVERYDAY LIFE

Mecca of the west

As capital of al-Andalus, Córdoba quickly grew to become one of the largest and most cultured towns of the age. Its wealth and beauty astounded Christian writers. An estimated half a million people lived there, though claims of Arab chroniclers that it had more than 113,000 dwellings, 3000 mosques and 900 bath houses were probably an exaggeration.

It was a great city, though, a place of astonishing prosperity and glamour with a high quality of life. Many of its streets were paved and at night its citizens enjoyed the benefit of the first street lighting in Europe. Order was maintained by the muhtasib or 'chief of police', who also oversaw weights and measures in the markets and standards of decency and dress.

If cleanliness is next to godliness, the Muslim world would certainly have put Christendom to shame. A visit to the hammam, or public hot baths, was a daily ritual for many, and this did much for both personal hygiene and public health.

Córdoba was a centre of scholarship, too, famous for its book trade and for the library of Caliph Al Hakam II which comprised some 400,000 volumes covering all branches of knowledge. And Córdoba was also noted for its music, thanks in large part to the work of Ziryab of Baghdad, who established himself here and helped to mould fashions in everything from food to etiquette.

The Great Mosque
Cultures collide in Córdoba's Great Mosque – Islamic, Visigothic and Classical elements came together to stunning effect. But the clash between Arabs and Christians would also have more destructive consequences.

received a ready response from Yusuf Ibn Tachfin, the leader of the Almoravids, a Berber movement dedicated to moral and religious renewal within Islam. Yusuf's forces streamed across the Strait of Gibraltar and into al-Andalus, where they prepared to engage the infidel in Allah's name.

BACKGROUND

Chess – the game of kings

Chess originated in India, from where it found its way via Persia to Arabia, arriving in the peninsula around AD 650. It was therefore just in time to be taken along on the epic journey to the west as the Arabs began their lightning campaign of conquest. To begin with, chess had mystic overtones in matching rival armies of 'good' and 'evil'; later, it became a straightforward game of war. The term 'checkmate' derives from the Persian-Arabic term 'al shah mat', meaning 'the King is dead'.

Chess match
In this 13th century miniature from the *Codex Alfonso*, a Christian knight and Moorish noble face each other across a chessboard. The green flag of the Prophet flies above the Arab-style tent.

For, fired up as they were with faith, the Almoravids did seem to be making progress. For a while, a series of victories looked like turning back the tide, but the Christian kings stood firm – in particular Alfonso VI, who by this time was fully reconciled with El Cid. Together, they proved irresistible. El Cid took the fight to the Almoravids, who with their supporters had taken power in Valencia in southeastern Spain. Over a 20-month siege, he starved the city into submission, then ruled there in King Alfonso's name. El Cid died in 1099 and a decade later Valencia was retaken by the Moors, who held on to it for another 125 years.

The Moorish 'minor kings' soon realised they had got rather more than they bargained for in the Almoravids – they had not been expecting their realms to be re-ordered along religious lines. Many of their subjects welcomed the newcomers, as the Almoravids insisted that only taxes specified in the Koran could be exacted, and scholars appreciated their narrow interpretation of religious laws. The kings stood to lose many privileges, however: some formed alliances with Christians – the devil they knew – while others gritted their teeth and made the best of it.

The fortunes of war see-sawed back and forth, but the Christian kings sensed that they were inching their way to victory. King Alfonso I of Aragon and Navarra joined battle against the Almoravids, making inroads deep into Moorish territory and winning for himself the epithet, El Batallador or 'the Battler'. In 1118 he conquered Zaragoza; a year later he took Tudela, in northern Navarra.

At this point Alfonso started receiving requests for help from far to the south. The easy-going atmosphere of al-Andalus had been changed completely by the coming of the Almoravid zealots, and Granada's Mozarabs were suffering under their intolerant rule. In a daring rescue mission Alfonso led an expedition deep into Andalucía, bringing back 10,000 Mozarabs whom he settled in the valley of the River Ebro. Alfonso I's military prowess won him the respect of his fiercest enemies, as an obituary by the Moorish chronicler, Ibn Al Athir, makes clear: 'No Christian prince was more courageous than he, or possessed such tenacity in battle against the Muslims… He slept in his armour… Through his death Allah allowed the Believers to breath freely again, liberated from his hammer blows.'

Alfonso of Portugal

One outcome of the Reconquista was the formation of a new state, which had its origins in a county called Portucalia. Situated in the north of what is now Portugal, at the beginning of the 12th century this was a possession of Castile and León. But as early as 1128, amid all the confusion of war with the Moors, the local lord, Count Alfonso 'the Conqueror', managed to liberate himself and his lands from his previous feudal dependence.

Eleven years later Alfonso won a great victory over the Moors at Ourique, a triumph for which the Pope himself proclaimed his gratitude. His fortunes riding high, Alfonso felt strong enough to assume the royal title of King Alfonso I; Castile and León had no alternative but to accept. He then embarked on military campaigns in the Moorish territories south of Portucalia, establishing his rule and raising taxes there. He took a number of towns and cities, though the most important prize, Lisbon, appeared beyond him, secure in Moorish hands.

Coincidence came to his assistance. In 1147 a Crusader fleet, 150 vessels strong, dropped anchor at Porto (now Oporto) en route to the Holy Land. The local bishop persuaded the Crusaders to join in the conquest of Lisbon, promising them the wealth of that city as their reward. The suburbs were soon taken, but the well-fortified inner city held out for six weeks, despite the ravages of hunger and disease. In vain did the attackers try to undermine the walls and break through with siege engines. Finally, a 25m (80ft) siege tower was built and pushed up against the city walls. With fearful losses, the Christians broke through, running through the city in an orgy of murder, rape and pillage. The power of the Almoravids was now broken, the territories of the Christian kings both massively enlarged and permanently secured. But even the achievements of El Cid and the Alfonsos did not mean the end of Moorish Spain. This suited Christian rulers well enough: the Moors made valuable trading partners, and they could always be raided for booty – or blackmailed for protection money. Not until the end of the 15th century would a Catholic fanaticism emerge to match Almoravid zeal and call for the eradication of Islam from Iberia.

Bread stamp
Ceramic stamps like this one were used by bakers in Mediterranean countries to mark their loaves of bread, declaring their provenance.

Alfonso I, the Conqueror
Through political acumen and military flair, Alfonso (1110-85) carved out the kingdom of Portugal. He declared himself king in 1139, and went on enlarging his kingdom thereafter, adding Lisbon with the help of Crusaders in 1147.

The rise of the kings of Denmark

Feared and hated for centuries as ruthless raiders and pillagers, the Vikings settled down to become successful farmers and traders. By the 11th century, King Cnut the Great had dreams of a Danish empire.

The word 'Viking' in Scandinavian usage meant simply someone engaged in an expedition for the sake of plunder. To the Vikings' hapless victims it meant fierce warriors who landed with lightning speed and rampaged through their coastal communities, killing people and animals, burning villages and making off with whatever valuables they could find. Then they were gone almost as quickly as they had arrived, their boats loaded down with booty, leaving their trail of devastation behind them. Thus the Vikings spread terror up and down the coasts of Europe.

Like their ancestors for countless generations, though, they were highly accomplished seafarers, their vessels built for manoeuvrability, speed and resilience. Denmark was a country inhabited by loose confederations of tribes, who all semi-independently sent out their young men on raids. For well over 250 years, this had been part of the Vikings' way of life, and they were feared far and wide. But when Gorm the Elder was crowned King of Denmark in 935, his ambition was for more than notoriety. He wanted to unite his country and he began by marrying a northern princess. By Gorm's day, many Vikings had already settled down as farmers, or plied the seas and rivers of Europe as traders rather than raiders. Gorm encouraged more men to give up the Viking lifestyle.

A state is born

Gorm the Elder aimed to build a new Denmark, a coherent kingdom like those to the south. His son, Harald Bluetooth, shared this vision. Evidence that theirs was a conscious project of state-formation comes from a pair of rune stones found on burial mounds in Jelling. On the first stone, King Gorm announces that he has erected the stones in honour of his wife, Tyra, and for the glory of Denmark. On the second, King Harald Bluetooth of Denmark proclaims that he has erected the stone in memory of his father, Gorm, and his mother, Tyra.

Ascending the throne in 945, and reigning until 987, Harald had himself baptised, but it appears that he embraced Christianity less through piety than his perception that the Catholicism of the age allowed the monarch to claim divine authority to rule. Christianity certainly helped to unify Harald's subjects when he took possession not just of the whole of Denmark but also of Norway. Harald did not believe in leaving such things to chance. The four great round fortifications

Memorial stones

These rune stones found at Jelling bear the names of the first king of Denmark, Gorm the Elder, his wife Tyra and their son, Harald Bluetooth. The stones also proclaim the formation and glory of the kingdom of Denmark.

Although Harald Bluetooth's predecessors accepted Christianity in 826 at the behest of the Carolingians, the Christianisation of Denmark really began with Harald's own baptism, c.965.

of Trelleborg, Fyrkat, Aggersborg and Nonnebakken were built about this time: anyone who held sway in them could call the surrounding region his own. The kings would have lived here, surrounded by their warriors.

The real strength of the Vikings, however, lay not in their fighting men but in their fleets. The longship was a thing of beauty, strength and speed. Its slender hull, gently curving, lay almost flat on the surface of the water. It had a stable keel, a large foldable sail and oars that made it fast and versatile in handling. With log rollers placed beneath, overland portages could be made with relative ease – invaluable for getting round obstacles on long-distance voyages inland by river. About 50 oarsmen could be seated in one of these 30m (100ft) ships, though they had little protection from the weather. At the prow of each ship reared up an impressive carved wooden figurehead which gave rise to the other name for these vessels: 'dragon ships'.

A lively town
The oldest significant town in Northern Europe, Haithabu was the largest market centre in the Viking period. Trade goods passed through here from Russia, Norway, France and southern Europe.

Dragon head
At the end of this 16cm (6in) bronze pin is the head of a mythical dragon, similar to those carved in wood that adorned the prows of Viking ships.

The longship was perfectly adapted to the Vikings' method of making war: the surprise attack and rapid withdrawal. Preferred targets were initially churches and monasteries; but even towns had to be prepared for Viking raids.

Haithabu – a thriving trading post

Away from the raids, however, a quiet revolution had been taking place in the north European economy, driven largely by technical innovations in shipbuilding since the 8th century. Trade between western Europe and Scandinavia had been growing fast and within a short time spread to the Slavic and Baltic Sea coasts. Before long more markets were needed, and this was the stimulus to the founding of towns like Haithabu in Schleswig-Holstein, a trading centre at the confluence of the rivers Schlei, Treen and Eider. Covering an area of about 50 hectares (125 acres), the settlement was fortified to landward – traces of a semi-circular wall can still be seen – but Haithabu lay open to the sea, the source of its prosperity. Excavations have revealed the remains of harbour installations and wharves with warehouses. Furs, hides, fish and luxury items would all have been traded through here, as well as slaves for selling on as far afield as Baghdad, Moorish Spain and Russia. A massive palisade wall in the harbour basin protected the settlement against robbers.

At its height, Haithabu was a densely populated little town in which almost 1000 people lived. There were workshops for bronze casting and for making shoes and combs. The houses stood on plots of ground with small sheds, or byres for livestock. Interior floors lay below street level, so that one stepped down into a house's living room as though into a basement. There were no windows, but there may have been a roof hatch, covered with a stretched pig's bladder. A simple hole in the roof let out smoke.

Haithabu could hardly have been more different from the Danish settlements of old: life positively pulsated in this bustling market centre. Traders travelled here from all over the known world. The Arab merchant Al Tartushi recorded details of a visit in 965, mentioning a freshwater fountain in the market place – a sensation in those times. He was also struck by the fact that both the men and women wore make-up to enhance their eyes. He was less impressed by their singing, reporting that he had never heard a people sing so horribly – more akin to growling, like the barking of dogs, only worse.

England and the Danegeld

During the 10th century, the Vikings continued to raid, but their tactics were gradually changing. They no longer returned home to the North with their loot, but saw out the winter wherever they found themselves. They occupied or laid siege to settlements or monasteries, demanding protection money from the inhabitants. Systematic extortion replaced the smash-and-grab tactics of the past.

This new strategy was taken to extremes in England by King Harald's son, Sven Forkbeard. His so-called 'Danegeld' was practically an official tax. By such methods the Vikings not only enriched themselves but consolidated their power across large parts of eastern England and laid the foundations for their later Dukedom of Normandy in France.

In 1000, having vanquished the Norwegian king, Olaf Tryggvasson, at the Battle of Svolder in the western Baltic, Sven Forkbeard was able to place himself on the Norwegian throne. His conquests did not stop there. Sven had long set his sights on England and now the English king, Aethelred II, offered extreme provocation. Instead of meekly paying the Danegeld, Aethelred had risen up against the Danish occupiers and had them put to death. Aethelred today is popularly remembered as 'the Unready', as though his preparations were at fault, but his Anglo-Saxon nickname 'Unraed' really meant something more like 'ill-advised'. Sven Forkbeard retaliated by launching a full-scale invasion, Aethelred was beaten

and Forkbeard became the first Dane to sit on the English throne.

The Danes had started to think on a grander scale – ad hoc raids were now a thing of the past. A sense of their military power can be glimpsed in the remains of their fortifications at Trelleborg, one of four surviving round fortresses of the Viking period.

The geometrical shape of Trelleborg has fascinated historians. It is situated on a tongue of land between two rivers, which affords good natural protection. Both a ringwall and a wide ditch encircle the fortress's interior, which is divided into four equal-sized quarters. A labyrinthine system of paths runs through the quarters, each of which has a gateway orientated towards one of the cardinal points. Four wooden houses of equal size were situated in each quarter. A further 16 fortified buildings faced inward from outside the quartered area. It is believed Trelleborg could accommodate some 1300 men.

Finely crafted gold and silver items have been found inside some structures, prompting the suggestion that the forts might have been work camps for prisoners. This would help to explain the separate arrangement of houses in the centre and around the outside edge, but it is impossible to say with certainty. What is clear is that Trelleborg was conceived not merely as a military headquarters but as a tangible sign of authority and strength.

Military camp or settlement?
The precise function of the Danish circular camps or 'castles', like the one at Trelleborg above, remains a mystery to this day. Archaeologists have so far uncovered only partial remains.

Dreams of empire

When Sven Forkbeard died in 1014, his kingdom was divided between his sons: the elder, Harald II, was given Denmark and Cnut or 'Canute', later called 'the Great', inherited the English throne. This was definitely the short straw, as many of Sven's conquests in England had been clawed back by Aethelred's son, Edmund II, 'Ironside'. Cnut set about reconquering the country: he and Edmund fought each other to a standstill, then agreed to divide the kingdom along the line of the River Thames. The peace agreement stipulated that if one of them died, his territories would be ceded to the other. In 1016, Edmund died – almost certainly of natural causes, though Cnut clearly benefited by his death as it left him the uncontested King of England.

To cement his claim to the crown, Cnut married Aethelred II's widow, Emma of Normandy, and made England the base of his North Sea Empire. In theory, his dominions included Denmark, Norway and parts of Sweden, but first he had to oust his brother Harald from the Danish throne. In 1019, he was able to proclaim himself King of the Danes.

Cnut the Great died in battle 16 years later and was laid to rest in the Cathedral at Winchester. His greatest achievement had been the unification of the Scandinavian countries under a single crown. Though he deserves credit for this, the empire he built did not prove enduring: the North Sea that separated the different countries was too wide and open to allow the formation and maintenance of a single realm. After Cnut's death, in 1035, he was succeeded by Harald Harefoot on the English throne, while Magnus the Noble stepped into his shoes in Norway. Denmark fell first to Sven II Estridsen, and then to Harthacanute (Cnut the Hardy) – and the dream of a North Sea Empire seemed lost for good.

Then something happened that was completely unexpected: in 1040 Harald Harefoot died of a serious illness, and two years later Harthacanute collapsed during a drinking bout. Whether it was murder or misfortune, both the English and Danish thrones were now unoccupied. Magnus of Norway had himself crowned in Denmark, but England seemed a kingdom too far. Edward the Confessor, a son of Aethelred II and Emma, was brought back from Normandy and crowned in Winchester Cathedral in 1042.

The gulf between Danish and Anglo-Saxon factions was still profound in England. Edward was a follower of the Danish line and Godwin, Earl of Wessex and a friend of Edmund Ironside, did his best to prevent him from installing too many Norman friends in positions of power. Edward sent him into exile, but when Godwin returned in force, Edward had to reinstate his lands and position.

When Edward died in 1066, Godwin's son Harold followed him onto the English throne as Harold II. But the wheel of fortune promptly spun again: that same year Harold lost the battle of Hastings to William of Normandy. Once again, England had a descendant of Danish-Norwegian Vikings on its throne.

The end of the Viking era

By the end of the 11th century the Vikings were no longer the threat they had been when they first charged onto the northern European stage. Now Christianised, they had created important settlements along many of the coasts around northwestern Europe, most famously Dublin in Ireland. In a classic example of poacher-turned-gamekeeper, the former plunderers were now traders dominating routes and markets from the fjords of Norway and the rivers of Russia to the ports of the Mediterranean.

A generous ruler
Edward the Confessor made a gift of gold and silver to fund the construction of Westminster Abbey in London, and was later buried there. He is regarded as a saint to this day.

Towards a united Hungary

Magyar horsemen were feared throughout much of
Europe because of their terrifying campaigns
of plunder. But a salutory defeat in 955
brought them a change of lifestyle and religion.

Saint Stephan's crown
The Hungarian crown is traditionally
held to date back to the saintly King
Stephan I in the 11th century, but it is
most probably of a later date.

On 10 August, 955, not far from the city of Augsburg
in southern Bavaria, the German ruler, Otto the
Great, brought together some 8000 to 10,000
armoured knights representing the main peoples
of central Europe – Franks, Saxons, Swabians,
Bavarians and Bohemians. This remarkable
show of unity, given the suspicion and
hostility that generally prevailed
among them, was an indication of
their fear of a common enemy: the
Magyars, or Hungarians.

The Magyars were nomadic
herdsmen and raiders who had
originated out in the Eurasian
Steppe, from where so many
tribes of mounted warriors had
come to afflict the western
world – including, of course,
the Huns, after whom the
Magyars' country would be
named. They had been led over
the Carpathian mountains by
their chieftain, Arpad, in about 895
and spilled out across the Danube
plains. Ferocious and formidable
on the field of battle, born to the
saddle and seasoned by a life of
war and hardship, they could gallop
and wheel at will, spraying deadly
arrows from their compound
bows – an elusive, mercurial force.
Even when massed as a large army,
the Magyars moved with all the
flexibility of a far smaller force.

At Lechfeld, however, the
tables were turned. Though
outnumbering the German army

fivefold, the Magyars badly misjudged their situation and found themselves in close combat with a heavily armed enemy. Many had broken off from fighting to plunder the German baggage train, which gave Otto a chance to rally his forces. He trusted in the 'holy lance' to make his decisive attack. In other circumstances, the lance would have availed him little, as the Magyars easily eluded the lumbering charges of armoured knights. Here on restricted ground, however, the lightly armed Magyars were at a disadvantage. The slaughter continued for almost three days.

The mighty brought low

Before the devastating defeat at Lechfeld, the Magyars had been feared far and wide. 'Save us, oh Lord,' householders had prayed, 'from the sharp arrows of the Hungarians!' They were not interested in gaining land, only in plundering gold and silver, so to keep these unbidden guests away from their borders, many a ruler had been prepared to pay tribute. Lechfeld brought the pride and power of the Magyars, and their time of rich plunder, to an end. The Hungarian leaders, Bulcsu and Lehel, were executed in Regensburg and the few survivors withdrew to the Danube plains.

Arpad's great-grandson, the Archduke Geza, made symbolic peace with the West

---

BACKGROUND

The crooked cross

St Stephan's crown has become a much-loved symbol of Hungarian nationhood, the bent cross on its top testifies to the traumas of the country's history. Originally, it is said, it was surmounted by a cross containing a relic, a fragment of the True Cross of Christ, but this was snatched by Queen Isabella, widow of King John I (John Zapolya), in the 16th century. By possessing the sacred splinter, she hoped to ensure the succession of her son, John Sigismund, to the throne. Scholars today believe that the crown was actually created rather later and that it may have been based on a Greek reliquary which was first made to house a skull.

---

when he had himself baptised by Bruno, Bishop of Sankt Gallen. Geza opened up his country to Christian missionaries and when, around 975, his own son Vajk was born, he had him baptised and given the Christian name of Stephan.

A replica of the 'holy lance' was given to the Hungarian kingdom by Otto III – both as a sign of welcome to the fold of civilised nations, and as a not-so-subtle reminder of defeat. It was hoped that the country's conversion to Christianity would make it a bridgehead into the pagan east: the Hungarian self-image was no longer about warlike prowess but about stability and civilisation. Geza's policy reached a high point in 997 with the marriage of his son Stephan to Gisela, sister of the later Emperor Henry II, the last Saxon king of Germany. The following year Geza died and was succeeded by Stephan I.

A Christianising king

In Stephan, Hungary had an energetic and decisive ruler. Like his father, he was a westerniser and ambitious for his people. He consolidated his kingdom, dividing it up into administrative counties, each governed by a count whose task it was to keep order and collect taxes. He also worked strenuously to Christianise the country: where his father's conversion had been one of convenience and he continued to worship pagan gods, Stephan was sincere. He had the entire population baptised and brought in Bene-dictine monks to develop an education system. He also established ten bishoprics, one for each county, and each was encouraged to found ten new churches.

The Hungarian horn
This piece of Byzantine ivory work is said to have belonged to the Hungarian leader Lehel, on the losing side in the battle of Lechfeld, in 955. At his subsequent execution he is said to have asked to be allowed to blow the horn one more time. Instead, he brought it crashing down on his would-be executioner's head, saying 'You will be my servant in the Beyond!'

Local sensibilities held little sway with Stephan. Key church posts were occupied by foreigners and there were stiff penalties for those who proved unwilling to go along with Christianisation. Stephan's order was clear: 'The priests and counts are to instruct the village heads to order everyone to attend church on Sunday. Anyone who negligently stays at home is to be beaten and shorn.'

Now all he needed to confirm Hungary's acceptance in the community of Christendom, and his own place in the brotherhood of kings, was some sort of confirmation from the Church. Thanks to the intervention of Germany's Otto III – whose plan was to create a universal Christian federation of states modelled upon the classical Roman Empire – Stephan was sent a crown consecrated by Pope Sylvester II. His formal coronation took place, according to some sources, on Christmas Day in the year 1000; others say it was on New Year's Day, 1001.

The new millennium marked the start of a new era for the Hungarians. In just half a century, a nation of ferocious raiders had been transformed into one of peaceful farmers and craftsmen. King Stephan I was canonised in 1083, giving Hungary its very own patron saint. A shrine in St Stephan's Basilica in the capital Budapest houses the King's 'holy right hand', and it is still revered as a sacred relic. 'He supported all the poor,' wrote a later chronicler. 'He went and looked after them with his own hand, which is why this compassionate right hand is displayed before the eyes of Hungarians to this day.'

A European bulwark

When Stephan died, in 1038, the succession to the throne was unclear, since his only son Emmerich had been killed in a hunting accident. But the structures he had built proved stable enough to weather the ensuing unrest; even two pagan uprisings, in 1046 and 1061, did not shake the country fundamentally. It was taken, briefly, under the sovereignty of the German Empire, but in 1077 a second saint-king, Ladislav I, revived Hungary.

Ladislav restored the unity of the state and reaffirmed the supremacy of the Christian monarchy with strict laws. His expansionist foreign policy saw Hungary extend its boundaries southwards to encompass an area including Croatia, Dalmatia and Slavonia. By 1102, Hungary was not just a kingdom but a European power, a force for stability on Europe's eastern marches. As a vital Christian bulwark against the pagan Turkic peoples, its importance would keep on growing.

Mobile marauders
This illustration shows Hungarian horsemen attacking a fortified town in the time of Henry I, founder of the Saxon dynasty in Germany. When the Magyars first raided Germany, Henry agreed to pay tribute to them in return for a nine-year truce. Raids resumed when he refused to renew the tribute, but Henry defeated the Magyars at Riade in 933 and his son Otto completed the job of bringing them to heel.

Byzantium – a great Mediterranean power

Under Emperor Basil II, Byzantium enjoyed a brief golden age. Time was fast running out for 'Eastern Rome', however, as religious disagreements and a catastrophic defeat by the Seljuk Turks at Manzikert began the long but irreversible decline of the Byzantine Empire.

When Emperor Romanos II died in 963, the hugely successful general Nikephoros was considered the obvious man to replace him. His first action on becoming Emperor Nikephoros II was to wed Theophanu, Romanos's widow, to secure his succession. More would be required, however, to hold on to popular support. So he launched a counter-offensive against Islamic advances, first winning back the island of Cyprus, then leading an army deep into Syria to take the city of Aleppo. His victories over the Arabs earned him the nickname, 'Pale Death of the Saracens'. Byzantium once again had a potentate to be taken seriously.

Nikephoros made this point forcefully when Emperor Otto the Great sought to marry one of the Byzantine princesses. The request was greeted with derision. And when a legation from the King of Bulgaria came to collect tribute, due under treaties agreed by Byzantium's rulers in times of weakness, the men were whipped and sent home with threats of worse next time. It was clear that times had changed.

Despite his strongman image, Nikephoros II was assassinated after only six years in power, but his successor, John I Tzimiskes, kept up the effort.

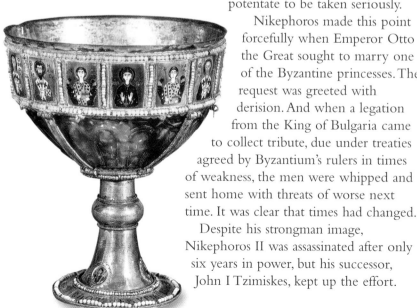

Imperial chalice
Made of gilded silver with onyx inlay and brightly enamelled images of saints, this magnificent Byzantine chalice was once the property of Emperor Romanos I. It is now in the treasury of Saint Mark's Basilica in Venice.

To the west he defeated the Bulgarians, and in the east he invaded Palestine. Byzantium was in the ascendant once again. 'Listen and hear of this great wonder,' John wrote to an ally, the Armenian king. 'All of Phoenicia, Syria and Palestine have been freed from the yoke of the Saracens, who now recognise the sovereignty of the Romans.'

It was no idle boast, and the Byzantine star was set to rise still higher when Emperor Basil II took power in 976. From the first, he showed himself adept politically, a clever statesman and strategist. All of his intellectual agility and cunning would be needed – not for nothing are labyrinthine intrigues now known as 'Byzantine'. Basil's battle for the imperial throne lasted three years. In the end it was the 6000 Varangian warriors, sent to him by Prince Vladimir the Holy of Kiev, who were decisive in his victory against rival emperor, General Bardas Skleros. The Varangians were Viking mercenaries who had enlisted in the service of the Kievan kings. They so impressed Basil that he made them the core of the elite imperial bodyguard, which was afterwards known as the Varangian Guard.

Divine blessing
The Byzantine emperors were believed to derive their legitimacy as rulers directly from God. This mosaic in Hagia Sophia, Istanbul, shows Emperor Constantine IX Monomachos and his wife Zoe being blessed by Christ himself.

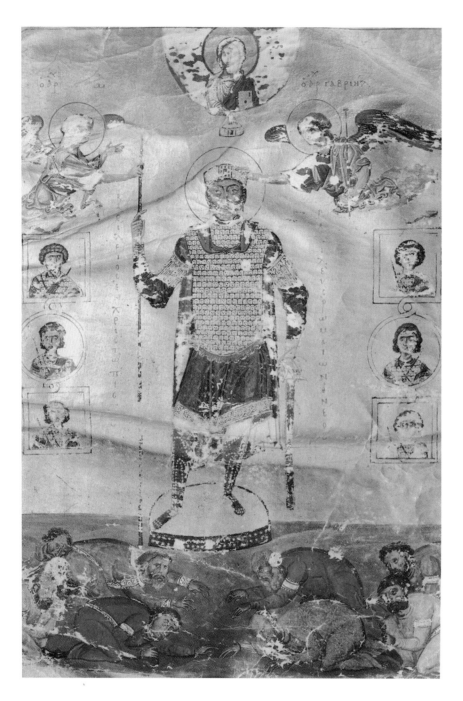

Basil the Bulgar-slayer
Reflecting his nickname, Emperor Basil II strikes a military pose in golden armour, commander's boots and purple cloak. Basil was prepared to lead his armies from the front.

districts under the rule of military governors. Country estates or small-holdings were handed out in return for military manpower. The wealthiest landowners provided the heavily equipped riders; the less well-off landowners would often join together to equip one rider. It all added up: during the 10th century, the eastern *themes* were able to provide the Emperor with about 70,000 cavalrymen.

The Bulgar-slayer

Basil II had struggled so hard to win his throne he was disinclined to tempt fate by shows of pomp: he became an ascetic, a loner who never married. All his energies were directed towards the greater glory of the Empire and the bringing down of its enemies, chief among whom were the Bulgarians. For three centuries, Bulgaria had been conquering vast tracts of territory in the region, most of it at Byzantium's expense. After the accession of Tsar Samuil in 976, that process seemed to accelerate: soon the Bulgarian Empire could eclipse Byzantium.

Basil resolved to turn the tide. In the year 1001 he embarked on a relentless campaign which earned him the nickname *Bulgar-aktonos*, 'Bulgar-Slayer'. He made his final breakthrough in 1014. Beside the upper reaches of the River Struma, he encircled and destroyed Tsar Samuil's army. Though the Tsar managed to escape, many thousands of Bulgarians were taken prisoner. Basil made a gruesome example of them by having them all blinded except one 'leader' in every 100, who was left with a single eye. They were sent groping and stumbling to Prilep, where their Tsar had fled. On seeing this wretched procession, he collapsed in shock and died two days later. Within four years, the Balkans were back under Byzantine rule.

Glorious Constantinople

The Byzantine Empire was now the strongest and wealthiest state in the whole of Christendom. Constantinople was its

Some sources describe the Varangians as 'wine skins' on account of their heavy drinking, but there was no doubting their loyalty or their effectiveness. They were joined in the imperial guard by Anglo-Saxons and southern Italian Normans: mercenaries made up the core of the Byzantine army, the *tagmata* or 'regiments', which were under the direct command of the Emperor. In addition, there were conscripts drawn from the Empire's different *themes* – the administrative

A manual for court ceremony

Constantine VII left a detailed account of the niceties of court ceremony and behaviour, including the titles and clothing of different dignitaries, the proper procedures for coronations, the furnishings and decorations in the imperial palace – and much more.

The Emperor's daily timetable began at six in the morning, when he was woken by three knocks on the silver door of his bedchamber. On rising, he went into the golden hall and prayed before an icon, after which he went to his golden throne where, having had breakfast, he received his foreign minister. This was followed by audiences with the highest officials and dignitaries of the Empire. During an audience, anyone who did not belong to the rank of senator had to lie down with outstretched arms on the floor in front of the Emperor, and kiss his feet.

Curtains of rich fabrics, concealing the raised throne, were opened for the visits of ambassadors from foreign rulers. An ambassador would step forward onto a disc made of porphyry that was set into the floor in front of the throne. There he would kneel down to greet the Emperor with due deference.

Symbols of power
This gold coin depicts Emperor Constantine VII Porphyrogenetus, the 'Purple-born', holding the imperial orb, one of the most important symbols of the Emperor's power. Constantine ruled from 913 to 959.

splendid centre. Founded in AD 330, by Constantine the Great, the city occupied a tongue of land on the Bosphorus and by the 11th century it had a population of half a million. The city was protected to landward by a triple wall some 8.5km (5½ miles) in length; the innermost band was 18m (60ft) high with 96 towers. The seaward side was fortified, too, and over the centuries the city's defences had proved impregnable.

The massive imperial palace lay close to the sea and not far away rose the city's greatest and most glittering church, the Hagia Sophia, as well as the impressive Circus, or Hippodrome. This was one of the few places in which the public were likely to catch a glimpse of their Emperor who, apart from important religious processions, appeared only at the chariot-races and other sporting events staged here. At his coronation, which was held at the Hagia Sophia, he appeared dressed in the Roman general's boots and purple cloak. The new Emperor was hoisted on to a shield for the admiration of the army, the people and the Senate.

The Emperor was the embodiment of social rank and temporal power. But he was also the highest Lord of the Church, and in this capacity he would name and appoint the Patriarch of Constantinople, the senior religious figure in the Empire. Despite a strict hierarchy, no real class system existed.

As in the ancient Roman Empire, an elaborate military and institutional administrative structure offered a ladder which could be climbed by those with the energy, talent and ambition. Occasionally, a man of modest background even rose to be Emperor.

An international trade centre

Unimaginable luxury and poverty existed side by side in Constantinople, which was thronged with people of the most diverse backgrounds. There were labourers and craftsmen (carefully organised into their own guilds), merchants, soldiers and officials. Many, in every walk of life, would have been slaves. Constantinople was a major trading centre, with contacts the

When Basil II died in 1025, he left behind an empire stretching from the Adriatic and the foot of Italy to Armenia and northern Syria, and whose cultural influence extended into the Germanic 'Roman' Empire. But this marked the imperial zenith – indeed that point may already have been passed. Basil had turned something of a blind eye to the tendency of larger landowners to annex small estates. This not only cut into tax revenues but impacted directly upon the military capabilities of the Empire, since it had been the small landowners whose joint contributions had done most to sustain the imperial army. In weakening authority at the centre, this tendency increased the strength of the provincial nobility – a recipe for insubordination and disunity. The problem grew in the reigns of Basil's successors, Constantine VIII (1025–8) and Romanos III (1028–34).

Schism splits the Church

In 1054, legates from Rome laid a papal bull on the altar of the Hagia Sophia, denouncing the pronouncements and actions of the Patriarch, Michael Kerullarios. The latter promptly issued his own attack on the papacy: what is known as the Western Schism was underway. It had been coming for quite some time: the eastern Church had for centuries disagreed with Rome on almost everything, from the marriage of priests to the position of the Patriarch. There were doctrinal

length and breadth of the Mediterranean and beyond. Furs, slaves and amber came from Russia and the Baltic; ivory and palm oil were brought from Africa; spices, precious stones, incense and indigo were shipped from as far afield as India and even China. Many of these raw materials were turned by the city's artisans and craftsmen into vessels, jewellery, tableware and clothing.

This trade and industry generated huge wealth, but enormous wealth was needed to cover the immense expense involved in maintaining a vast army and bureaucracy and the opulent imperial court. There were other great costs, too: Byzantium often bought peace along its frontiers. Huge amounts of gold were needed to keep the ship of state afloat, but Byzantine emperors did not need to fear ruin since taxes on land ownership, grazing and other items swelled coffers already amply filled by customs duties and tribute from defeated enemies.

Treasured reliquary
Holy relics were vital to Byzantine spirituality. This detail is from a container specially made to house seven fragments of the 'True Cross'. The figures represent the Archangel Gabriel and John the Baptist.

differences, too, especially on the Trinity: Rome believed that the Holy Spirit derived at once from the Father and the Son, whereas, for eastern Christians, the Spirit originated solely in the Father. The repercussions of this split have still not been resolved.

At the time, the Emperor Constantine IX had more pressing concerns. A group of nomadic raiders from the Steppes, the Petchenegs, had crossed the Danube into Byzantine territory in 1048, and imperial forces had been unable to eject them. Constantine's representatives had attempted to recruit the Petchenegs as a mercenary army, but they had taken the money and carried on pillaging as before.

Danger from the East

To the east, a greater storm was brewing: the Seljuk Turks were advancing on the Empire. Under the warlord Tugril Beg, they had already conquered large parts of the Middle East; now his nephew Alp Arslan, the 'Mountain Lion', was pushing on into Asia Minor. By 1067, the Seljuks had taken Caesarea Cappadocia (Kayseri).

Emperor Romanos IV raised an army, mostly of mercenaries but with the Varangian Guard and Tagmata cavalry at its core. Along with this fighting force came thousands of servants, a mighty baggage train and several siege engines. Things did not begin well. As the army set out, an argument blew up over division of spoils after the conflict, and a battle within the army was only narrowly avoided.

On August 19, 1071, the two armies met near the Armenian town of Manzikert on Lake Van. The Seljuks, employing a ruse, pretended to retreat before the enemy advance. Byzantine discipline broke down as they set off in headlong pursuit. Triumph turned to consternation as a rumour spread that the Emperor had fallen, and the imperial army was gripped by fear and indecision.

The Turks were quick to take advantage and launched a devastating counter-attack which soon brought about total victory. Romanos IV was taken prisoner and led before Alp Arslan, while the remnants of the imperial army fled in panic. Though treated honourably by the Sultan, the Emperor's power was broken. 'The army is to the state as the head is to the body,' Emperor Constantine VII had commented a century earlier. The aftermath of Manzikert bore this out: the destruction of the Byzantine army left the road into Asia Minor wide open for the Seljuk Turks.

World metropolis
This 15th-century miniature represents Constantinople, with the great church of Hagia Sophia dominating the city and an equestrian statue of Constantine the Great raised on high.

The kingdom of Kiev – origins of Russia

Under the rule of its grand dukes, Kiev grew into a bustling centre of trade and power, almost rivalling Constantinople.

The treasure of Gnezdovo
This collection of gold and silver jewellery and other precious items comes from a treasure horde found in a fortified settlement not far from Smolensk. It is the largest medieval treasure so far unearthed in Russia.

On his way home to Kiev in 972, after a humiliating defeat in his Balkan campaign against the Byzantines, Duke Svyatoslav I and his men were ambushed by a group of Petchenegs – nomadic horsemen who were supposed to have been Svyatoslav's allies. The Duke never reached Kiev, where news of his death sparked off a vicious power struggle. Not until 980 would a clear successor, Vladimir, ascend the Grand Duke's throne.

Kiev had always been a rough-and-ready sort of place, its foundation closely connected with the Vikings who had sailed down the rivers of Russia to the south and east. Along the way, they had 'traded' with Balts and Finns around the Baltic coast, and with the Slavs in the forests and steppes which lay beyond. Whilst these adventurers did exchange goods with the wealthy and powerful chieftains they came across, they raided defenceless villages and extorted furs from riverside communities. The Finns called these foreigners Ruotsi, or 'oarsmen', a word which evolved into the Slavic Rus. Hiring themselves out to wealthier chiefs as 'Varangian' mercenaries, they involved themselves in local disputes and soon made themselves a part of the Slavic scene. The differences between Rus and Slav became increasingly blurred as a hybrid Scandinavian-Slavic culture began to emerge. Among its most important centres were the old town of Ladoga, on Lake

Ladoga, and Novgorod to the south with its mixed population of Slavs, Finns and Scandinavians. These towns, situated on the river banks, were protected by a surrounding earthen wall topped with wooden fortifications. Slav settlements in the forests around looked much the same.

The conquest of Kiev

Kiev, in the land of the Polyane, was one such small fortified Slavic settlement: it is thought it had been founded by the brothers of a Polyane prince, Kij, and named in his honour. According to the medieval *Chronicle of Nestor*, it was under the rule of Khazar nomads when the mid-9th century brought sudden change.

Around 862, Slavs and Finns living in northwest Russia asked a Rus named Rurik to be their new prince. Rurik based himself in Novgorod, from where his followers ventured south, eventually establishing a new headquarters in Kiev. 'They assembled many Varangians around them', continues the Chronicle, 'and began to rule over the land of the Polyane.' Rurik's successor, Oleg, took personal charge in Kiev, which meant that the two most important cities in the land were now firmly in the control of Rurikid rulers. Though the origins of Kiev are shrouded in legend, there is every reason to believe that the Rus did indeed have an important part to play in its development.

Conversion to Christianity
The baptism of Grand Duke Vladimir, shown here in a miniature from a 15th-century copy of the *Radziwill Chronicle*, a rare account of medieval Russian history. Vladimir's conversion in 988 marked the start of Orthodox Christianity as the state religion of the Kingdom of Kiev. To seal the contract the Byzantine Emperor, Basil II, gave his sister Anna to Vladimir in marriage.

The influx of Scandinavian Varangian mercenaries continued unabated, and Kiev grew in power as well as size. The grand dukes extended their area of influence across vast areas of Russia, violently extorting tribute from the Slavic tribes. They also maintained close relations with the Byzantine Empire. For centuries, the Scandinavian Rus had been travelling downriver to the splendid city of Constantinople, which they knew as Miklagard, 'the great city'. To the Kievan Rus it was Zargrad, source of the most desirable luxuries in the world, such as the silks and jewellery they bought with furs and slaves.

But contacts were not always peaceable. On a number of occasions, fleets of longships attacked Constantinople. The Byzantines came to appreciate the warlike capabilities of the Rus and a great many Varangians were taken into Byzantine service. In return for the hand of Anna, the Emperor's sister, Grand Duke Vladimir sent 6000 men to Constantinople: they

EVERYDAY LIFE

Olga comes to Constantinople

Duchess Olga converted to Christianity long before her grandson, Vladimir, and was invited to Constantinople by the Emperor as part of his trade and diplomatic efforts. Her conversion probably contributed to a new warmth in relations. A chronicler recorded the meeting: 'The Duchess entered together with her relatives ... She walked ahead of her women ... [and] stopped on the spot where the chancellor usually stood to ask questions. After her came the ambassadors of the Russian princes and the merchants ... On the Sunday a banquet was given in the Golden Palace, and the Emperor sat down at table with the Rus.'

became the core of a permanent Imperial Varangian guard. When it seemed that the Emperor might be having second thoughts about sending his sister, Vladimir conquered Kherson, a Byzantine colony on the Black Sea coast. The princess was promptly despatched to Kiev.

Religion also played a key part in the relationship between Constantinople and Kiev: Vladimir's conversion to Christianity was a prerequisite of his marriage to Anna. The Byzantines wanted a Christian ally on their northeastern frontier and Vladimir saw faith as a useful bargaining tool. But if his conversion reassured the Byzantines, it also strengthened his position at home. Under the Orthodox Christianity which was now Kiev's state religion, the Grand Duke was the Lord's 'anointed one'. The Church proved an invaluable support, especially after 1037 when Kiev was made the seat of a metropolitan, or archbishop.

Through the efforts of Byzantine missionaries the Slavs also obtained their own Slavic script, which partly derived from the Greek. The new script was disseminated widely through the reading and copying of Christian texts. To this was added the first written summary of Russian laws, the *Russkaja Pravda*.

A growing metropolis

Kiev was now an international trading centre and one of the foremost cities in Europe. Its merchants ranged as far afield as western Europe and the Arab countries. The Black Sea was their highway, so much so that, at certain periods, it was widely referred to as the 'Russian Sea'. Foreign merchants streamed into Kiev and found a fast-growing, increasingly impressive city.

Kiev's Golden Gate
This imposing portal, carefully restored, was the main entrance to Jaroslav's city. To the right a portion of the old wood-and-earth wall has been reconstructed.

Kiev was divided into two parts: warehouses, workshops and quays crowded the river bank, while the Grand Dukes' Kremlin, or stronghold, stood on the hill above. In all, the city covered an area of approximately 400 hectares (1000 acres), and up to 50,000 people lived there. Both in the lower city and the Kremlin, people lived in wood-block houses; each section was surrounded by an earth-and-timber wall. Among the first stone buildings, erected with the help of Byzantine craftsmen, were several palace structures, the great Sophia Gate and the Church of the Tithes, completed in 996. This took its name from the fact that Grand Duke Vladimir funded its construction with a tax of one-tenth of every householder's income.

Kiev's era of glory

Kiev reached its zenith in the years after 1019, under the rule of Grand Duke Jaroslav the Wise, one of Vladimir's younger sons. Jaroslav extended Kiev's upper town, surrounding it with a wall some 3.5km (2 miles) long and 16m (50ft) wide. There were three monumental entrances to 'Jaroslav Town': the Polish, Jewish and Golden Gates. At its centre stood the splendid Cathedral of St Sophia, which was commissioned by Jaroslav; its interior was adorned with precious mosaics, frescoes, icons and columns topped with marble capitals. The cathedral library contained almost 1000 volumes. Jaroslav, a highly cultured man, hoped to make Kiev a rival to Constantinople and he worked an extraordinary transformation.

Jaroslav won respect for Kiev internationally, cultivating regular diplomatic relations not just with the Byzantine Empire but with the rulers of Scandinavia, the German Empire, Poland, Bohemia, Hungary and France. To secure his southern frontier, Jaroslav built a line of fortified settlements as a barrier against the nomadic tribes of the steppe. A mark of the popularity and respect that Jaroslav commanded at home is shown by some contemporary graffiti in St Sophia's Cathedral mourning 'the death of our Zar on February 20, 1054'.

Apostle of the Slavs
Cyril, or Kyrill (right), together with his brother Methodios, developed the Glagolitic script, the first form of what has come to be known as 'Cyrillic' writing, which was widely employed in the Kingdom of Kiev.

Cluny – fount of monastic reform

At the beginning of the 10th century, the Benedictine Abbey at Cluny in France became the centre of a reform movement that would sweep the whole of Europe.

Father of monasticism
Ora et labora – 'pray and work' – was the essence of the rule of St Benedict of Nursia and the founding principle of monasticism. Here, he is shown handing over his book of rules to his followers. On joining a community, a monk took a vow of poverty, chastity and obedience to his abbot.

Duke William I of Aquitaine was known as William the Pious and fully deserved his nickname, but this did not blind him to the failings of the clergy. On the contrary, the Duke felt that far from being directed to the business of prayer and the work of God, too many monasteries had become the possessions of important churchmen or temporal rulers. Accordingly, in 910, William founded a new abbey at Cluny in western Frankish Burgundy. Here, free from worldly interference, the monks would be able to re-dedicate themselves to the ideals of St Benedict of Nursia who, in the 6th century, had set down the Benedictine Rule, the template for monastic life ever since. Benedict envisaged that monks would follow a life of quiet contemplation, moulded by useful work and peaceful prayer. His community at Monte Cassino was an inspiration to the Christian world.

Soon after his death, his monks left their monastery and set out to spread the Benedictine way all over Europe. Wherever they went, they established new monasteries, schools and libraries: Western civilisation is forever in their debt for their contributions to the arts and sciences. But their place in mainstream medieval culture inevitably involved a conflict of interest – what had become of the commitment to an inward, spiritual life? Concern had been growing for some time: almost a century before William's initiative, the Carolingian Emperor, Louis the Pious, had sought to reform the monasteries and ensure strict enforcement of the Benedictine Rule.

A crisis in monasticism

Louis's intervention had come at the wrong time. Civil wars had weakened the once mighty Carolingian Empire to such an extent that in 843 it had to be divided. Simultaneously, from north and south, the Normans and the Saracens attacked. The very existence of the monasteries was threatened. Abbeys were burned and plundered; monks murdered or driven away. The monasteries' worldly strength turned out to be their salvation. It was not prayer and contemplation but institutional resilience that saw them rising again. Could they really be blamed for having favoured structures over spirituality, work and discipline over inward exploration?

When peace returned, there was a sense that the monastic system had been vindicated, though the problems that had worried Louis the Pious still remained. Concern grew through the decades, though, and by around 900 many monks themselves were conscious of just how far they had departed from the Benedict's original intentions.

Life in the newly founded abbey of Cluny was actually stricter than Benedict's regime: the monks lived largely in silence and ate only the plainest fare. Days of prayer and fasting were rigorously observed and the highest moral principles adhered to – but young men took to this austere code with enthusiasm, even joy. Physical work, a key component in Benedict's rule, was seen at Cluny as a potential distraction: where possible, it was to be carried out by servants and lay brothers. The duty of the monks was to praise God day and night and to offer prayers for the souls of all humanity.

The spread of monastic reform

Whenever worldly rulers wanted to reform an old monastery, or found a new one, they contacted Cluny for help. Monks who were sent out as advisers in this way carried the Cluniac message far and wide: soon several hundred reformed monasteries were answerable directly to the Abbot of Cluny. The result was a family of monasteries and congregations all offering mutual support, but also keeping an eye on one another to prevent backsliding. Reforming zeal spread across the whole of Europe.

The influence of Cluny was not restricted to the monasteries. Cluny had set new standards, shaking up the complacent and shaming the corrupt. Many bishops and cardinals (even several popes) started their careers at Cluny: the monastery's influence touched every aspect of religious life. The Cluniac reforms affected even temporal rulers like Henry III and moulded the life and thought of the Middle Ages.

In the meantime, Cluny itself was losing sight of its founding ideals, perhaps understandable given the fame it had now

Golden treasures
Among the Benedictines were many artists and craftsmen, who made precious decorations for their churches and abbeys, such as this jewel-encrusted statue of Saint Faith.

achieved. Just a small farmyard and chapel when founded by William the Pious, the Abbey of Cluny was now the largest and most splendid monastery in the whole of Europe, grown fat on praise and donations from its admirers. The Abbey owned extensive estates, its monks celebrated lavish masses in a splendid church, and still the believers streamed in, still their gifts swelled Cluny's coffers. In 1077, Pope Gregory VII declared at the Council of Rome: 'Of all the abbeys north of the Alps, Cluny occupies the first position.'

True enough, but as Christianity's founder had said: 'The first shall be last, and the last shall be first.' Ideals of poverty and asceticism could be no more than pretence amidst such wealth. Much the

The Abbey of Cluny
Cluny experienced its most successful period in the late 11th century under Abbot Hugo. The Abbey complex had to be extended as the number of monks grew from 60 to 300.

The monks came together twice daily in the refectory, where they ate in silence.

Every day, after early mass, the monks assembled in the chapter hall, to discuss any concerns of the Abbey community.

The Romanesque chapel at Cluny was for centuries the world's largest church. Its many decorations included beautiful frescoes.

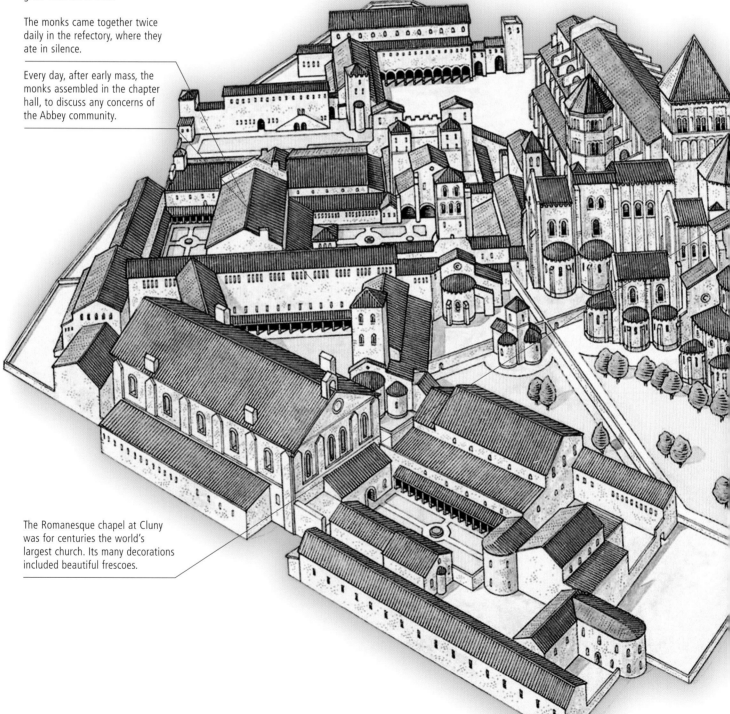

same was happening at other reformed monasteries, such as Molesme in Burgundy. Within 20 years of its founding in 1075, Molesme had grown into a wealthy abbey with more than 30 successful subsidiary foundations. Abbot Robert saw no other option but a radical new beginning, in order to reassert adherence to strict Benedictine rules.

New orders

In 1098, Robert led the foundation of a new monastery in the wilderness of Citeaux. This marked the beginning of the Cistercian order. Though the Pope ordered Robert to return to Molesme, his brothers would succeed in building the independent monastery of which he had dreamt. However, it would take the energy of the Abbot, St Stephen, and the vision of a pious young nobleman destined to be one of the great luminaries of the medieval Church to achieve it.

Bernard, a son of Tecelin, Lord of Fontaines, and his wife Aleth of Montbard, turned up at Molesme one day with 30 of his friends, seeking admittance to the community. Three years later, in 1115, Abbot Stephen sent Bernard with a group of monks to found a new monastery at Clairvaux, about 150km (95 miles) away. Prayer and scripture study were to take precedence in the daily schedule here, but emphasis was also laid on useful toil. With new buildings to be constructed and lands to be cleared for cultivation, there was no question of anyone avoiding physical work. So heroic was the effort involved that it nearly killed Bernard, weakened as he was by the asceticism of his regime.

There would be no let-up in the labour: all donations and endowments given to the community were directed into the purchase of more land. A clear Cistercian style was emerging: mass was celebrated with extreme simplicity; Cistercian architecture was austere. From 1118, Bernard of Clairvaux was the leader of the Cistercian order, viewed not just with admiration but affection by his followers. He wrote hymns of touching depth and sincerity, composed inspiring sermons and travelled throughout Europe to speak before popes and kings. It was an impassioned speech by Bernard which sparked off the Second Crusade of 1147–9; its disastrous failure would come back to haunt him.

Over time, the example of Clairvaux Abbey in turn began to pale. Farming and administration were taking up more time than prayer and contemplation, and not much was left of the ideal of poverty. A new sort of Christian community now arose: the Franciscans and Dominicans. These orders outlawed all possessions. Their monks – or friars, as they were called – lived by begging and from charitable donations. This was a shockingly radical requirement, but it caught the Christian imagination. Young men of talent and commitment flocked to join, and eventually famous scholars came from their ranks – like Albertus Magnus and Thomas Aquinas, who would have a profound influence on the development and history of Christian spirituality.

The Norman kingdom in Italy

Oriental and European influences came together under Norman rule to create a flourishing hybrid culture in Sicily.

Towards the year 1000, southern Italy was spiralling into instability – a situation soon to be exploited by the battle-ready knight-adventurers known as the Normans. The region had for some time been divided up into different spheres of influence, whose rulers may have squabbled and sparred with one another, but seemed to take little interest in the running of their realms. Benevento, Capua and Salerno were principalities of Lombardy, far to the north; Apulia and Calabria were under Byzantine sovereignty; a few smaller states, including Naples and Amalfi, were independent. Life here felt precarious: pirate raids were frequent. With the ruling powers so remote, there was little sense of authority or order; rather, there was a feeling that this was a land up for grabs.

It was potentially a prosperous country, however, and this was noticed by the large numbers of pilgrims from the Duchy of Normandy as they passed through on their way to the ports from which they would set sail for the Holy Land. In 1016, a group of Norman pilgrims, reaching Salerno, were asked to help to defend it against an Arab attack. They did so and were richly rewarded.

Composite of cultures
Built by King Roger II, the Cathedral in Cefalú shows the full cultural diversity of Norman Sicily. The towers are reminiscent of minarets, the main building is in the Romanesque style, and the mosaics inside are Byzantine in inspiration.

On their return to northern France, news rapidly spread of this land of milk and honey, where the prospects were bright for a young man skilled in arms. Soon, warlike bands of landless or impoverished noblemen were leaving Normandy for this 'El Dorado', hoping to be hired as mercenaries and ultimately to make their fortunes. The virtual anarchy that they found in Italy suited such adventurers down to the ground: they would fight for anyone who promised them a generous portion of the spoils of war.

By about 1030, some of them had succeeded in creating a small Norman area of rule in Aversa near Naples. But their great opportunity came in 1037, when a large number of Normans enlisted with a Byzantine force sent to dislodge the Arabs from Sicily. The Arabs had kept a firm hold on the island since the middle of the 9th century and had made its capital, Palermo, one of the grandest cities of the Mediterranean. Mosques dotted the town and people from many countries thronged the streets. Just as they had in Spain, the Arabs had also enhanced an

On his high horse
Roger I, King of Sicily, is depicted on this coin as a typical Norman knight with a long, triangular shield and conical helmet.

already fertile country with a sophisticated irrigation system and had introduced a similar range of new crops – cotton, sugar cane and mulberry trees (to feed silk-worms for silk production). Initially successful, the invasion faltered when the Byzantine general George Maniakis upset his Norman mercenaries, who withdrew to the mainland; it collapsed altogether when the Emperor summoned him home.

Fit for a king
This ivory-inlaid and painted oak casket is from Palermo at the time of Norman rule in Sicily.

The Normans were profoundly impressed by what they had seen in Sicily, and before long they were back on their own account. Among them was a knight called William 'Iron Arm', who in 1024 had gained the title of Count of Apulia. He was soon joined by his younger half-brother, Robert Guiscard 'the Resourceful', who, it was said, would shrink from no crime or dishonour. With the immense political skills for which he became notorious, Robert managed to secure Pope Nicholas II's recognition of his conquests. His Holiness proclaimed him Duke of Apulia, Calabria and of Sicily – even though the last of these had not yet been conquered.

The conquest of Sicily

His new title and friendship with the Pope gave Robert an advantage over other Norman warlords in the race for the wealth of southern Italy. He set about seizing all the Byzantine possessions in the region. Bari fell in 1071 after a three-year siege, bringing Byzantine rule in Italy to an end, but still Robert's lust for power was not satisfied. 'The Terror of the World', as he was called on his tomb, crossed the Adriatic and attacked the Byzantine Empire through the Balkans.

Meanwhile, with his younger brother Roger, he had launched a Norman

invasion of Sicily: they took Messina in 1060. The conquest of the whole island would take many years, but the brothers pursued domination in what amounted to a war of attrition.

By 1088, Roger I was Lord of Sicily. Despite the bitter resistance they had met with, the Normans were accepted readily enough once they were firmly in power. It helped that they had taken care not to alienate the island's Arab-Greek population. The Arabs and Jews had to pay special taxes, but apart from that were left alone and even allowed to make many of their own laws. Beyond a desire for power and wealth, Roger had no real agenda: so the existing system of administration and land-ownership was left intact.

Absolute rule

In fact, Roger showed more respect for the ways of his new subjects than he did for the feelings of his fellow-Normans, who looked askance at his adoption of Byzantine ceremonies and court protocol. Norman rulers had traditionally been first among equals, but Roger's power was now absolute. When he died in 1112 his son, Roger II, picked up where his father had left off.

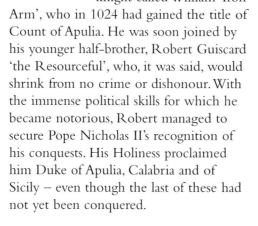

By Norman standards, Roger II was remarkably well-educated; he spoke Greek and Arabic, among other languages. He was extremely intelligent and energetic: it was said that he 'could achieve more while asleep than others could awake', and the Arab influences among which he had grown up were reflected in his rule. His court included a harem, his chief minister had the resounding title 'Emir of Emirs', and Roger gave himself an oriental potentate's grand airs. Underneath the show, however, he was as down-to-earth, tough and ambitious as any other Norman leader. Though ruling over only Sicily and Calabria to begin with, he soon extended his power over the whole of southern Italy and even into North Africa. On Christmas Day, 1130, Pope Anaclete II crowned him King of Sicily in the Cathedral of Palermo. To this title Roger swaggeringly added 'King of Africa'.

Multicultural Sicily

This Norman kingdom was now one of the richest and most powerful states in Europe. Its wealth was based on its trade in grain and on the production of luxury goods, such as silk. Its fleet, crewed mainly by Greeks, ensured security and affluence; both Arabs and Normans served in the land army.

Palermo, with its numerous palaces, was the administrative centre of the kingdom and a truly multicultural capital. Roger II admired learning and expertise wherever he found it: Greeks and Muslims worked as administrators, physicians and scientists, and he even had a water clock made for him by an Arab craftsman. Roger was fascinated by the sciences, especially geography and astronomy. The renowned

Arab geographer, Al Idrisi, was resident at his court, where he compiled the *al-Kitab al-Rujari*, or 'Roger's Book'. With over 70 chapters and 71 maps, this was a summation of everything known at that time about the geography of the world, including distances, zones of the Earth and a great deal more.

Norman Sicily was now a cultural crucible mixing Arab, Byzantine-Greek and western European-Latin influences. This was reflected in the architecture and art of the period, as can still be seen in buildings such as Palermo's church of San Giovanni degli Eremiti. Commissioned by Roger II, this church with its five red domes at once resembles a Christian church and Muslim mosque.

Historically and culturally, the Norman kingdom of Sicily was a remarkable phenomenon, but it was also a fleeting one. Roger died in 1154 and, within less than half a century, the line of Sicily's Norman dynasty was over and Germany's Hohenstaufen kings reigned in their place.

A royal mantle
The Arabic influence on the culture of Roger II's Norman Palermo is clearly displayed in his gold-embroidered coronation cloak: in the centre is the Tree of Life, a palm, flanked by oriental motifs of battling animals.

The Normans conquer England

After William the Conqueror's successful invasion, the Normans ruled over England for almost a century. The changes they brought to the language, law and land-use have influenced English society ever since.

Battle tactics
Norman cavalry and archers attack the English wall of shields in this scene from the Bayeux tapestry. Dead and dying men lie strewn about the field.

When William, Duke of Normandy, set sail across the English Channel in September 1066, he had with him an invasion force of 7000 men, 3000 horses and tons of supplies. It was the end of many years of bitter frustation. At last he was to fight for what he considered was rightfully his: the English crown.

It was a long and roundabout journey that had brought him here. Two centuries earlier his Norman ancestors had been Norsemen, better known as Vikings, spreading terror down the coasts of western Europe. Many had settled in northwestern France where, in 911, their right to stay had been agreed by Charles III, 'the Naïve', who signed a treaty with the Norman Duke Rollo, acknowledging the integrity of Normandy. In return, France's new citizens pledged loyalty to the King as their feudal overlord and converted to Christianity. As time passed, the Duchy of Normandy became a powerful force in France.

William was only seven years old when his father, Robert I, died in 1035. Despite being Robert's only son, he was not his lawful heir – Herleve, his mother, had been the daughter of a tanner, and William 'the Bastard' would always carry the stigma of his illegitimate birth.

Inevitably, his claim to rule had been challenged, but with the support of his royal feudal lord, King Henry I, William was ultimately able to emerge as victor in the battle for succession in Normandy. Soon he went on to conquer the county of Maine as well as Brittany, and made himself the most powerful prince in northern France. But now he wanted to be King of England, too.

Rival claims to England's crown

Edward the Confessor, who came to the throne in England in 1042, was related to the Norman ducal family on his mother's side. Edward was childless and had declared William his successor as early as 1051. Others disagreed – King Harald Hardrada of Norway for one, who stated his intention of resuming Scandinavian rule over England. And Harold Godwinson, the Anglo-Saxon Earl of

Effective protection
William had three horses killed under him in the course of the Battle of Hastings, but thanks to his chain mail he himself came through unscathed.

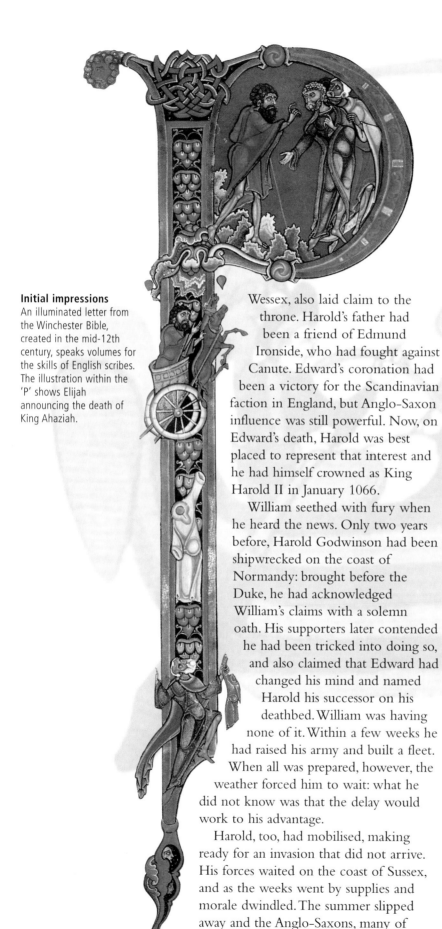

Initial impressions
An illuminated letter from the Winchester Bible, created in the mid-12th century, speaks volumes for the skills of English scribes. The illustration within the 'P' shows Elijah announcing the death of King Ahaziah.

Wessex, also laid claim to the throne. Harold's father had been a friend of Edmund Ironside, who had fought against Canute. Edward's coronation had been a victory for the Scandinavian faction in England, but Anglo-Saxon influence was still powerful. Now, on Edward's death, Harold was best placed to represent that interest and he had himself crowned as King Harold II in January 1066.

William seethed with fury when he heard the news. Only two years before, Harold Godwinson had been shipwrecked on the coast of Normandy: brought before the Duke, he had acknowledged William's claims with a solemn oath. His supporters later contended he had been tricked into doing so, and also claimed that Edward had changed his mind and named Harold his successor on his deathbed. William was having none of it. Within a few weeks he had raised his army and built a fleet. When all was prepared, however, the weather forced him to wait: what he did not know was that the delay would work to his advantage.

Harold, too, had mobilised, making ready for an invasion that did not arrive. His forces waited on the coast of Sussex, and as the weeks went by supplies and morale dwindled. The summer slipped away and the Anglo-Saxons, many of them farmers, fretted to think of the harvest going ungathered in their fields. Harold had no choice but to stand down his army and return to London – only to hear alarming news from Yorkshire, 350km (220 miles) to the north: King Harald Hardrada of Norway had landed near Scarborough with a huge army, laid waste to the surrounding area and was now marching on the city of York. Harold urgently recalled his men and set off to repel the invaders. On September 25, 1066, the two armies met at Stamford Bridge. Harald Hardrada was killed and his leaderless troops took flight.

It was a remarkable victory, but the Anglo-Saxons could not celebrate for long. Just three days later William and his invasion force finally landed at Pevensey on the Sussex coast. He met with no resistance – only a few fishermen had seen the enemy fleet arrive in the dawn light. Even so, the early omens did not seem promising. Leaping ashore at the head of his force, William is said to have stumbled as he landed. Legend has it that he pulled himself upright clutching a fistful of pebbles and reassured his disconcerted men by crying out: 'See, already I hold England in my hand!'

The battle of Hastings

Harold had no alternative but to march south with his exhausted soldiers as swiftly as possible to meet William and his army head-on. Just a fortnight later, on October 13, they were in Sussex, about 10km (6 miles) inland from Hastings, camped on Sentlach Ridge. It was the perfect position, straddling the northward route to London and commanding the valley floor. Here, Harold would arrange his shield wall, which William's Normans would have to attack uphill, across boggy ground.

Battle was joined on October 14, and for most of the day the outcome seemed evenly poised. William's men, though fresh, were at a disadvantage on the terrain. Harold's choice of ground, as he had hoped, seemed to have neutralised

William's greatest asset, his heavy cavalry. Again and again the Normans charged the Saxon shield wall, but were beaten back each time. Finally William saw that he was wasting his strength, so he ordered his men to pretend to flee. The English threw caution to the winds and pursued them down the slope. Hardly had the Normans reached level ground than they turned abruptly and did battle anew – this time on much more favourable ground.

William's cavalry now came into its own: protected by chain mail tunics that came down to their knees, they could range almost at will, cutting down the English infantry. Even so, the fight went on until, in late afternoon, King Harold was killed – struck in the eye, tradition has it, by a Norman arrow. The Anglo-Saxons had fought bravely, but now they broke and ran: William's invasion had acquired unstoppable momentum.

Within a week, William had taken the vital south coast ports, so that supplies and reinforcements from Normandy could be safely landed. On Christmas Day he had himself crowned in Westminster Abbey.

He was now King William I, but could not yet claim to be master of all England: it took a further five years to subjugate the country as a whole. In many places, Yorkshire in particular, the Normans met with bitter resistance. And not until 1072 did William secure his northern border

with a war against Scotland. Even then, he could not afford to rest on his laurels. The Danes were threatening England all over again while, back home in Normandy, his absence had bred unrest and uprisings flared.

The Domesday Book

William was able to secure his territories, but the military campaigns involved were very costly. So he decided to secure his finances with a fundamental reform of taxes. To make a new system effective, he realised, he would first need to know exactly what was in his lands, so he ordered a comprehensive registry of land ownership to be made, with a complete inventory of the country's wealth. In 1086 he dispatched officials to every corner of his kingdom to ascertain which village belonged

---

TIME WITNESS

The Bayeux tapestry

This famous tapestry has the life and energy of a medieval cartoon strip. It sets out the story of the Norman invasion of England in vivid pictorial scenes embroidered on linen with remarkable skill. Beginning with Edward the Confessor's promise to proclaim Duke William his successor, the narrative reaches its climax in the events of the Battle of Hastings. It ends with the flight of the English before William's troops.

The Norman sympathies expressed in the tapestry are

never in any doubt, but it is unclear who commissioned the work: it may have been William the Conqueror himself, but it is perhaps more likely to have been his half-brother Odo, Bishop of Bayeux, for whose cathedral the tapestry was destined.

More than 70m (230ft) long and about 50cm (20 inches) deep, the tapestry was created around 1070, probably in southern England – perhaps in Canterbury. Unknown stitchers worked on it for about ten

years, among them maybe even William's wife.

The tapestry was regarded as a treasure in its own time: it appears to have been displayed only on special occasions. More usually it was kept carefully rolled up, safely away from dust and sunlight, so it survived for centuries with little damage and its colours have hardly lost any of their original brilliance. The tapestry can be viewed by modern visitors in a special museum in Bayeux, Normandy.

Vivid chronicle
This scene from the Bayeux tapestry shows a mother and child fleeing their home as the Normans destroy their village. The ships used in the invasion (background) were a reminder of the Normans' Viking ancestry.

to which lord, and to assess the value of every item. 'Not one ox nor one cow nor one pig' were to be missed, and though there were some significant gaps, most of the country was surveyed in impressive detail. The figures were carefully recorded, enabling William's clerks to calculate just how much he could raise in taxes and how many men could be conscripted for military service.

Succession struggle
This medieval book illustration shows Stephen of Blois with a pet falcon. Stephen became King when Norman nobles refused to accept his cousin Mathilda as Henry I's rightful successor. The two cousins wrangled over the crown for years. Stephen won, but only by conceding the succession to Mathilda's offspring.

Not surprisingly, there was widespread resentment of William's information-gathering, and before long the records produced came to be known as the Domesday Book, named for the Last Day at which the souls of all would be weighed in judgment. There was indeed something awesome about the scope, speed and detail of the survey – perhaps the greatest administrative feat of the Middle Ages. It was certainly a triumph of bureaucratic efficiency, and showed just how quickly and completely William I had replaced the old Anglo-Saxon order with the Norman system.

Since the conquest, many of William's soldiers had settled in England and been rewarded with estates confiscated from the old Anglo-Saxon nobility. Before long,

only about 8 per cent of the land remained in Anglo-Saxon hands. In a country of roughly 1.5 million Anglo-Saxons, about 10,000 Normans represented a very small but powerful and privileged minority. The Normans had brought with them the continental-style feudal system, in which local lords held their lands from the King, to whom they owed military service in return.

William probably did not live to see the completion of the Domesday Book. In 1087, further uprisings in Normandy forced him to return to his homeland to reassert his authority. While there, he had a riding accident and died a few weeks later of his injuries. He left Normandy to his oldest son, Robert Curthose, while his second-born son, William Rufus, became King of England.

A lasting legacy

The Anglo-Saxons may have groaned under the financial burdens that William laid upon them, but there would be many positive consequences of Norman rule. The English language, for instance, was profoundly enriched by the influence of French, the tongue spoken by the new aristocracy. French became the language of culture, education and government, and to this day, much legal terminology is French in origin; so too are many everyday words like 'table' and 'chair'. By the time French ceased to be the language of officialdom three centuries later, English vocabulary and grammar had evolved irrevocably. A Latinate-French element now leavened the Germanic-based Anglo-Saxon to produce a rich, flexible and subtle modern language.

There were more visible signs of the Norman presence, too: William's architects set new standards in building in England. His most famous monument was the White Tower of the Tower of London, built in 1078. It was the largest stone-built secular building since Roman times. Massive walls and a deep ditch provided defences for the Tower, which was continually extended until it reached its present form in the 14th century.

The female line

Norman rule in England lasted barely 100 years. William Rufus died mysteriously in 1100, killed by an arrow while hunting in the New Forest. He was succeeded by his younger brother, King Henry I. A highly competent ruler, Henry brought Normandy back under the direct rule of the English crown. Like his conquering father, Henry was determined to make himself master in his kingdom. He worked hard to establish an effective centralised government administration and it was he who, in about 1118, set up a central treasury to take overall charge of the finances of the state.

But the orderly realm that Henry had built came close to falling apart after his death in 1135. With no male heir, he had declared his daughter, the Empress Mathilda, as his successor. She was the widow of the Ottonian Emperor, Henry V; her father made his nobles swear to accept her rule.

There was no precedent for a woman ruler, however, which left Mathilda's position vulnerable. She then wed Geoffrey of Anjou, an enemy of the Normans, which made matters worse. Her cousin, Stephen of Blois, claimed that he should be England's King. Many among the nobility agreed and he was crowned.

A period known as 'The Anarchy' ensued. It stopped just short of civil war, but unrest smouldered on for almost 20 years. Though he was able to see out his reign, Stephen was forced to concede that Mathilda's descendants from her second marriage would inherit his crown. Geoffrey of Anjou had a habit of always wearing a decorative sprig of broom (*genista*) on his helmet, from which came his familiar nickname, 'Plantagenet'. When Stephen died in 1154, it was Henry II, Geoffrey and Mathilda's eldest son, who ascended the throne and founded the house of Anjou-Plantagenet.

From palace to prison
William I built London's White Tower as his personal fortified palace. In time it became a prison for the nation's traitors.

Pope and King in conflict

Relations between Europe's temporal and spiritual rulers broke down in the so-called 'Investiture Contest'. In dispute was the question of who held the authority to appoint bishops.

Since the time of Otto I, Germany's rulers had allied themselves closely with the Church in order to control a wayward aristocracy. The Church had benefited in its turn: under this *Reichskirchensystem*, it had a real stake in the power and prosperity of the Empire.

By the 11th century, however, times were changing, the system was coming in for increasing criticism, and stresses and strains were beginning to sour the relationship. Henry III's interventions in the politics of the papacy had ruffled feathers in Rome and also affronted the growing numbers of Christians who, swept up in the spiritual revival unleashed by the Cluniac reforms, felt that religion and politics should be strictly separate spheres.

In 1056, Henry IV became Emperor. He was determined to strengthen the role of the monarchy: the issue he chose was the matter of Church appointments. The precedent established under the *Reichskirchensystem* was for the King to appoint his own candidate by giving him the spiritual symbols of the ring, a sign of marriage with the Church, and the crozier as a sign of his duties as shepherd. The King thus simultaneously bestowed on a bishop his spiritual office and the secular powers which he would exercise in the name of the King. Henry considered he was within his rights to appoint his own bishops and abbots, but this was not the best time to be insisting on that privilege.

A reformist movement within the Church was demanding the 'free election' of church officials by church members: the bishop by his clergy, the abbot by his monks, the Pope by the College of Cardinals. In 1059, a Roman synod laid this system down as Church policy – a confrontation was inevitable.

One of Henry's most vociferous critics among the reformers was a monk named Hildebrand, who ascended St Peter's throne as Pope Gregory VII in 1073. As uncompromising and self-confident as Henry, two years after his election Gregory proclaimed his *Dictatus papae*, in which he put forward his view of the papacy in 27 principles that boiled down to just one thing: the precedence of spiritual over secular power. Gregory scornfully rejected the great legitimising claim of the German emperors – the idea that they enjoyed divine sanction for their power. He proclaimed that secular rulers were subordinate in the eyes of God and insisted that the Pope even had the right to depose them if so minded. Charging Henry with disobedience, he threatened him with excommunication – expulsion from the community of the Church.

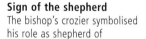

Sign of the shepherd
The bishop's crozier symbolised his role as shepherd of his Christian flock.

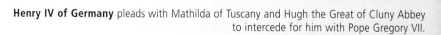

Henry IV of Germany pleads with Mathilda of Tuscany and Hugh the Great of Cluny Abbey to intercede for him with Pope Gregory VII.

Personal humiliation or political gambit?

Henry IV's penitential journey to beg absolution from Pope Gregory VII at Canossa, stronghold of Mathilda of Tuscany, sent shockwaves through the whole of Europe. Such humiliation for a King chosen by God was unimaginable: his degradation went to the core of the medieval psyche.

In more prosaic terms, too, there was a political price to be paid: even a military defeat could hardly have been more damaging. That Henry should abase himself so abjectly before the Pope seemed an igmonious surrender for one who had been so adamant in his stance of absolute power.

Yet was this reverse really so desperate for Henry? Contemporary chroniclers were in no doubt, but recent historians have begun to see an alternative interpretation. They point to the tactical subtlety of Henry's actions, which were timely in preventing a coalition between the various malcontents around him at home. It was also a dramatic public assertion of piety in a Christian world.

In the short-term, at least, Henry's overt submission achieved his aim: the Pope's absolution took the political pressure off him at home, and bought him valuable time.

The longer-term consequences are less clear: arguably, it dented the sacral aura of the King and gave the impression that he ruled only with the Holy Father's blessing. In the end, however, it was his own son Henry V, not the Pope, who forced him to stand down from his throne.

Flight from Rome
This book illustration from the 12th-century chronicle of Otto of Freising shows Henry IV and his antipope, Clement III, banishing Pope Gregory VII from Rome. Gregory died in Salerno in 1085.

Mutual depositions

Unconcerned by this outburst, Henry did what his predecessors would have done: he called together his bishops for a synod in the town of Worms. They did what he expected them to do by deposing the Pope and his leading cardinals. Problem solved – or so Henry hoped. Gregory's response was to depose Henry in return. He absolved 'all Christians from the bond of the oath of allegiance they had made' to Henry, then carried through his threat of excommunication. From a modern perspective, Gregory's proclamation was little more than bluster: he could hardly eject Henry from his throne. But in the Middle Ages, the Pope's denunciation left Europe genuinely awestruck.

An outcast among Christians, Henry found his authority seeping steadily away. His noblemen flexed their muscles, and rival claimants jostled for position: his very throne was under threat. Finally, he accepted that he would have to sue for peace with Gregory, who saw no reason to make it easy for him. So it was that for three whole days and nights, in the icy cold of January 1077, Henry waited barefoot in the snow outside the Tuscan castle of Canossa in the rough shirt of a penitent, seeking the Pope's absolution.

Two popes

Conflict with the Church had severe consequences for the King, whose leading nobles now appointed Rudolf of Rheinfelden as a rival king. This plunged the Empire into civil conflict, worsened by Gregory's second excommunication of Henry and recognition of Rudolf. Henry responded by declaring Gregory deposed again and had his own 'antipope', Clement III, proclaimed.

The pressure on Henry eased when he killed Rudolf in battle and hacked off his right hand. This was regarded as a potent omen, given that it was the hand with which Rudolf had once sworn his oath of

allegiance to the King. His authority thus renewed Henry IV marched to Rome, where he enthroned Pope Clement III, who promptly crowned Henry as Emperor. The Norman Robert Guiscard came to Gregory's military aid and they escaped from the city, but the dispute was set to smoulder on. Two popes – Victor III and Urban II – would be elected outside Rome, while the 'antipope' Clement occupied the papal seat.

In 1105, Henry IV was forced to abdicate by his son, Henry V. He had the backing of a new pope, Paschal II, who regained Rome after Clement's death. If anything, however, Paschal was to find Henry V more intractable than his father. A compromise was finally reached at the Concordat of Worms in 1122, where it was agreed that priests and monarchs would keep to their own spheres. Kings could no longer install their own bishops or abbots, who instead would be invested by the Church in the presence of a royal ambassador. The King kept the right to be consulted, but could not impose his will.

Victory for the Church

Though both sides had made concessions, this was clearly a victory for the Church: after 50 years of struggle, royal power had been radically curtailed. But it had also clipped the wings of reforming zealots within the Church who had harboured hopes of a Christian theocracy under papal rule. The Church and the feudal monarchy were the two most powerful institutions in medieval Europe, and competition between them was an inescapable feature of medieval life. There would be further flare-ups in the centuries to come but, for the moment, an accommodation had been reached.

An exalted seat
This splendid bishop's throne stands in the cathedral at Canossa. Pope Gregory VII believed the Church, not kings, should appoint bishops. He set out his views of the papacy and its powers in his *Dictus Papae* (extract in background, above).

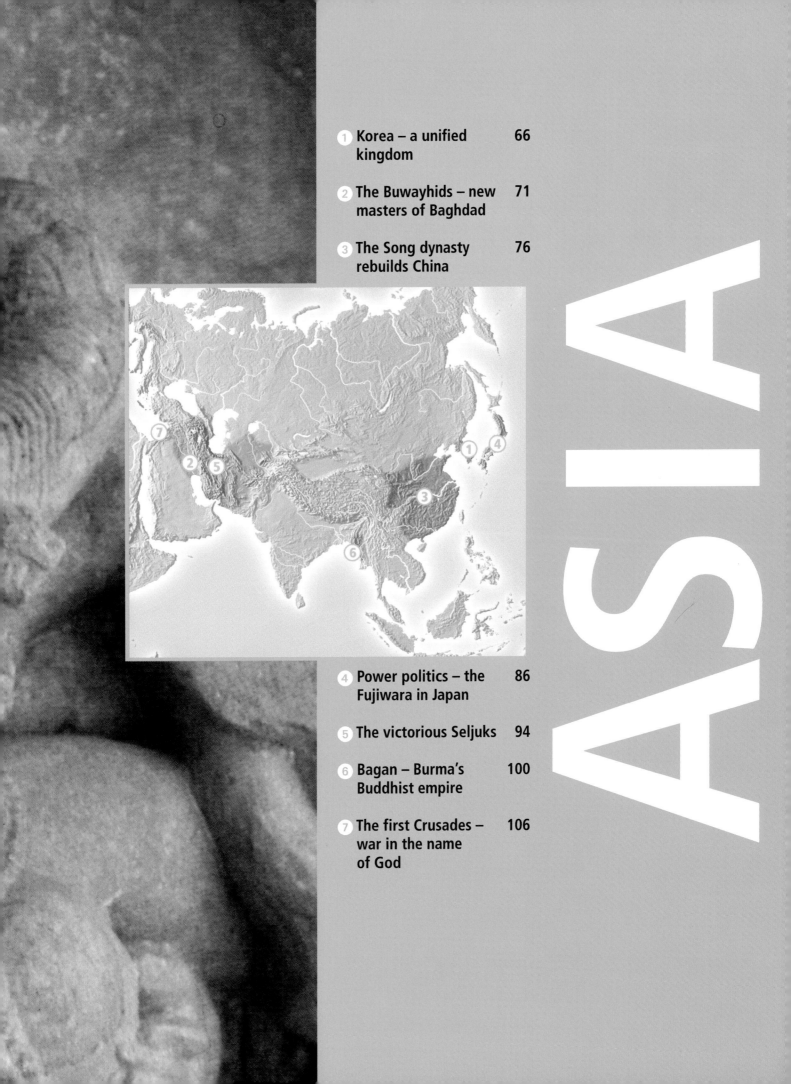

1 Korea – a unified   66
   kingdom

2 The Buwayhids – new   71
   masters of Baghdad

3 The Song dynasty   76
   rebuilds China

4 Power politics – the   86
   Fujiwara in Japan

5 The victorious Seljuks   94

6 Bagan – Burma's   100
   Buddhist empire

7 The first Crusades –   106
   war in the name
   of God

ASIA

Korea – a unified kingdom

The decline of the Great Silla Kingdom saw Korea disintegrate into anarchy. The country was unified once again by warlord Wang Kon, who established the Koryo dynasty and ushered in two centuries of prosperity and peace.

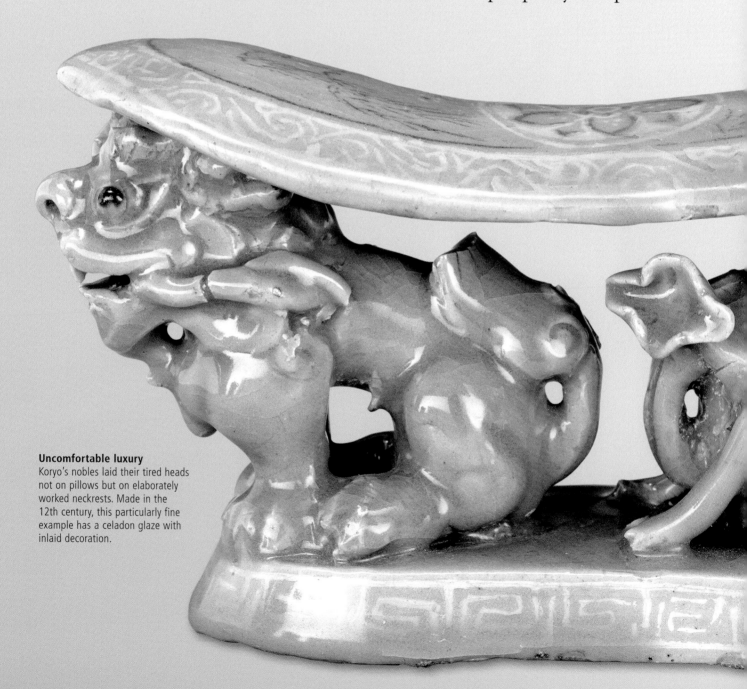

Uncomfortable luxury
Koryo's nobles laid their tired heads not on pillows but on elaborately worked neckrests. Made in the 12th century, this particularly fine example has a celadon glaze with inlaid decoration.

The Great Silla Kingdom had reached its zenith in Korea during the 7th and 8th centuries. By the beginning of the 9th century, however, this cultural and economic golden age was over and the country had broken up once more into three smaller states, corresponding roughly with the three kingdoms of Korea's earlier history: Silla in the southeast, Paekche in the southwest and Koguryo in the north. The re-emergence of the three kingdoms did little to halt the descent into chaos and confusion. In-fighting gripped the ruling families, unrest was widespread among the peasants and the country was carved up into fiefdoms by local warlords. Among these was Wang Kon, a man of high ambition born into a leading clan of Songdo (modern Kaesong, in North Korea).

In 918, Wang Kon declared himself King of Koguryo: the name would be contracted to 'Koryo', which eventually gave the country its modern name of Korea. Under Wang Kon, Koguryo came to control the whole peninsula. Wang was treading in the footsteps of King Mumnu, creator of the Great Silla Kingdom and an enormously charismatic figure. Despite the instability which had brought down his unified kingdom, Mumnu's memory was still revered and he was regarded as the protector of Korea. Legend had it that on his death he had been transformed into a dragon, to watch over his country in perpetuity – although so far that protection seemed to have left a lot to be desired.

By 935, Wang Kon had taken both Paekche and Silla; by its meek surrender Silla saved its magnificent capital, Kyongju, from destruction. Its status was about to fade, however: Wang Kon wanted to base himself where he felt most secure, and made his hometown of Kaesong his capital. He poured vast resources into enlarging and improving Kaesong, consulting special experts versed in the ancient Chinese art of feng shui. He wished to find the most propitious site for a new royal palace that he hoped would announce the power and prestige of his new kingdom to the world.

An Eastern approach to architecture

As elsewhere in eastern Asia, the underlying intention of architecture in Korea was to find a form that would reflect the harmony of the Universe. Koreans did not view their buildings as self-contained structures, imposed on their surroundings, but as elements in the more complex overall scene.

Sheer elegance
Korean ceramics were justly famed. Artisans were under pressure to find new styles and refinements to delight their aristocratic consumers. This celadon glazed vase is from the 13th century.

Serene sculpture
In its original conception, Buddhism had no gods. In popular belief, however, a large collection of bodhisattvas or 'enlightened beings' emerged, who were worshipped almost like deities. This 10th-century marble bodhisattva was from the Hansong-sa temple

It was essential that the built environment should resonate with Nature. Water courses and protective hills or mountains were considered especially important – both were believed to help to ensure good fortune. Once an appropriate site was identified, architects would take account of the existing landscape in their designs, including such apparently minor features as rocks and trees. This approach contrasts starkly with the Western way of imposing man-made forms on nature – and even with the Japanese practice of fashioning natural landscapes into perfect idealised gardens.

Covering more than 100 hectares (250 acres), the gigantic palace complex of Kaesong was built under the protection of a nearby chain of hills. At its centre stood two vast, colourfully decorated pavilions in which royal audiences and religious ceremonies could be held: both pavilions had elegantly curving roofs. To the west was the palace proper and the living quarters of the country's queens; royal princes had their own accommodation to the east. Covered galleries connected the different buildings.

Hugging the hillside below the royal residence were the houses of wealthy artisans and merchants. These had decorative red-and-white patterned walls, with additional splashes of bright colour provided by flowerpots and climbing plants that trailed picturesquely across the roofs. Inside, the houses were luxurious – they even had the benefit of under-floor heating, as pipes carried warm air from the ground-floor kitchen to the living rooms and bedrooms above, then out via a tall chimney.

Artistic ceramics

Kaesong's craftsmen and artisans were so wealthy because the luxury goods they created were in great demand among the kingdom's affluent ruling class. Beautiful, well-crafted items were sought-after not only by the royal court and the warrior-aristocracy but also by the Buddhist temples in which they worshipped.

Wang Kon's diplomats took expensive gifts with them when they went to visit foreign rulers, advertising Koryo's wealth, and the skill of its craftsmen, to the wider world. Wealthy Koreans had always loved to surround themselves with pomp and luxury – in the days of the Great Silla Kingdom, a porcelain-like stoneware with a distinctive greenish glaze had been particularly popular. This glaze was later called 'celadon' in the West. The vogue strengthened during the Koryo era: some 260 state factories were opened to make celadon pottery during the 10th century. Craftsmen displayed great imagination and ingenuity in the designs of their ceramics. Vases and bowls with flower-like lobes and shapely, slender-necked 'plum blossom' vases all echoed the cherished concept of harmony with Nature.

Archaeologists investigating the Koryo kingdom have found a range of different types of ceramic bottle, pointing to a taste for a variety of alcoholic drinks. Particularly sought after, it seems, were jugs in the shape of pomegranates, melons or double gourds. With these was often found a thin celadon bowl in the shape of a lotus leaf, thought to have been used for gently warming the wine, which was best served at about body temperature. Towards the middle of the 12th century, skilled Koryo potters developed the technique of inlaid celadon. Scratched indentations in the unfired vessels were filled with white kaolin or a black clay mass to enhance the decoration. Once the object had been covered with its greenish glaze and fired, the pattern would shine through; occasionally items were painted with copper oxide or iron before the glaze was applied. Where figurative designs were used, the dragon motif was a favourite, thanks to its association with the semi-legendary King Mumnu.

A flourishing trade in lacquer

The use of techniques involving lacquer also enjoyed an upsurge in the Koryo period. Lacquer is made from the resinous sap of the tree *Rhus vernicifera*, which is native to East Asia. Chinese craftsmen had understood its properties from as early as 1000 BC. Resistant to moisture, heat and even acid, properly applied lacquer made a beautiful and highly durable coating for wooden and metal objects of every sort. Korean craftsmen made exquisite lacquer boxes, often inlaid with tortoiseshell or mother-of-pearl: these were used for storing sacred Buddhist texts.

Much to the satisfaction of Korea's merchants, trade in laquer items flourished too. Some made their way via the caravan routes of Central Asia as far as the Mediterranean world. Of more significance, however, was the brisk commerce with China and Japan. Silk textiles, porcelain, musical instruments, books and writing implements were exported – wealth (and cultural influences) flowed the other way. Only very gradually did a monetary economy become established in Korea, however. It was not until 996 that the first iron coins were minted. Alongside these, silver coins and, above all, Chinese coins circulated freely. The government did its best to encourage the use of metal currency, paying its civil servants and soldiers in coins, but for a long time, bartering remained important.

Buddhism a basis of power

During a reign lasting 25 years in all, Wang Kon laid the foundations for a strong and efficient state. He began by improving the condition of the peasantry: the almost incessant unrest in the country was not surprising, given the crippling level of taxes. Wang Kon eased the burden, thus removing the biggest threat to the stability of his kingdom. He also worked skilfully to bind the Silla nobility to his cause. Although he deposed the last Silla king, he gave him a key government post and also married a princess from the Silla royal family. Those who had helped Wang in his ascent to power – old comrades among rebel leaders and local magnates – were given government positions and grants of land. He built an impressive state apparatus, founded on loyalty to himself as King, but with a well-organised system of civil servants.

Sweet scents
Incense is an indispensable element of Korean Buddhism. During religious ceremonies, aromatic herbs were burnt in elegant bronze vessels such as this. In the background are coins and metal ornaments, which were sewn onto clothing as decoration.

Colourful mask
During the late Koryo period, masks like this one were worn at carnivals held to honour special gods. Such masks are still carved today, faithfully copied from the ancient originals.

Buddhism was the state religion in the Koryo kingdom, just as it had been during the Great Silla period. Wang Kon and his successors established a series of splendid new state temples and monasteries throughout the land and a member of the royal family entered each new foundation. Each year, moreover, the King and his family took part in elaborate religious ceremonies in the palace city of Kaesong. The ruling dynasty thus wove itself into the fabric of Korean society, with a major role to play in the country's spiritual life and a presence in every corner of the kingdom. Some Buddhist monks, for their part, became crucial to the running of the state: special schools were set up to train them in administration. Under the aegis of the state, other monks made copies of the sutras, texts of Buddhist teaching, embellishing them with splendid illustrations. The Koryo government thus clothed itself in religious garb.

Pious works for peace

In the early years of the 11th century, King Hyunjung gave his monks a spectacular commission. After a long period of peace, Korea was for the first time being threatened by external enemies. So significantly had Wang Kon enlarged the realm, it now bordered on the lands of the Asian nomads. Now the Khitan Tartars were making inroads into the Korean kingdom: before long, they were drawn up right outside the gates of the capital, Kaesong.

In this hour of desperate need, King Hyunjung was forced to look for desperate remedies: with no obvious military option available to him, he turned to divine remedies and ordered that 80,000 wooden printing tablets be prepared to facilitate the dissemination of the key Buddhist texts and bring blessings on the country.

Down the centuries, wandering far and wide, wayfaring monks had collected holy Buddhist scriptures, copied them down on palm leaves and carefully preserved them in baskets. By tradition there were three baskets containing, respectively, monastic rules, doctrinal lectures and commentaries. Collectively, they were called *tripitaka*, literally 'three baskets'. It was this important body of Buddhist learning that Hyunjung had carved into wooden tablets, and made into 5000 volumes for distribution. Momentous in the history of Buddhism in the country, it was also something of a turning-point for the Koryo state: in 1022, a permanent peace was achieved with the Khitan.

Threat from the north

Yet as time went on, attacks by other groups of steppe nomads only increased. From 1104 onwards, the Jurchen raided deep into Koryo territory, year after year. It showed the desperation of the Kings that, once the construction of state temples and the reproduction of religious texts no longer seemed a sufficient deterrent, they started pressing Buddhist monks into armed service.

The deteriorating security situation was not without consequences for Koryo's internal politics: serious faction-fighting broke out within the ruling caste. Top civil servants were playing an increasing part in decision-making, not just in civil but in military matters, and the traditional warrior elite were not pleased.

Under King Yidshong, who reigned from 1146, a bloody military rebellion broke out, which ended in the banishment of the monarch. Such was the shambolic end of the mighty state founded by Wang Kon: Korea's great and glorious Koryo dynasty was no more.

The Buwayhids – new masters of Baghdad

Overlordship by the Iranian Buwayhids meant ignominy for the once-proud Caliphs of Baghdad, but it fostered an extraordinary flowering in science, scholarship and artistic culture.

Dance of the stars
For centuries, the Islamic world was far in advance of the West where astronomy was concerned. This illustration, from the 10th-century *Book of the Stars*, shows a constellation called 'The Dancer'.

By the beginning of the 10th century, the once powerful Abbasid Caliphs of Baghdad were no more than puppets in the hands of their military commanders and high officials. These soldiers and civil servants had become the 'shadow rulers' of the Abbasid Empire, appointing and deposing Caliphs as they pleased. To add insult to injury, many of them were drawn from the class of Turkish slaves. Slave status had never been a bar to success in Islamic societies, but still their ascendancy represented a humiliating fall for such a great dynasty.

The fate of Caliph Al-Qahir was not untypical: deposed, grotesquely disfigured and blinded by his tormentors, he had been set 'free'

Built for eternity
Fellow-Persians and contemporaries of the Buwayhids, the Samandis ruled in eastern Iran and Uzbekistan. The Ismael Somani Mausoleum at Bukhara is one of their most splendid structures.

to scavenge through the city for a living. But he was lucky to be alive: these were difficult times for the Abbasid Caliphs.

Down from the mountains

The enormous extent of the Abbasid Empire had for some time masked a power vacuum at its heart. The weakness of the Caliphs was exploited by a number of different local dynasties, including the Buwayhids, who had taken the city of Isfahan in 935 and made it a centre for their further conquests in the region.

The Buwayhids' original homeland, south of the Caspian Sea in the Iranian province of Dailam, lay in such remote and inaccessible mountains that the Arab campaigns of conquest had largely passed it by. Its inhabitants had stayed closely connected with more ancient Iranian traditions, and though they had embraced Islam, they tended towards its Shi'ite form. Hardy warriors, they had been much sought-after as mercenaries by the Samanid rulers who had established an all but independent dynasty in the eastern region of Iran. Others had enlisted in the service of the Baghdad Caliphs, in many cases rising to positions of great importance.

The founder of the Buwayhid line was Buyeh, or Buwayh, who claimed descent from Iran's pre-Islamic Sassanid emperors. With the support of their Dailamite followers, his three sons – Ali, Hasan and Ahmed – began to carve out their own independent kingdom in western Iran. Pushing steadily southwards, they occupied the important province of Fars, with its city of Shiraz, before striking north against Isfahan. Annexing Khuzistan and Kerman gave them control of most of western Iran – and brought them to the very doorstep of the Caliphs.

The Buwayhids made two unsuccessful bids to take Baghdad, then in 945 the city fell without a fight. Caliph al-Mustakfi found himself so badly beset by his Turkish emirs and generals that he was compelled to ask Ahmad to help him enforce his rule: he got what he wanted – but at a price. Ahmad was given the title 'Emir of Emirs'. He was also given the honorific Mu'izz ud-Daula ('He who increases the wealth of the Kingdom') whilst his brother Ali became Imad ud-Daula ('Pillar of the Kingdom') and Hasan was Rukn ud-Daula ('Support of the Kingdom'). With these imposing titles came equally impressive powers: in effect, the brothers were given what amounted to dictatorial authority. Within a year, al-Mustakfi managed to offend his new masters and Mu'izz ud-Daula had him deposed and blinded.

Brothers in power
The kingdom of the Buwayhids was divided into three: Imad ud-Daula ruled western Iran from Shiraz; Rukn ud-Daula ruled over Isfahan and Raiy; and Mu'izz ud-Daula ruled central and southern Iraq from Baghdad, but the old imperial capital was no longer so central in the new scheme. Imad ud-Daula, took precedence over his younger brothers: 'Mu'izz ud-Daula', says a chronicler, 'kissed the ground in front of him. Imad ud-Daula wanted him to sit beside him, but the latter would not.' Although the Buwayhids

---

BACKGROUND

'Caliph' vs 'Emir' – what's in a title?

The position of *Caliph* or 'Successor' was held by the line of men who followed on from Muhammad as leaders of Islam, inheriting both the Prophet's religious and political authority. The first caliphs were elected, but the principle of the hereditary caliphate soon asserted itself. As time went on and the Islamic world expanded, different dynasties rose and fell and caliphates existed in Baghdad, Córdoba and Cair. From 1517, the Ottoman Sultans claimed the honour of being caliphs, until the title was dispensed with after their fall in 1924. The term *Emir*, in contrast, is a purely secular Arab title denoting a ruler, provincial governor or military general.

---

themselves were Shi'ites, they never felt quite confident enough to do away with the office of the Sunni Caliph, though they did have Shi'ite festivals incorporated into the calendar, and had their own reigning titles read out alongside those of the Caliphs at Friday prayers. They also had their own names stamped on the coinage of the realm – till then the sole prerogative of the Caliph.

Culture and science
Buwayhid power reached its peak in the reign of Adud ud-Daula, son of Rukn ud-Daula, who around 977 gained control of the areas ruled by rival branches of the family. Taking on the ancient Persian title Shahan Shah, 'King of Kings', he not only asserted his pre-eminence but also underlined the Iranian identity of his empire. And what a glittering empire it was. Under Adud ud-Daula and his successors Islamic scholarship, the sciences, art and literature

Attentive audience
The Greek philosopher Aristotle – shown here expounding his views in oriental dress – was highly respected in the Islamic world and his writings had a great influence on their philosophy and science. The illustration comes from a 13th-century Seljuk Turkish manuscript.

Advanced medicine
A European view of Avicenna, better known in his own country as Ibn Sina, an important protégé of the Buwayhids. It was through Avicenna's writings that the medieval West first gained access to the wealth of medical lore so painstakingly put together over hundreds of years by Arab and Asian scholars – and to the long-forgotten heritage of ancient Greece. Here, we see him in a pharmacy, surrounded by assistants. The background image shows medical instruments used in Avicenna's day.

service with the Emir, I owned a mat, a cloak and my writing implements. Today I am an equal of those in power with respect to money, possessions and slaves.' Lavish banquets and parties were held – at one the tables had huge sugar palaces as centrepieces, from which, at a given signal, dancing girls burst forth.

Religious tolerance

Court ceremony was designed to drive home the awesome majesty of Buwayhid rule. Guests who were invited for audiences had to throw themselves down in front of the Shah. When foreign ambassadors were received, triple rows of guards with splendid weapons and costumes lined their route all the way from the River Tigris to the foot of the throne.

Adud ud-Daula kept up diplomatic relations with Byzantium, the Egyptian Fatimids and Yemen, among others. He was as broad-minded as he was outward-looking: his religious tolerance extended to having a Christian vizier to whom he gave explicit permission to reconstruct ruined churches and monasteries and to build new ones. Other Christians were in important positions, too: Adud ud-Daula appreciated the fact that they did not get themselves involved in Islam's various internal arguments.

The Buwayhid rulers lived surrounded by every conceivable luxury, their palaces bedecked with precious brocades, furniture and rugs. Some 800kg (1750lb) of wax is said to have been used for lighting each month. Gazelles roamed freely through the ornamental grounds

all flourished. Magnificent mosques and public buildings were built to proclaim the power and glory of the realm, and splendid residences were constructed for the ruling family. In Baghdad, Mu'izz ud-Daula had already built a vast palace complex with gardens, spaces for playing polo and open esplanades for military parades. Famous architects and craftsmen were brought in specially from Mosul and Isfahan: the cost of the project was astronomical, but the ruler raised it easily by confiscating the private assets of his wealthiest officials. By their own admission, they could afford it: as one civil servant records, 'When I entered into outside. In their treasuries, prestigious weapons, gold-studded belts, jewels, gold and pearls were piled high. The Buwayhids did not travel light, even on military campaigns: one magnificent tent is said to have had room for 500 people.

Medical progress

Some of this prosperity trickled down to improve the conditions of the masses. The irrigation channels on which agriculture depended were renewed. And in 982, Adud ud-Daula had a famous hospital built in Baghdad, equipping it at a cost of 100,000 dinars. The hospital had a permanent staff of 24 doctors, who also taught as medical professors, as well as apothecaries, storekeepers, doormen and overseers. The Buwayhids proved to be benevolent patrons of medical research: it was under their sponsorship that Ibn Sina (980–1037) became the most famous physician of the Islamic world. He would later be celebrated in Europe where he was known by the name of 'Avicenna'. The Buwayhid Empire became a cultural crucible in which Greek and Persian-Indian scientific traditions mingled, to the ultimate advantage of both East and West.

Adud ud-Daula's son and successor Sharaf ud-Daula had a particular interest in astronomy and so he ordered the construction of a major new observatory. While it was being built, he had his astronomers base themselves in the palace gardens to record exact observations of the courses of the seven known planets. And it was not just the Buwayhid rulers themselves who bought prestige by endowing such projects. In 993, the vizier to Sharaf ud-Daula's successor, Samsam ud-Daula, had a great library built in Baghdad to house a collection said to number more than 10,000 volumes.

Feuding and failure

In the background, however, while this wonderful flowering of culture and advancement of science was taking place, political manoeuvring and in-fighting

went on as usual under the Buwayhids. Like the Caliphs before them, they faced a never-ending struggle to keep a large body of key soldiers and civil servants happy, without encouraging them so much that they were tempted to bid for power themselves.

There were external enemies as well, such as the Hamdanids who came from around Mosul in northern Iraq, a warrior clan, just as the Buwayhids themselves had been. With the support of their loyal Dailamite infantry and the Turkish military slaves who comprised their cavalry, the Buwayhids did succeed in holding the Hamdanids in check. The costs of keeping up their armies were enormous, though, and more land and power had to be handed out to generals to keep them loyal. In addition, they had to deal with raids by Bedouins, Kurds and rebel Turkish mercenaries. On top of all this, internal family feuding – always a feature of Buwayhid rule – was becoming ever more bitter, and almost continuous, distracting the dynasty at what could not have been a worse time.

Objects of desire
Conspicuous consumption was a feature of life under the Buwayhids, both in the royal palaces and in the houses of the upper classes. This early 12th century blue-glazed ceramic bowl bears a design of extravagant golden arches.

For advancing out of the steppes were the Seljuk Turks under the leadership of the warlord, Tugril Beg. The Seljuks had already cut a swathe through Central Asia and a divided Buwayhid Empire could not resist them for long. In 1055, they duly took the city of Baghdad.

The Song dynasty rebuilds China

'The Five Dynasties Period', 'the Ten Kingdoms of the South' – the terminology of 10th-century Chinese history tells a story of disunity. The great challenge facing the Song dynasty was to rebuild China as a single, stable realm.

On the morning of February 2, 960, General Zhao Kuangyin, commander of the palace guard, was rudely awoken when a band of his officers burst into his chamber. 'We want you as our Emperor!' they cried, bundling him into the yellow robe which was to mark his elevation from the kingdom's highest military officer to its monarch. The existing monarch, Zhou Gong Di, was a boy barely nine years old and there was little loyalty to him.

Since the collapse of the Tang dynasty 53 years before, southern China had fractured into the Ten Kingdoms, while five short-lived dynasties had ruled in succession in the north. Nomads from the steppe were encroaching on the Empire's northern margins: China was in danger of extinction. The boy-emperor's father Chai Rong, his predecessor in the later Zhou dynasty, had made a brave start on restoring China to greatness, but completing the work required a man not a boy. Zhao Kuangyin was convinced he was the man for the job. He would rule until 976 as Emperor Taizu, or 'Great Ancestor', the first ruler of the Song dynasty.

Zhao had not actively schemed for this new status, but he accepted it when it came, then protected it zealously. The decay of the Tang and his own elevation had taught this son of a military official that the power of the generals had to be curtailed, and as Taizu he knew just what to do. One evening, in the course of a banquet, he began to reminisce with his companions about their shared experiences on campaign. To the astonishment of all, he ended by raising his wine goblet and congratulated them on the completion of their careers. Henceforth, he informed them – all smiles and bonhomie – they would enjoy a worry-free retirement in the capital, Kaifeng. His companions, stunned, could only stammer out insincere expressions of gratitude – and curse inwardly to find themselves so deftly outmanoeuvred.

Power reforms

Taizu had expansionist policies, but he preferred to pursue them through diplomacy rather than force. When he did call his forces into action, he lead from the front: there was never any doubt of his courage or resolve. Within a few years he had succeeded in

Precious headdress
The state mines under the Song dynasty produced more than 2000kg, or 2 tonnes, of silver annually. In the hands of outstanding artisans, it was fashioned it into luxury items like this gilded crown.

reunifying northern and southern China under Song control. Always feeling that he had more to fear from his own military than from any external enemy, Taizu determined to break its power for good. He reformed the administrative system, placing the army under the control of his central civilian bureaucracy in Kaifeng. He started limiting the authority of his top generals,

and made sure they were regularly moved around the country from one command to another. And, recognising that it was almost an invitation to set up a provincial power base in opposition to the Emperor, he abolished the position of military

At full gallop
Her arms waving, her body gracefully swaying, her clothing streaming out behind her in the wind, this wood carving of 'Genius on a spirit horse' – created during the Song dynasty – personified freedom. The reality for Song women was very different: they were hidden away as valuable property, and the cruel practice for footbinding was beginning.

The Iron Pagoda
So-called because of the reddish colour of the ceramic tiles used to make it fireproof, this 11th-century pagoda of the Youguo Temple in Kaifeng replaced an all-wooden one which burned down after being struck by lightning. The Iron Pagoda has stood firm for almost 1000 years, surviving winds, earthquakes and devastating floods.

governor. Gradually he changed the army from one of conscripts, rooted in the regions, to one of mercenaries, loyal to their paymasters in Kaifeng. Taizu also brought in the best-trained military units to reinforce his palace guard.

Taizu put himself at the centre of an Empire-wide web of surveillance and control. Government offices and secret-service posts in every town meant very little happened without the Emperor getting to hear of it. High officials were not allowed to gain too much power, either: authority and responsibilities were strictly regulated. Central administration was structured into three main sections. One department dealt with the military; the second with the administration of justice and matters of personnel; the third functioned as a treasury, responsible for overseeing the economy and the gathering of taxes. In what was becoming an unabashedly bureaucratic society, the Emperor took to referring to himself not as the ruler but as the 'administrator' of his Empire. The result of all these reforms was a strong, reunified empire with internal political stability. The power of the military elite had been broken, and a highly efficient bureaucracy was ready to take the country into a new and more successful era.

Education and printing

For all his controlling instincts, Taizu was tolerant towards intellectuals: he recognised the vital role of education in producing the capable bureaucracy that he hoped to build. He looked to Confucian tradition to nurture the sort of civic-minded young clerks the Empire needed. This made sense: the 1600-year-old philosophy of Kong Fuzi (Confucius) called for the moral self-perfecting of each individual and his induction into the skills that would make him useful to the state. Those skills included patience, discipline and accomplishments in several fields.

The ideal educated person would not only be able to recite and discuss an ancient text, but could shine as an artist or calligrapher. He would have read widely among the books already printed and published in large numbers in the years before the accession of the Song, thanks to the introduction of block-printing techniques. The invention of moveable type towards the middle of the 11th century considerably simplified the

■ Extent of the Song Empire

● Main towns and cities

Liao

Beijing

Xi Xia

Huang He

Northern Song Kingdom

Kaifeng

YELLOW SEA

Chang Jiang

Hangzhou

Southern Song Kingdom from 1127

Guangzhou

Xi Jiang

Annam

production of templates for printing. In the new method, a soft mass of wax, resin and ash was inserted into an iron frame which was then heated till the filling was tacky. The letters were set into this base to make up a page. After this was printed, it could be dismantled again and the letters recombined to make new texts.

Technological progress

With unity, peace, security and a well-ordered administration in place, the foundations for progress had been laid. The result was a technological revolution. The metalworking industry, for example, was transformed by improved techniques and processes. Coal replaced charcoal as a fuel for smelting; hydraulic machines were used to drive the bellows. The use of explosives made the mining of ore much easier and the mining industry expanded rapidly. In southern China in particular, numerous enterprises sprang up for the extraction of ore. By the middle of the 11th century, the Chinese were producing 13 times the amount of copper and 14 times the amount of iron than they had 250 years earlier. In 1078, for example, cast-iron production came to an estimated 114,000 tonnes – an industrialising England managed only 68,000 tonnes in 1788. Other sectors thrived as well, including construction and shipbuilding.

Economic growth stimulated the demand for luxuries. Silk textiles, cotton and woven hemp were sought after; so, too, were lacquered goods and fine furniture; householders spent more money on tea, salt, spirits and other products. Technological advances raised standards in manufacturing. Craftsmen formed guilds, separated according to increasingly specialised skills, which encouraged both professional pride and practical support in difficult times; each guild had its own shrine, where offerings were made to the tutelary divinity of the profession. The activities of the guilds were restricted to the local level, however, so they would not accumulate political power.

An economic boom

As professions and trades became more specialised, individual regions of China acquired reputations for particular products. Iron came from Hebei in the north, for example; cane sugar from Fujian in the south; paper and printed products from Zhejiang, another southern province. The individual regions profited, but so, too, did China as a whole, riding high on an economic boom. Newly wealthy regions were able to trade with one another along a well-maintained and much-extended network of waterways.

At the heart of this network were the great rivers running from west to east: the Chang Jiang (or Yangtze) in central China; the Huang He (Yellow River) further north; and the Xi Jiang in the south. But a chain of canals linking the larger and smaller

Sky guide
A model of Su Song's masterpiece, the first astronomical clock driven by water. The original, completed in 1088, was over 10m (33ft) tall. The sky globe showed the position of the constellations at any given time: celestial bodies could be located with its help.

tributaries to provide the north–south connections that the river system lacked had been growing for over a thousand years. Neglected when the Tang dynasty entered its decline, this was restored and rapidly expanded under Taizu. There were sea links between coastal regions and to neighbouring countries: millions of tonnes of rice went from south to north around the coast each year. Floating trading posts grew up along the Chang Jiang River and its estuary – 20km (12½ miles) wide – was a meeting point for shipping.

Sea-going ships for precious goods

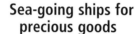

Ceramics, in particular, flourished under the Song, and were exported to eager markets across the known world. Song ceramics were stunningly beautiful,

Superb ceramics
Chinese pottery reached new heights under the Song with shapely forms, elegant decoration and lustrous glazes. Much was made for export, but the higher social circles at home also loved fine ceramics. The jar below and the golden cups in the background are examples of the popular red stoneware.

and productivity was soaring as large numbers of factories sprang up with the sophisticated kilns needed for the best pottery and highest-grade glazes. Some turned out rustic ware for everyday use, but carefully regulated state-run enterprises also produced pottery of astonishing elegance and technical perfection. The celadon ware which had taken the Great Silla Kingdom of Korea by storm had originally been developed by Chinese potters. Now it was brought to new heights of refinement, beautifully shaped and painted with delicate designs. One vogue was to treat vessels with special glazes before firing: the resulting 'distressed' or antique look was much valued. Along with ceramics, silks were the most important exports, shipped from ports in Zhejiang and Fujian provinces to Asian neighbours and even to Africa.

To transport all these goods Song China had the world's largest fleet, which plied more than 50,000km (31,000 miles) of shipping routes. Trading voyages were made in ocean-going junks – China's first genuinely ocean-going craft – that confirmed the reputation of the Chinese as master-shipbuilders. The largest junks held up to a thousand men. They unfurled as many as twelve sails from up to six masts, and the sails pivoted so a junk could sail close to the changing wind. They had an innovatory 'sternpost rudder' that was really a keel as well: it extended well below the line of the hull, providing not only steering but stability, which was enhanced by the use of ballast in the hold. A V-shaped hull ensured manoeuvrability and speed. Mariners had compasses and charts to enable them to navigate at sea, and they could also draw upon the reports of earlier sailors.

The overland trade was important as well: tea, salt, textiles and metal were transported along land routes to the north and along the Silk Road through Central Asia to the Middle East. Trade within China had grown so much, meanwhile, that even the merchants organised themselves into guilds. As commerce grew, so did the cities which were the market centres. With over a million inhabitants, Kaifeng was bursting at the seams, but even the smaller regional centres were growing: 30 other towns had populations of between 40,000 and 100,000. There were also numerous medium and smaller provincial towns. An estimated 6 million people were urban-dwellers, but this was still only 5 per cent of the population.

Kaifeng – urban crucible

China's growing towns were taking on a very different character: previously, they had been administrative centres. Now they were centres of commerce, culture and entertainment. Cities were filled with bustling life and colour; people of all classes mingled in the streets. Kaifeng, as imperial capital, was home to hundreds of high-ranking bureaucrats and military officials, and thousands of civil service staff lived here with their families as well.

Even the landowning elite had homes in Kaifeng, far from their rural estates. Many had posts in government departments, but the bulk of their income no longer came from the rents on their lands and the produce of their harvests – much of their wealth had been invested in large-scale trade. The profits they made were generally used to buy more land, as landownership was still the benchmark for social prestige. The persistence of this attitude meant that there was no sense that trade, or capitalism, might in itself be a valid way of life for the well-born.

The new urban-dwellers enjoyed their wealth, the luxuries it could buy and the new amenities on offer in the towns. Many pursued the arts: there was a vogue for painting (especially landscapes); some

turned to writing and the study of history – even archaeology. Others became students of philosophy, the natural sciences, mathematics, astronomy and geography.

Further down the social scale, craftsmen and tradesmen, manufacturers and merchants were all thriving, too: struggling to keep pace with the demand created by the cities. There, buoyed up by the new consumerism, trade was starting to liberate itself from the old rules which had constrained economic activity for so long.

In 1063, for instance, Kaifeng removed the curfew which, till then, had limited business to the hours of daylight: now small traders could stay open all night. Restrictions on movement within the cities were also lifted, along with an array of local laws confining particular trades to particular parts of town. Cities became vast, sprawling, open-air markets, with stalls selling all manner of produce and manufactured goods springing up along all the main routes in from the country. Porters hurried here and there, heavy loads hanging from poles across their shoulders. The administrative authorities still had their own designated area of town, where they could work undistracted by all this hubbub – but the price they paid was that they now seemed marginalised, out of the mainstream swim. Amidst the stalls and the strolling pedlars, showmen, storytellers, jugglers, dancers and puppeteers all found places to perform: many made a living as professional entertainers. Swindlers and criminals of every kind found rich pickings: peasants streamed into the city with their savings, ripe for exploitation. Employment agencies were set up to help newcomers to make the most of the opportunities; others established old people's homes to look after their elderly dependants.

The first banknotes

All this buying and selling of goods and services created a need for a suitable form of payment. The first Song emperors cast

---

TIME WITNESS

China's first historian

Sima Guang will always have a place in Chinese folk tradition as the boy who, when young, fell into a deep vat and started to drown, but had the presence of mind to pick up a stone and break the vessel, releasing the water and saving his own life. He has a place in Chinese history, too, as one of the first scholars to start writing that history down. His great book was called *Zizhi Tongjian*, which roughly translates as *A Comprehensive Manual to Aid Government*. It was one of Sima Guang's insights that the past could offer lessons for civil servants in the present. He saw, too, how the same event might be open to different interpretations, and was strikingly modern in many of his judgments.

---

large quantities of copper coins. By about 1000, though, many of these had been dispersed to foreign countries, while demand, from both traders and government, still rose at home. For a time the mints tried to meet this demand using silver, lead and iron, but all these metals weighed far too much and the coins they made were too bulky.

So the government introduced a system offering so-called deposit certificates by way of payment. These could be taken elsewhere and exchanged for money at a fee of 3 per cent, or used on the open market instead of coins. They were, in fact, the first banknotes in the world. The system was a huge success, despite the fact that the paper crumbled easily and that a note only remained valid for three years. In a parallel development, certain merchants were given permission to create a kind of bill of exchange for business transactions taking place over long distances.

In contrast with previous dynasties, the Song took a keen interest in monetary policy and responded imaginatively to changing times. For example, flexible duties on shops, goods and trade traffic replaced the conscription of craftsmen's labour, to the benefit of both individuals and the state. The government gained further income from its monopolies on salt, tea, alcohol and perfumes as well as from customs duties, poll tax and taxes on land. Money was soon pouring in.

Peasants – the losing class

Back in the countryside, however, the boom was by-passing China's peasants and small farmers. As incomes fell, driven down by competition with the big landowners, the Emperor's tax-collectors

Hard at work
This wall painting from northwest China's Mogao caves represents the reality of life for rural peasants during the Song dynasty – never-ending toil. Many peasants left the land for the towns in search of a better future.

were increasing their demands. This was ironic, as it was the peasants who had done so much to increase the prosperity of China as a whole by adopting a new variety of rice, originally brought from Champa in what is now Vietnam. The new strain grew quickly, with a cultivation period of only two to four months, allowing several harvests a year. Moreover, it was so hardy hitherto marginal areas could be brought into production: in the space of a few years, the area under rice cultivation doubled. These developments massively augmented cereal yields that were already rising thanks to improved irrigation systems. With water-powered threshing and milling, the increased availability of food helped to promote a rise in population, from 53 million in the 8th century to 100 million by the 13th.

But the peasants could not match the scale or technological improvements of the big producers. Their circumstances desperate, many small farmers were forced to sell their land to the great estates and work as tenants. The new owners of their land would take up to 70 per cent of the harvest as rent. Many drifted away to find work in the cities.

A weakening giant

In the long term, the state suffered: the flight from the land meant a slump in government revenues, worsened by the large-scale tax evasion of the land-owning class. By the mid-11th century, only about 30 per cent of agricultural area under the Song was yielding taxes; yet outgoings continued to increase. An opulent imperial court and expanding government and administrative structures swallowed up enormous sums of money.

The greatest drain of all, however, was the army. For good reasons, the Song emperors had dropped conscription in

Holy helpers
Serenity and goodness radiate from these 10th-century carved wooden bodhisattvas. It was believed that 'enlightened beings' like these chose to remain in the suffering world in order to help humankind.

Laughing Buddha
People queue up to rub the plump belly of the Laughing Buddha, carved in stone in 11th-century Hangzhou. The statue symbolised abundance, prosperity and a full stomach.

favour of mercenaries: conscript forces were generally apathetic, and China's troops before the Song had become the private armies of their generals. A paid army would not only be more professional in its attitudes, but feel a clearer loyalty to its imperial paymaster. But paying them was the problem: the army had more than 1.25 million men and their upkeep devoured more than three quarters of all state incomes. Increasingly, China found it was getting very little in return: the state was bankrupting itself to support an army of ill-trained, ill-equipped and ageing time-servers. Lacking in horses, discipline and fighting spirit, this was not a force to strike fear into the Empire's enemies.

There was a marked 'technology gap' between China and its neighbours: the Song could deploy treadmill-driven ships at sea, and on the battlefield could call on catapults, repeating crossbows, smoke-bombs, flares and explosive grenades. But no amount of sophisticated weaponry could invigorate an over-sized but under-motivated military: the Chinese lion was toothless, as all could see.

In the northeast, the Khitan had not been slow to take advantage: former nomads from the steppes, they had now built a kingdom called Liao. In the northwest, meanwhile, the kingdom of the western Xia was becoming stronger under the rule of the cattle-breeding Tanguts.

Already strapped for funds, the Song had been obliged to buy peace for their kingdom, paying expensive tribute to what should have been insignificant foes. In 1004, for instance, they signed a treaty with Liao agreeing payments in silver and silk. In time, they would have to pay tribute to the Tanguts too.

New policies create unrest

When the young Emperor Shenzong ascended the imperial throne in 1068, he found himself beset with problems from the very first. Military failure, financial crisis, a flight from the land and rampant corruption − and no one around him, it seemed, had the vision to make things better. A year after ascending the throne, he decided to take a more radical step and called Wang Anshi, governor of Nanjing, to Kaifeng.

A leading writer and scholar, Wang had a more practical side as well and a longstanding interest in policymaking. At 47, he was already an experienced and effective public official, so the 20-year-old Emperor was prepared to accept his advice and give him a free hand. Wang tackled the problems head-on. His first priority was to improve the lot of the small farmers, peasants and traders, with the long-term goal of strengthening the state. He helped those working on the land with training in the latest agricultural techniques, an important investment in China's long-term farming future. More immediately, though, he came to their rescue by granting them easy credit to see them through sowing time, with debts to be settled after the harvest. Wang even set up state pawnbrokers as an alternative to the profiteering money-lenders.

A new registry of land ownership was compiled to prevent the big magnates from evading taxes. Wang went further, controlling the price of cereals. He stopped monopolies by large traders, freed trade by curtailing the anti-competitive power of the guilds and helped smaller merchants to build up their businesses by granting loans. Wang also reintroduced the old system of peasant militia to fortify the military. He broadened the training of prospective civil servants, to take in economics, law, geography and medicine.

Beginning of the end

Although with hindsight Wang's reforms seem sensible, at the time the very highest in society saw them as a direct attack. The big magnates in the regions had led charmed lives for many decades. Now they made common cause with the Empire's most senior civil servants, and together they obstructed change at every step, saying that Wang was leading China into disaster through his un-Confucian greed for profits. Wang saw himself as a high-minded, committed Confucian, and was stung by the criticism.

Who knows what benefits the Wang revolution might have brought, had vested interests in China given it a chance? Instead, beleaguered by public abuse and behind-the-scenes intriguing, Wang lost the will to drive his reform programme through and turned his back on politics. He died in 1086, by which time his younger master had already been dead a year. Shenzong's successor Zhezong was to fare no better in his attempts to curb the power of the old elites. This was unmistakeably an empire on the slide. From 1101 to 1125, inefficiency, disorder and corruption reigned as

the artistic and sensitive but totally ineffectual Emperor Huizong looked on helplessly. The final blow was dealt by a former Song ally: the Tanguts were on the rise. Expanding eastward to begin with, they overran the Khitan kingdom of Liao before pushing south into the Empire. In 1127, Kaifeng fell and the last Emperor was captured. Although the Song were able to hold onto power in the south, the Tanguts took over northern China.

The written word
It was under the Song dynasty that the first books were printed using moveable type − four centuries before Europe produced the Gutenberg Bible. Printing could never replace the ancient art of calligraphy, however, and elegant handwriting is a living tradition in China to this day.

Power politics – the Fujiwara in Japan

Despite controlling the fate of Japan for centuries, the Fujiwara dynasty showed no interest in the title of Emperor, preferring to manipulate events from behind the throne.

When Michinaga died, at the age of 62, the news spread like wildfire through Japan. The shadowy Fujiwara patriarch had not appeared in public for several years, yet there was not a child in the land who did not know of him by name. His life had been one of priestly retreat, yet its simplicity was deceptive: nothing happened at the imperial court, or indeed in the country at large, without Michinaga's knowledge. He had been father-in-law to four emperors and a crown prince; two emperors and two regents numbered among his grand-children. As *kampaku*, head of the imperial administration, he had dominated Japanese political life for decades and influenced just about every aspect of the kingdom's culture. His death, in 1028, was a significant blow to a clan not immune to internal feuding and faction-fighting. But Michinaga had prepared well: his son, Yorimichi, would carry on the Fujiwara tradition.

The Fujiwaras had been Japan's most important clan for generations, manipulating imperial power from behind the scenes. Their influence had grown steadily since the 7th century, but it was not until 866 that Michinaga's ancestor, Fujiwara no Yoshifusa, made himself *sessho* – the title given to the regent of a child-emperor – and the extent of their ambitions became apparent.

Power-bases and marriage bonds

Yoshifusa had already been given extensive powers when Emperor Montoku had made him chancellor, a title not previously awarded for 88 years. During that time, Japan's emperors had preferred not to concede too much power to potential rivals, but these were strange times and the Fujiwara an unusual clan. For a long time, its members had been building a network of contacts at court, steadily extending their influence through the country's ruling circles.

The Fujiwara comprised four large families; of these the northern line had shown remarkable energy and skill in expanding its power-base at court. Unlike other nobles, however, they had never actually sought for themselves the title of Tenno, or Emperor. They were content to trade the trappings of office for the reality of power, and this strategy was successful. Many Emperors valued the Fujiwara as advisors, and so Yoshifusa was rewarded with the post of imperial chancellor.

The heads of the other great families looked on, half admiring and half envious,

Wedded rocks
According to traditional Shinto belief, these two rocks near the town of Futami symbolise the unity of man and woman in marriage.

Woman of words
Murasaki Shikibu was the most celebrated of a remarkable generation of Japanese women writers. Creator of *The Tale of Genji*, she was arguably the world's first novelist.

Artistic inspiration

The *Genji Monogatari* was more than a literary landmark: it was an inspiration to countless Japanese artists, including the creator of this painting. The Fujiwara enjoyed power during the Heian period of imperial rule, and they fostered the political and economic stability that encouraged the flowering in the arts. Both the painting below and the silk fan (background) are from this Heian period.

The world's first novelist

As a lady-in-waiting to the Empress Akiko, Murasaki Shikibu had an insider's view of the imperial court. She also possessed an acutely observant eye for social manners, a grasp of human psychology, creative flair and awesome energy. Her *Genji Monogatari* (*The Tale of Genji*) ran to 54 volumes in all, and is widely considered to be the first novel in the history of literature.

Born in 978, Murasaki Shikibu is believed to have written in the early years of the 11th century, which makes her masterpiece almost exactly a thousand years old. It tells of the loves and adventures of Genji, a prince blessed with both beauty and talent, and his generally unlucky son, Kaoru, at court.

The novel is unabashedly romantic – some 800 poems are interwoven with the narrative to maintain the lyric mood. It is also rich in descriptive detail, offering an unrivalled window on the medieval Japanese court – its fashions, customs, attitudes and assumptions.

A minor member of the Fujiwara clan, Murasaki Shikibu had secured her place at the palace through the intervention of Michinaga himself after her husband's death. This led to persistent rumours of a liaison between the author and the great Fujiwara *kampaku*.

as the Fujiwara skilfully eased their way to power. Having secured the Emperor's political dependence and personal trust, Yoshifusa cemented the connection by contriving the marriage of his daughter, Akiko, with Emperor Montoku. Political loyalties may change, but blood ties are indissoluble and enduring: Yoshifusa thus bound the fortunes of the monarchy inseparably together with those of his own Fujiwara clan. To begin with, Montoku had shown no interest in the match: he was already married, with three children, and had no reason whatever to complicate his domestic – or dynastic – arrangements further. Yoshifusa was persuasive, however. Not only did Montoku marry Akiko, but when he died he bequeathed his throne to her son, Seiwa.

Yoshifusa was now the Emperor's grandfather, and as Seiwa was only nine years old, it seemed natural that he should have the assistance of a *sessho* to help him reign. The fact that this was the first *sessho* not to have been drawn from the imperial family itself raised a few eyebrows, but Yoshifusa was too powerful a figure to be

challenged. Seiwa grew to adulthood and Yoshifusa showed no signs of stepping down, his role modulating imperceptibly from *sessho* to *kampaku*. In theory, the title *kampaku* suggested nothing more than a sort of chief counsellor to the Emperor. In practical terms, however, it amounted to a regent's authority over the reign of an adult ruler. The Fujiwara clan would make the office their own for almost three centuries.

Consolidating power

The Fujiwara did not, of course, enjoy their ascendancy unopposed; nor did they escape the envy of rival clans. The warlike Taira and Minamoto families in particular resented the Fujiwaras' hold over the Emperor – much later, indeed, they would bring about the dynasty's downfall. For the moment, however, these aristocratic rivals to the Fujiwaras kept their heads down, all too aware of the risks involved in any attack on the ruling clan.

The Fujiwara did not need to resort to violence to get the better of an incautious enemy – a 'promotion' to some post in the provinces might suffice to finish a court career. Emperors, too, learned the futility of attempting to resist Fujiwara dominance: in any struggle between Tenno and *kampaku*, the former usually lost. The Emperor's nominal authority was as nothing against the power of a political force whose reach extended far beyond the imperial court. The Fujiwara had been adept in making marriage alliances with other leading families, and were themselves among the richest of the country's clans. They had accumulated enormous areas of land which the state could neither control nor tax, and their wealth bought them power. From the Emperor and his court to the lowliest local officials, the Fujiwara had a hold over the main mechanisms of government in Japan.

But even such consummate operators had a weakness: internal rivalry brought particular difficulties. One such rivalry erupted shortly after Michinaga's birth. In 967 two ambitious brothers, Kanemichi and Kaneye, started vying with each other for power. From 968 the feud deepened until it threatened to engulf the whole Fujiwara family. Finally, Kanemichi gained an edge over his brother and emerged the winner. Accordingly, he assumed the authority of *sessho* over the Tenno – still a minor and, in the best Fujiwara tradition, Kanemichi's grandson.

Of Emperors and daughters

Yoshifusa's formula for success had not been lost on his descendants. In every subsequent generation, the head of the Fujiwara family would ensure that one of his daughters married the Emperor. After the birth of a grandson he would then force the incumbent Tenno to abdicate, taking over the regency for the successor, who was still a minor. By the time the latter ascended the throne, a few years later, he would have been fashioned into a fully serviceable instrument for his Fujiwara masters.

It was essentially a simple system, and it was extremely effective in perpetuating Fujiwara power. The reign of the great Michinaga saw it at its triumphant height. Initially, he too had to assert himself against the ambitions of his brothers in the sort of internal family feud that had always dogged the dynasty. Once his rivals were successfully eliminated, he married

his oldest daughter to the Emperor Ichijo, who had been crowned in 987 at the age of only seven. When Ichijo died in 1011, Michinaga had his successor prepared, and he was duly married off to Michinaga's second daughter. Five years later, this successor went blind and had to abdicate, dying soon after, but Michinaga was quite undaunted by this apparent ill-fortune. He had at his disposal a seemingly inexhaustible supply of marriageable daughters, and he still had plenty of political ingenuity up his sleeve. In no time at all, he had lifted his nine-year-old

Rival interest
Shigemori, head of the Taira dynasty, was one of the Fujiwaras' most dangerous foes.

grandson, Go-Ichijo, to pre-eminence. Michinaga ruled on Go-Ichijo's behalf during his minority, then married him off to his third daughter. The destinies of the present generation now decided, Michinaga could look to the future. He married his fourth daughter to the younger brother of the newly proclaimed Emperor; though Michinaga would not live to see it, in 1037 this brother too would be elevated to Emperor in his turn.

By 1018, when Michinaga retired from politics to dedicate himself to the studies and devotions of a Buddhist priest, he had fully prepared his son Yorimichi for the succession. It proved a good choice, as Yorimichi would uphold the dignity of the dynasty to the full. In a career of almost 50 years he 'served' as *kampaku* to three emperors, none of whom were under any illusions as to where the real power lay. Yorimichi was also the father of numerous daughters, whose marriages would maintain the might of the Fujiwaras for decades to come.

The Heian cultural awakening

The name of Fujiwara is forever linked to a particular concept of permanent, intelligent participation in political power. But it also stands for a great cultural

period in Japan's history. The Fujiwara were no philistines and they presided over an era of incredible artistic creativity. Michinaga in particular encouraged the arts. Under his regency, Kyoto – then called Haiankyo, 'capital of peace and tranquillity' – became an important centre for artistic excellence and innovation.

What is now known as the Heian period saw Japanese art breaking free of the Chinese influences which had, until then, predominated. The mood of self-confidence was expressed in strong colours, bold brushstrokes and indigenous Japanese themes. Towards the beginning of the 11th century, painted figures were fixed in sequence to rolls called *makimono*, so entire stories could be set out in pictorial form. This 'comic-strip' style of art was very popular among the ordinary people, most of whom were illiterate.

A writing revolution

The skills of reading and writing may have been confined to the aristocratic elite, but change was afoot here too. New developments in the visual arts went hand in hand with an outpouring of literary creativity, in

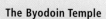

The Byodoin Temple
One of Japan's most famous shrines, Kyoto's Byodoin Temple was built in the 11th century by the Fujiwara. It represents Heian architecture at the height of its glory.

which the noble ladies at the imperial court led the way. As so often in artistic history, a hitherto marginalised group found itself better placed than the mainstream to move things forward. The long-established male scribe class used the traditional Chinese script. The ideograms were impressive, but as they offered a separate symbol for every concept, they were difficult to learn and unwieldy. They were hallowed by tradition and their use lent an aura of stately authority to what was written, but the writer was restricted to thoughts and images that had been rehearsed before.

The ladies employed a new script known as the *hiragana* or *onnade*, 'the woman's hand'. Rather than representing concepts, the symbols represented syllable sounds. This proved to be far more flexible and unleashed an astonishing surge of imaginative energy. To begin with the new penmanship was viewed with disdain by the artistic establishment, but the stream of literary masterpieces that emerged made it impossible to ignore. The place of honour among the new generation of female poets was held by Murasaki Shikibu, author of the much-read tale of a fictional prince, Genji. Another very popular writer was Sei Shonagon, a former lady-in-waiting to the Empress Sadako who delighted all with her *Makura-no-soshi*. Known as the 'Pillow Book' after the way she acquired the books to write in – 'Let me make of them a pillow' – Sei presents amusing observations and anecdotes of court life in an easy-going, even chatty style.

Music also played an important part in court life during the Heian period. Anyone with any claims to breeding or accomplishment was expected to play an instrument such as the lute or flute. As in fine art and literature, a new sense of cultural confidence found expression in more assertive Japanese styles.

Buddha from Byodoin
This cult figure occupies an honoured place inside the Byodoin Temple. The Fujiwara were avowed followers of Buddhism.

A Nara monk
The remarkable realism of this wooden sculpture illustrates the accomplishment of Japanese artists, who flourished during the Fujiwara dynasty.

Religious merger

Religion, and Buddhism in particular, was increasingly influencing output in the arts. Two different sects were competing at this time. First there was the Tendai School, founded as early as the 9th century by the monk Saicho, who built his monastery on a mountain called Hiai, near Kyoto. Laying great emphasis on public duty and respect for authority, Tendai teaching appealed to the imperial court – and to the Fujiwara, the power behind the scenes.

But enormous attention and interest were also commanded by the Shingon School, founded by a theologian called Kukai. Shingon was a more mystic creed, with a strong inclination towards the esoteric, so on the face of it, it could hardly have been more different to Tendai. Yet the withdrawal of its followers from worldly concerns meant that they were no more threatening to the political and social status quo than the eager conformists of the Tendai School.

Not surprisingly, by the end of the 10th century, the two schools had come together. Merged with older, indigenous elements, they formed the 'Ryobu Shinto', still practised in Japan to this day.

Yet all the illustrious achievements under the Fujiwara – in the arts, in literature, in religion – masked a dynasty in decline. Slowly but surely it became evident that the Fujiwara were past their peak: the all-encompassing authority of Michinaga was never quite recaptured.

A dynasty adrift

Tensions and discontent within the state were growing. What did the elite in Kyoto know of the lives of the wider population? What did the court care for the sufferings of the peasantry? Who was going to protect the people from increasing attacks by foreign raiders? Having long since ceased to look to their Emperors for guardianship, the Japanese directed their resentment towards their real rulers, the Fujiwara dynasty. Soon dissatisfaction was flaring up into actual resistance.

The sporadic outbreaks of unrest were easily enough put down. Far more alarming was the way a spirit of insurrection seemed to be spreading. Worse still for the Fujiwara was that the Emperors, previously puppets, seemed to be gaining in self-confidence. Was not the Tenno supposed to be an imperial ruler? And if so, should he not enjoy imperial authority? Why should an adult emperor have a regent, as though he were a child? Why should he be swayed by his chancellor, even if the latter were his own grandfather and father-in-law?

Several Tennos opted simply to remove themselves from the oppressive hold of a Fujiwara *kampaku* by abdicating – technically relinquishing their thrones. Their name and status still sufficed to command obedience and support in the country, however, so they could organise a system of government from which the Fujiwara were excluded.

With their authority visibly ebbing away, the Fujiwara found themselves having to contend with rivals. Right across the country, the rural warrior nobility was on the rise. Seen amid the splendours of the capital, the Fujiwara seemed undiminished in mastery and magnificence, but in the provinces, country-dwellers were looking to local magnates for leadership. Two families in particular rose to prominence towards the end of the 11th century, calling on all to make a stand against the old regime.

Almost imperceptibly, in eastern Japan, the warlike Taira clan had been building up a power base; and in the north the Minamoto had been growing steadily in strength. The latter had actually been in the service of the Fujiwara in Kyoto for some time, but sensing that their chances

of further advancement were limited, they had withdrawn to the provinces. The situation was volatile. The two clans may have shared a common goal of over-throwing the Fujiwara and their clique, but neither clan had any interest in sharing the spoils of victory. Violence buffeted the land as the two families fought for supremacy, and Japan threatened to sink into the chaos of civil war.

Reduced to the status of spectators, the Fujiwara looked on helplessly, kept in power only by the divisions among their rivals. A spent force, they could not hope to withstand the military might of the Taira or the Minamoto. And they were weakened still further by their own internal conflicts.

The bitter end

The Fujiwara dynasty's final collapse was a surprise to no one: the decisive moment came in 1156. After the death of Tenno Toba, the warriors of the Taira and Minamoto fought one another for supreme rule. Though the Taira had the upper hand to start with, the Minamoto eventually prevailed: a new era began for Japan with the foundation of Shogun rule.

Firing the palace
Go-Shirakawa's palace goes up in flames in 1156 during an internal Fujiwara feud over the imperial succession. This image of insurgents plundering the palace is from a 13th-century war-scroll.

The first samurai
The leader of the Minamoto clan in full warrior regalia. He is held to be the model for the traditional samurai fighter.

The victorious Seljuks

The 11th century saw the Middle East transformed, as a group of Turkic nomads known as the Seljuks pushed into Asia Minor. They came as feared conquerors, but won respect as rulers and as protectors of Sunni Islam.

Over the centuries, the cities of Europe and the Middle East had suffered a series of raids and attacks by warlike people from the Asian steppe. The Scythians, the Parthians, the Huns – all had been nomadic pastoralists first and foremost, roving the steppe in search of grazing and water for their flocks. Raiding was a profitable sideline, resorted to when times were hard, and westward migrations were sparked by scarcities and political instability at home. Now it was the turn of the Seljuk Turks.

Home for the Seljuks was the Syr Basin, an area of steppe to the north and east of the Aral Sea. They took their name from Seljuk, tribal chief of the Turkic confederation of the Oghuz, whose territories extended westward towards the shores of the Caspian Sea. In the later part of the 1st millennium AD, these peoples had moved southwards seeking better grazing; now they were centred on the areas around Bukhara and Samarkand, where the nomads' warlike temperament and fighting skills had made

them indispensable allies to the local rulers. According to Turkic tradition, Seljuk himself had aspirations of imperial conquest: he had seen himself in a dream, urinating fire over the world. In fact, the Seljuks would probably have remained content with their regional significance on the southern steppe had it not been for their conversion to Islam.

Muslim missionaries and traders had for some time been wandering the outer peripheries of Iran, bringing the teachings of the Prophet to the peoples of the steppe. When Seljuk and his clan were converted, they forsook the Oghuz Confederation and struck out alone; they had found a cause in Sunni orthodoxy. Sunni Muslims follow the *sunnah*, the customs and rituals of religious practice exemplified in the life of Muhammad and recorded by his followers as a code of law. They reject the claims of Shi'ites that only the Prophet's son-in-law Ali and his descendants were the rightful Imams or rulers of the Islamic world.

Around 1040, Seljuk's grandsons, Tugril Beg and Chagri, led the conquest of the Ghaznavid territories to the south, thrusting west into the heartland of Iran. Here, the Shi'ite state of the Buwayhids was soon toppled, as province after province fell to the Seljuks' swift advance. Establishing himself first in Rayy, just south of Tehran, Tugril Beg then set himself up as ruler in Isfahan, at the same time proclaiming himself protector of the 'rightful' Sunni caliphs in Baghdad.

A warlike people
Local princelings skirmish in the presence of the mighty Seljuk ruler, Malik Shah, in this miniature from a 16th-century manuscript.

The fortress of Aleppo, a stronghold of Seljuk power in Syria.

Seljuk warriors
The Seljuks were feared as fighters, not just as mounted archers. Their infantry wore chainmail tunics and conical helmets and were skilled with the sword and shield.

Terror centre
The Assassins operated out of fortified strongholds in Iran, Syria and Lebanon: they may have numbered as many as 60,000 at their height. Their main fortress was Alamut in Iran's Elburz Mountains.

The taking of Baghdad

This new development suited the caliphs, and they willingly recognised Tugril Beg's rule over his new territories. In return, he felt duty-bound to come to Caliph al-Quaim's aid when the latter came under pressure from his Buwayhid masters. The conquest of Baghdad in 1055, however, could not have been less dramatic: the Seljuks simply marched into the city. Not a drop of blood was shed.

Tugril Beg reinstated the spiritual authority of the Caliph, but wrested the secular authority from the Buwayhids for himself, taking the name of 'Sultan of the Eastern and Western Worlds'. This separation and reconciliation of the spiritual and secular spheres was sealed by a double marriage contract. The Caliph was to marry a niece of Tugril Beg and the Sultan would wed one of the Caliph's daughters. But before he could keep his side of the deal Tugril Beg died, in 1063, leaving his followers wondering how to administer their new territory.

The sudden acquisition of Iran and Mesopotamia presented the Seljuks with severe problems. As uneducated nomads, they felt ill-equipped to govern such great and sophisticated civilisations. They were pragmatic, however, and content to leave the old administrative structures in place: as long as their own ultimate authority in the land was acknowledged.

Iranian civil servants found their position strengthened, if anything, under the Seljuks; the vizier, as head of the civilian administration, became the most influential person in the land. Persian remained the official language and as attempts to integrate the nomads with the settled population largely failed, social structures in the new empire remained much the same as before.

Murder most effective – the Assassins

A radical Shi'ite sect, the Ismailites, won dubious notoriety throughout both the Islamic world and Christendom. Ferociously opposed to the Sunni Seljuks, but equally conscious of Seljuk strength, they resorted to methods that we would now call 'terrorism' in pursuit of their cause. In 1090, under their Persian leader Hasan as-Sabbah, the Ismailites conquered the mountain fortress of Alamut in the Elburz Mountains. They made it their base for a sustained campaign of harassment, disruption and murder.

From Alamut, Hasan's followers ventured forth – often in disguise – to make their way to the courts and cities of the Seljuks. Becoming ever bolder, they carried out countless politically motivated murders. Vizier Nizam al-Mulk, Sultan Malik Shah and Caliph al-Amir all fell victim to Hasan's Assassins, along with many other Sunni dignitaries. Christian Crusaders were another target for the killers – men like the Margrave Conrad of Montferrat and Count Raimund II of Tripoli.

Rumour had it that hashish was used to ignite fanaticism in the hearts of these 'fighters for Allah'. Although there was never any historical evidence for such claims, the notion held sufficient weight at the time for the group's members to be dubbed *hashshashin* – 'hashish-eaters'. Contracted to assassins, the term has been applied to political murderers ever since.

Tools of the trade
The Assassins took pride in their murderous work, regarding richly decorated knives and swords as status symbols. These have iron blades and bone handles decorated with silver.

Alp Arslan's 'divine mission'

Tugril Beg's nephew and successor as Sultan, Alp Arslan, was a charismatic personality. He was tall, it is said, and of extraordinary strength. His black moustache was so long he could tie it in a knot at the back of his neck. He was a daring rider, courageous in the field of battle. Yet this figure of warlike prowess also had a more thoughtful side: he became a keen student and active patron of science and the arts. Under him, the Seljuk Empire once more expanded vigorously. First he pushed westward, taking Byzantine territory in Asia Minor. Next he thrust further south, invading Syria and Egypt, both controlled by his enemies, the Shi'ite Fatimids. Alp Arslan conducted these campaigns under the cloak of religious duty: both Christians and Shi'ites were 'infidels' as far as the Sunni Seljuks were concerned.

Alp Arslan also had the blessing of the Caliph in Baghdad as Chief Commander, responsible for 'everything beyond the gates of the Caliph's palace', so his wars were seen as being fought in Islam's name. Having 'liberated' the holy cities of Mecca and Medina from Fatimid rule, he went on to capture Jerusalem and the important northern Syrian town of Aleppo in 1071.

Victory over the Byzantines

That same year, Alp Arslan's armies came face to face with those of the Byzantine emperor, Romanos IV, at Manzikert, beside Armenia's Lake Van. Romanos had marched to the eastern border of his empire with 200,000 men to cut off the Seljuk supply line into Egypt. Yet his hastily assembled army of mercenaries was clearly no match for Alp Arslan's battle-hardened Turks: many abandoned Romanos on the day of the battle. The Seljuks won a resounding victory and Romanos was led before the Sultan in chains – an outrageous humiliation for a proud empire and emperor.

The defeat represented a grievous wound for Byzantine power in Asia Minor. Turkic tribes streamed into what had been a Hellenistic land. Nomadic raiders were quickly followed by permanent settlers of Turkic descent, displacing a Christian population already depleted by emigration.

enjoyed an economic upturn and a flourishing trade developed with Europe via the ports of Palestine and Syria.

One of the most formative figures of the time was Nizam al-Mulk, vizier to both Alp Arslan and Malik Shah, who helped to determine the destiny of the Empire over a period of more than 30 years. Nizam was not only an important statesman, but a poet of high repute and compiler of an influential handbook about the art of government. He invited other literary luminaries to the Seljuk court, among them the poet Omar Khayyám, whose *Rubayat* was to become well-known in the West. Omar was, in fact, a scientist first and foremost: among other duties, he headed an observatory from which were made the observations which supported the calculation of a calendar. Nizam worked hard to encourage education throughout the realm. It was on his initiative that the so-called madrassahs, religious institutes of higher education, were established. The first was founded in Baghdad, but others followed in Basra, Mosul, Isfahan and Herat.

The assassins strike

The Seljuks' strict enforcement of Sunni orthodoxy inevitably alienated the Shi'ite population. One radical sect, the Ismailites, also known as the Assassins, fought the sultans with all the means at their disposal. In 1092, Assassins in disguise killed Nizam al-Mulk; later that same year they murdered Malik Shah. His death was also the death knell for the Seljuk Empire.

Turkic tradition ordained no clear rules for the succession – they had been, after all, free-ranging nomads of the steppes. So any male relative of the deceased chief could make his claim to rule: the man

Sufi at sea
The Persian mystic Abu Said, the founder of Sufism, is depicted on board a ship in this illustration from the 13th-century Arabic manuscript known as the *Maqamat Al-Hariri*. A mystical form of Islam, Sufism seeks unity with God through asceticism and contemplation. Its followers wear a penitent's robe of wool, *suf* in Arabic, from which comes the sect's name.

Gold dinarius
The earliest coins of the Seljuk period were minted in Nishapur and Merw under Seljuk's grandsons Tugril Beg and Chagri. This coin was minted in 1056-7, in the reign of Malik Shah

The 'Islamification' of those who remained progressed with surprising speed. Since these lands had formerly belonged to the Roman Byzantine Empire, its inhabitants came to be known as Rum-Seljuks.

By the time of his death, in 1072, Alp Arslan's empire extended from Afghanistan to Egypt. In his son, Malik Shah, it was to have its ideal ruler. Like his successors, Malik was a great admirer of Iranian culture and an eager patron of architecture, the arts and literature.

Imperial splendour

The Seljuk sultans built their residence at Isfahan in great splendour. They also rebuilt the city's Great Mosque on an impressive scale and in innovative style: it took the form of four buildings, clustered round a central court, and was reborn as a centre not just for prayer, but for spiritual and secular teaching. The marvellous domed hall, with its mihrab or prayer niche, is one of the architectural masterpieces of the age. Towns along the Empire's main commercial routes also with the most aggression and natural leadership would win. It may have worked well for nomads, but in the context of a settled society this was a recipe for chaos, and so the Empire began to disintegrate after the death of Malik Shah.

Pulling the Empire apart

Malik's son, Sandshar, could hold on to only Khorasan, in eastern Iran. The rest of the country was carved up between a snarling, squabbling pack of rival rulers. Some set up as sultans in Syria, Iraq and the regions of Asia Minor. The kingdom of the Rum-Seljuks was especially strong: as the centuries went by it would prove a headache for both Byzantium and the Christian crusaders.

In Syria, too, independent princedoms formed, the most important being centred on Aleppo and Damascus. The son of an insubordinate emir of Malik Shah, Imad ad-Din Zengi, created an empire of his own amid the wreckage of the Seljuks' empire in Syria: he played a key role in mobilising Muslim resistance to the Crusades. His son, Nur ad-Din, succeeded in uniting all the Seljuk princedoms from Mosul to the borders of Egypt. Nur ad-Din's nephew, Salah ud-Din, or Saladin, was serving

the last Fatimid Caliph of Cairo as vizier when he overthrew his Shi'ite master in favour of the Sunni Caliph of Baghdad. Saladin himself took over secular power in Egypt, establishing a new dynasty, the Ayyubids. In Iran, the centre of Seljuk power, the reign of Shandshar only postponed the inevitable: after his death in 1157, affairs deteriorated rapidly.

Seljuk princes had nominally ruled in the provinces, but they did so under the control of their Atabegs, or provincial governors – again, the sultan was subordinate to his supposed servant. In the confusion that followed the empire's collapse, new dynasties rose and fell with bewildering rapidity. One seemed destined for glory: in Khwarezmia, south of Lake Aral, Ala ad-Din Muhammad built an empire which, by 1205, held sway from Anatolia to India. But his Khwarezmid dynasty was to have only the merest taste of power before being swept away in the terrifying onslaught of the Mongols.

Symbol of Islamic power
The Great Mosque of Isfahan is among the most important monuments of the Seljuk era. It became a model for Muslim architects of later centuries.

Bagan – Burma's Buddhist empire

In the space of a few years, Burma grew from a small state into a mighty empire. Successive kings constructed extravagant temples as an expression of their greatness, leaving behind an awesome monumental legacy.

The great reliquary
With its shimmering central stupa of gold, Bagan's Shwezigon Pagoda is said to have been built to house a piece of the forehead and a tooth of the Buddha himself, given to Anawratha by the Sri Lankan King Vijayabahu.

Burma's rise began modestly. When, in 1044, Prince Anawratha ascended the throne of Bagan, a tiny city-state, no one would have guessed that he or his kingdom was destined for such great things. In fact, Anawratha was about to embark on an unprecedented campaign of military expansion which would ultimately bring all Burma under his rule. He started out by subjugating the smaller principalities adjoining his own, specially the important rice-growing areas of Kyauske and Minbu, to the south. Those aims successfully achieved, he set about protecting the northern flank of his new kingdom by fortifying existing defences and adding new ones. Then he secured his eastern frontier by making marriage alliances with the rulers of the Shan.

Bagan had been founded several centuries before by the Pyu, a tribal group with origins in Yunnan in southern China. Settling across the centre of what is now Myanmar, in the region of the Chindwin and Ayeyarwady rivers, the Pyu had made these arid lands productive by creating sophisticated irrigation systems. Even the *tattadesa* or 'dried up land' around Bagan itself was now fertile, thanks to the industry and ingenuity of this people.

The Burmese people also came from China, though they were more recent arrivals: from the 9th century onwards they had migrated into the region of Kyauske, south of present-day Mandalay, before following the River Ayeyarwady southwards. At last they, too, arrived in Bagan, where they learned about irrigation and wet rice-cultivation from the Pyu. They also became Buddhists.

Religious wars

Bagan was growing in importance but was still a pigmy-power beside a major southeast Asian kingdom such as Mon, in southern Burma. So when Anawratha took Thaton, the Mon capital, in 1057, it was a stunning coup – a complete reversal of the political pecking-order. For Bagan, though, there was no looking back: during the following 250 years, only the Khmer kingdom of Angkor would prove to be a rival of equal standing.

Anawratha claimed his conquests were motivated by religion. According to tradition, the King had been converted by

Shin Arahan, an orthodox Buddhist monk of the Theravada school from what is now Sri Lanka. Theravada – literally, 'The Way of the Elders' – is the oldest and most conservative form of Buddhism and lays emphasis on the individual's responsibility for his or her own salvation.

In Theravada the Buddha's words, as passed on orally then faithfully written down in the Tripitaka, are regarded as the only true and permissible Buddhist doctrine. Mahayana Buddhism, in contrast, allows for the mediation of bodhisattvas – Buddhist 'saints' immortalised through their own enlightenment. More accommodating of local traditions, this version was taken up quickly and extensively across much of southern and southeast Asia around the turn of the millennium. Anawratha's embrace of Theravada was exceptional, and

Burmese bodhisattva
Statues of gilt-covered wood and stone were placed in many Mahayana temples. Bodhisattvas represented enlightened beings prepared to help others.

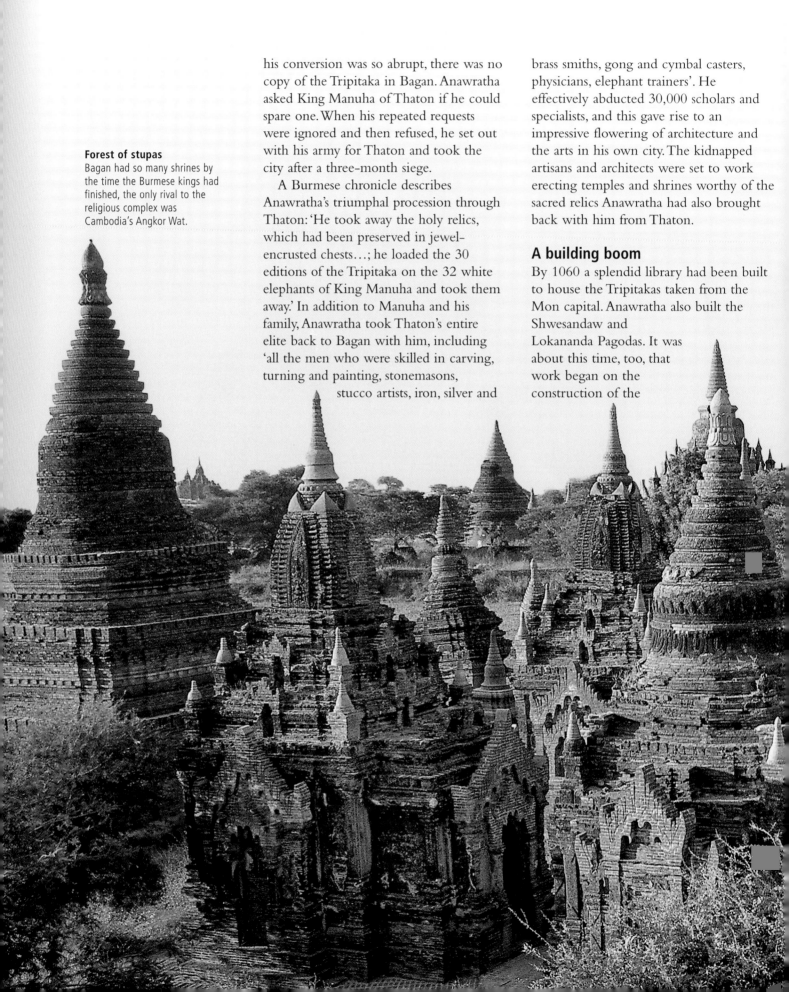

Forest of stupas
Bagan had so many shrines by the time the Burmese kings had finished, the only rival to the religious complex was Cambodia's Angkor Wat.

his conversion was so abrupt, there was no copy of the Tripitaka in Bagan. Anawratha asked King Manuha of Thaton if he could spare one. When his repeated requests were ignored and then refused, he set out with his army for Thaton and took the city after a three-month siege.

A Burmese chronicle describes Anawratha's triumphal procession through Thaton: 'He took away the holy relics, which had been preserved in jewel-encrusted chests…; he loaded the 30 editions of the Tripitaka on the 32 white elephants of King Manuha and took them away.' In addition to Manuha and his family, Anawratha took Thaton's entire elite back to Bagan with him, including 'all the men who were skilled in carving, turning and painting, stonemasons, stucco artists, iron, silver and brass smiths, gong and cymbal casters, physicians, elephant trainers'. He effectively abducted 30,000 scholars and specialists, and this gave rise to an impressive flowering of architecture and the arts in his own city. The kidnapped artisans and architects were set to work erecting temples and shrines worthy of the sacred relics Anawratha had also brought back with him from Thaton.

A building boom

By 1060 a splendid library had been built to house the Tripitakas taken from the Mon capital. Anawratha also built the Shwesandaw and Lokananda Pagodas. It was about this time, too, that work began on the construction of the

Shwezigon Pagoda, its great central stupa a shimmering blaze of gold. The building programme inaugurated by Anawratha gathered momentum under his successors. The next two centuries saw the creation of literally thousands of pagodas and temples up and down Burma: 'The towers are built out of stone and one of these was covered in gold at least as thick as a finger,' a Chinese visitor would afterwards report, his account eagerly recorded at secondhand by the Venetian traveller Marco Polo. 'Another was covered in silver in the same manner: the kings had these towers built to demonstrate their greatness, but also for the salvation of their souls. They really are one of the greatest sights in the world … when the sun shines on them, they glow visibly across the land.' Even today, some 2500 sacred structures still rise above the plain of

Bagan, silent witnesses to the former splendour of that kingdom.

This frantic building boom paid dividends in the aura of saintliness that it conferred on the King. To prove his own piety and to encourage the spread of a teaching which upheld his reputation, he felt called upon to build temples and establish monasteries. Others, too, stood to gain by making donations. The whole of society was caught up in a great collective building project, from the royal house right down to the working poor. Temple inscriptions provide evidence that donors could share the spiritual rewards with others, or even transfer them entirely.

Thus Rajakumar, son of King Kyanzittha, paid for the construction of the Kubyaukgi Temple in Myinkaba, south of Bagan, in gratitude for his father's recovery from illness.

Despite his assertions of religious motivation, Anawratha's expansion into southern Burma was almost certainly for economic reasons. His kingdom straddled one of southeast Asia's most important trading routes. Goods were already being brought to Bagan from Bengal and western China in the north. By taking control of Thaton and the other Mon ports Anawratha gained a gateway on the Indian Ocean, as well as the overseas trade with eastern China, the East Indies, India and with Sri Lanka, soon to be Burma's most important commercial partner and political ally.

Anawratha's successors

In 1077, Anawratha was killed by a wild water buffalo. His son, Saw-lu, found it harder than his father had done to hold on to power: his reign saw a series of insurrections among the Mon and the loss of much conquered territory. In one of these rebellions, King Saw-lu himself was killed. One of his generals, Kyanzittha, seized power.

Kyanzittha reigned for 30 years, expanding the realm to cover most of modern Myanmar. He sent out ambassadors to China to encourage trade, and with the same sense of public piety as his predecessors, supported the renovation of the Mahabodi Temple at Bihar in India. This was where Prince Siddhartha was said to have become the Buddha, so Kyanzittha's work here won him the approbation of the entire Buddhist world.

Like Anawratha, Kyanzittha was an active, energetic king. Always on the move, he took personal charge of construction and irrigation projects and the administration of justice. A patron to monasteries and shrines all over the country, he completed Bagan's Shwezigon Pagoda and also built the famous Ananda Temple. As ever, piety served political ends: a golden statue of Kyanzittha in the temple made clear his claim to rule.

When Kyanzittha died, in 1113, the succession skipped a generation: he had asked that his grandson, Alaungsithu, should follow him on to the throne. His own son, Rajakumar, was a studious and contemplative recluse, whereas his grandson had already proven himself a tough and skilful military commander. Alaungsithu became known as 'the Long-lived King' because he reigned for more than half a century, till 1167, and under his rule the Burmese kingdom had its heyday of wealth and power.

Reflecting the kingdom's new self-confidence, Burmese replaced Mon as the official language of administration. In architecture the Mon influence began to

Sacred statuary
These figures from Bagan's Ananda Temple represent the Buddha and one of his teachers, Alara or Uddaka.

ebb away: the Burmese preferred the Pyu style of building, topping cylindrical towers with bulbous domes, rather than the more angular, pyramidal structures of the Mon. All areas not under the direct control of the capital were compelled to pay handsome tribute. Like his grandfather, Alaungsithu was a practical ruler who travelled widely throughout his realm overseeing important projects and initiated reform of weights and measures to simplify administration.

Alaungsithu left behind a stable and wealthy kingdom, but his successors were not to prove his equals. For a time the kingdom prospered well enough – in some ways it improved. Reforms to the administrative system enhanced both the hold of the state and increased its revenues: women were now treated as feudal subjects and taxed as such.

The appointment of inspectors in every village allowed imperial power to extend into the heart of every household. The ruler rewarded these officials with special insignia and privileges. Gifts of containers for betel nuts were made – an important status symbol; betel nuts were popularly chewed for their mildly narcotic effects. Among other privileges, it was in the power of the King to grant the right to ride on an elephant, to wear silk or jewellery, or to have a certain seat in the audience hall. The granting of such favours, like the awarding of feudal land, constituted a connection between the King and his official. They also reminded the subject of the power of the royal whim, since they could be withdrawn at will by the King or a successor.

The downward slide

The problem with such a system is that it institutionalises pride and pomp, almost ensuring the inflation of empty gesture over action. There was more than a hint of absurdity and decadence creeping into the manners of Burma's ruling caste. The risks of this sort of arrogance had been seen even in Alaungsithu's reign when, in 1164, he had mistreated a legation from the Sri Lankan King, Parakramabahu I. A Sri Lankan expeditionary force was dispatched and severely chastised Burmese forces – no lasting damage was done, but the humiliation was keenly felt. The final end of Bagan came in response to an even worse display of arrogance when a later king had Mongol ambassadors killed. In 1287 the Mongols overran Bagan.

Scenes from the Buddha's life
The elaborate wall paintings in the Lokahteikpan Temple served as subjects for religious contemplation and for teaching. They show events from the Buddha's life, as well as his followers worshipping him.

The first Crusades – war in the name of God

At the end of the 11th century, western Christendom took up arms to liberate the holy city of Jerusalem from its Muslim rulers, triggering a 200-year confrontation.

The gathering of church leaders and their lay supporters at the Council of Clermont in November, 1095, took a decidedly dramatic turn when Pope Urban II stood up to address the convention. Trembling with emotion, he launched an impassioned and eloquent appeal on behalf of the suffering Christians of Palestine. The godless Saracens, said the Holy Father, had over run the eastern outposts of Christianity.

'Penetrating deeper and deeper into the land of these Christians,' he declared, his words recorded by the chronicler Caplan Fulcher of Chartres, 'they have beaten them seven times in battle, have killed a great number of them or taken them prisoner, have destroyed churches and laid waste to the land.' They had captured Anatolia and stood on the very banks of the Bosphorus, at the threshold of Christian Europe. The Pope pleaded with those present for their support.

'This is why I am begging you and urge you – no, not I, but the Lord Himself begs you and implores you, as the heralds of Christ, the poor as well as the wealthy, to rush and drive away this mean rabble from the regions inhabited by your brothers, and to bring rapid relief to those who worship Christ.'

His audience recognised the challenge in his words, but they were ready to respond with their very lives: thousands of voices repeated the cry, '*Deus vult!*' – 'God wills it!' They threw themselves to the floor before the papal throne and afterwards, to mark their commitment to this almost militarised pilgrimage, pinned crosses of red fabric to their clothes. The great adventure was set for the following year; it would begin on August 15, the Feast of the Assumption. What more auspicious day could there be for so sacred and ambitious an undertaking than the anniversary of Our Lady's transportation, body and soul, from earth to heaven?

Salvation through soldiering

Urban II's inflammatory speech mobilised all Christendom. Thousands flocked to make the journey to the Middle East – not just knights and their armed retinues but also merchants and tradesmen of every type, and a rag-tag army of peasants, apprentices and vagabonds. Motivations were varied: some sought glory and adventure, while others saw the possibility of plunder, but the part played by spiritual

Church militant
A cross in one hand and a sword in the other, Pope Urban II calls on the faithful to enlist in the First Crusade.

Christian soldier
The Crusaders saw their mission as part pilgrimage, part military campaign. An illustration from a 12th century manuscript captures both of these aspects. The orders of the Knights Templars, the Knights of St John and the Teutonic Knights were actually armed priests.

fervour should not be underestimated. The sense of religious duty was strong in the Middle Ages, as was the Catholic custom of offering sacrifices of prayer or service for some specified 'intention' – the easing of a sick relation's sufferings, or the repose of a departed soul. In this case, there was the clear promise of heavenly reward. Not wishing to rely too much on Christian commitment, Urban had made it clear that participants in his 'crusade' could expect 'indulgence' on Judgment Day – the pardoning of their sins, and accelerated passage into Paradise.

Political realities

The huge groundswell of support seems to have far exceeded Urban's expectations, since his actual aims were much more modest. His speech at Clermont had been prompted by a message from the Byzantine Emperor, Alexius I, handed to him at the Council of Piacenza a few months earlier. The Emperor had

TIME WITNESS

The massacre of Jerusalem

The Christian conquest of Jerusalem on July 15, 1099, began with a wholesale massacre. 'No one had ever heard of such a bloodbath among pagan peoples as this one,' Archbishop William of Tyre reported. Thousands of Jews and Muslims – men, women and children – were put to the sword.

'If you had been there,' wrote Fulcher of Chartres, 'you would have seen our feet discoloured to our ankles in the blood of the slain. ... None of them were left alive; neither women nor children were spared.'

Raimund of Agiles wrote 'Countless Saracens were beheaded or hurled to their death from the towers.'

informed His Holiness of the invasion of Asia Minor by the Turkish Seljuks and requested his help in defending Christian Constantinople.

For decades, Europe had been caught up in a great struggle for supremacy between Europe's spiritual and temporal powers. Urban saw Alexius' letter as offering an opportunity to break this stalemate and press home his supreme authority as leader of the world's Christians. He hoped that it might also enable him to heal the rift between the Church in the East and the West which had existed since the schism of 1054. Islam offered a convenient 'other' against which a divided Christian Europe could unite; the Crusade was a cause to give quarrelsome rulers common ground.

Initially, Urban and Alexius had envisaged only a very limited force recruited in the south of France, an elite troop to be deployed at Constantinople under Byzantine leadership. But for all its many glories, Constantinople did not fire the western imagination in anything like the way that Jerusalem did: many medieval maps placed Jesus's city at the

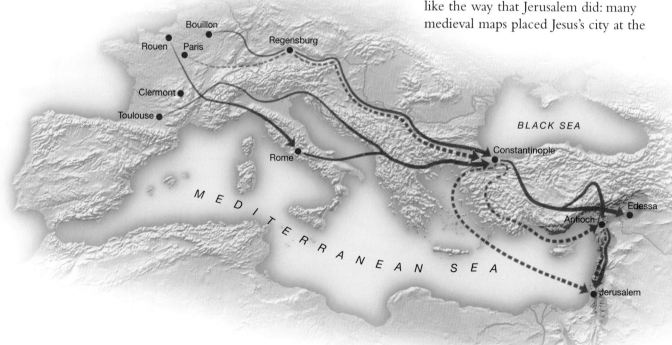

Crusader states

First Crusade 1096-1099

Second Crusade 1147-1149

Main towns and cities

centre of the world.
Jerusalem awoke deep
feelings in the mass of the
population. Despite the fact
that these 'Holy Places' had
been in Muslim hands for
some four centuries, all of a
sudden Christendom
decided to feel outraged.

The great adventure

If piety played its part in
this mass movement, so too
did a spirit of escapism
fostered by a range of
economic and social
problems. The medieval
masses were economically
exploited and politically
oppressed, and their feudal
masters were in a state of
unrest. Despite their
comparatively privileged
position, minor knights and
nobles felt trapped, caught
up in conflicts over which
they had no control. Famines afflicted
France; there was a sense of stagnation.
The Crusade offered an escape from what
was often a grim routine.

Their fervour could not be contained:
well before August, the first impetuous
hordes were setting out, often under
extremely dubious leadership. The most
influential of these self-appointed Crusade
leaders was a wandering preacher called
Peter of Amiens, better known to history
as Peter the Hermit. Riding on a donkey,
like Christ Himself in his humble
triumph in Jerusalem, Peter went from
place to place denouncing pagans and
infidels and announcing the advent of
Heaven on Earth. As he went, he gathered
an enormous army of enthusiastic
followers – up to 100,000 strong –
convinced that they were enlisting under
a saint. Packing their belongings and
children into ox carts they left their old
lives behind them, eager to follow Peter
wherever he might lead.

The people's pogrom

The so-called 'People's Crusade' soon
degenerated into a murderous pogrom.
Why travel hundreds of miles to face an
unknown foe when Christ's killers were
to be found right here at home? An
ever-increasing mass of people travelled
through Lorraine, headed for the Rhine –
actually away from Jerusalem – and forced
their way into the cities of Aachen and
Cologne. Jews were massacred and
synagogues burned down – in Mainz,
Worms and Speyer, too – before these
'crusaders' made their way towards
Constantinople. Robbing, murdering and
raping as they went, they moved on
through Hungary and the Balkans.

Alexius I was appalled at the mob
which eventually arrived outside his city
in the summer of 1096. He ordered that
they be sent across the Bosphorus to Asia
Minor without further ado: there they
proved easy prey to the attacks of the
Seljuk Turks.

A fight to the death
Jerusalem's Muslim defenders
fought desperately to save the city,
and their fears of the Crusaders
were to prove well-founded. The
frenzy of killing is captured in this
illustration from a French
manuscript of the 14th century.

Bitter conflict

The fury of the fight for the Holy Land was fuelled by cultural differences as well as rival religious enthusiasms. The clash of civilisations is depicted in this illustration from a French book of the late 11th century.

Krak des Chevaliers

The Knights of St John obtained possession of this formidable stronghold in 1142. Still the best-preserved of the Crusader Castles, it could house an occupying force of 2000 men, along with all the provisions they might need for several years.

Square and round towers were built into the castle's 9m (30ft) high curtain wall. There were slits for arrows and spouts through which hot pitch could be poured on attackers.

Between the outer and inner walls lay an open area with a moat.

An aqueduct fed the moat, which was both a defensive barrier and water source.

Suspect motives

The Emperor was not much more favourably impressed by the real Crusader army, which began to arrive in August 1096, just a few weeks after Peter's rabble had appeared.

It was not the strength or determination of the force he doubted: it numbered some 50,000–60,000 well-armed and experienced fighting men, as well as innumerable attendants, porters, priests and female followers. The problem was rather the commitment of the Crusaders.

For a start, they were overwhelmingly French – already excommunicated by the Pope, the German Holy Roman Emperor, Henry IV, had shown no interest in what had been very much a papal initiative. By the spring of 1097, the cream of French nobility had gathered, including such powerful lords as Count Raimund of Toulouse and Count Hugo of Vermandois, brother of King Philip of France. Count Robert II of Normandy was here, as was his fellow-Norman, Boehmund of Tarent, who had brought along his nephew, Tancred of Lecce, destined for epic fame as a warrior against Islam. Every bit as illustrious was Godfrey of Bouillon, the Count of Lorraine, who had travelled with his brother, Baldwin of Boulogne.

Alexius could hardly reject the Crusaders' assistance, but he insisted that they swore an oath of loyalty, promising to return all the lands they conquered back to the Byzantine crown.

Mixed fortunes

It was not long before the Crusaders registered their first success, conquering the Seljuk capital of Nicaea on Lake Iznik

and fighting their way over the Anatolian mountains into northern Syria. But poor preparation and inadequate logistics turned triumph into disaster over the course of the relatively short but desperately gruelling march to Palestine. A gigantic army – not just men, women and children, but also horses and beasts of burden – had to make their way across arid terrain in a season of scorching heat. Many thousands died in great suffering: of the 100,000 who set out, only 40,000 arrived, exhausted, at the gates of Antioch.

As the strategic centre of Syria, the city of Antioch was heavily fortified: undaunted, the Crusaders settled down for a prolonged siege. After seven long, hard months, Bohemund of Tarent talked the city's Christian inhabitants into betraying their fellow-citizens and opening the gates: on June 3, 1098, Antioch was taken. Buoyed up by this success the Crusaders were able to hold on to their prize, fighting off a Turkish relief force led by Kerbogha of Mosul.

VIEWPOINT

Liberators or conquerors?

The inhabitants of the Holy Land viewed the invasion by the European Crusaders in different ways. In northern Syria and northern Mesopotamia, a predominantly Christian population of Greeks, Syrians and Armenians welcomed them. They were delighted to be delivered from the Turkish yoke by their co-religionists. Likewise, it was at the entreaty of the city's Christian Armenian community that Baldwin of Boulogne took Edessa. In Antioch, too, Christian inhabitants collaborated with the Crusaders, opening the gates to let them in.

In southern Syria and Palestine, the coming of the Crusaders was regarded very differently: to the majority Muslim population they were barbaric invaders. Outraged by the sacking of Jerusalem and the accompanying slaughter, they seethed with anger and schemed for the recovery of the city.

The word *jihad*, assumed by many non-Muslims to mean 'Holy War', is far too narrow an interpretation of a concept that embraces spiritual 'striving' or 'struggle' of every sort. It was at about this time, however, under inspired leaders like Nur ad-Din and Salah ad-Din (Saladin), that the idea of an Islamic counter-crusade began to gain strength.

The battle for Jerusalem

After resting in Antioch, the Crusaders continued on their way to the Holy City. On June 7, 1099, they gazed upon Jerusalem for the first time. Since they had set out on their march, the situation in the city had changed: Arab Fatimids had driven out the occupying Seljuks, and

Different types of tower were constructed in the inner fortifications. The Grand Master of the Knights had beautifully furnished living quarters in the southwest tower.

At the heart of the castle was the so-called 'Great Hall' with a richly decorated antechamber. Close by there was a military chapel.

The only access to the castle was through the East Gate.

Together again
Crusading campaigns could go on for years, and many who went would never return. The happy homecoming illustrated by this late 12th-century statue was the exception, not the rule.

they were not going to give up their conquest lightly. Jerusalem was every bit as sacred to the Muslims as it was to the Christians. Their name for the city, al-Quds, meant 'sacred', for it was from the Temple Mount that Muhammad was held to have been borne up to Heaven by a host of angels in a vision one night; he had left behind his footprint, which is venerated in the Dome of the Rock. Beside it stands the al-Aqsa mosque, known throughout the Islamic world as a centre for worship and for religious learning.

Military skirmishes and the rigours of the climate had continued to wear down the Christian forces, which now numbered no more than 20,000 men. Not surprisingly, the first bid to take the city failed. Morale among the attackers was soon flagging – it took a vision to renew the Crusaders' courage. A priest named Peter Desiderius reported a dream in which a divine plan of action had been revealed to him. The Crusaders were to fast, before marching barefoot around the city in solemn procession; nine days later, he said,

Jerusalem would fall. The plan was clearly based on the biblical story of Joshua at Jericho – and it was to prove just as successful. Praying and singing, the army marched around Jerusalem three times. The assault itself began on the night of July 13, 1099. After much ferocious fighting, a group led by Godfrey of Bouillon managed to break through the wall from a siege tower.

Division of the spoils

The next task was to secure the conquered sites. Four 'Crusader States' were established in Palestine: the kingdom of Jerusalem, the principality of Antioch, and the counties of Edessa and Tripoli. Baldwin of Boulogne had broken away from the official Crusader force as early as spring 1098 to establish his own state on the upper Euphrates at Edessa – now Urfa, Turkey, but then in northeast Syria. Bohemund of Tarent had also defected, remaining in Antioch when the Crusade moved on: having masterminded its capture, he regarded the city as his personal property. In the same way, Godfrey of Bouillon saw Jerusalem as his spoils of war. In a show of humility, however, he refused the title of king, and called himself 'Advocate of the Holy Sepulchre'. Baldwin, his brother and successor, was to show no such modesty: he chose Christmas Day 1100 for his coronation, and held it in Bethlehem's Church of the Nativity.

Baldwin then expanded his kingdom to include the coastal cities of Acre (now Akko), Beirut and Sidon. Raimund of Toulouse, who had so far been left with nothing, defiantly obtained for himself a zone of power between Antioch and Jerusalem with a capital at the seaport of Tripoli in Lebanon, though his son Bertrand would not finally make the realm secure until 1109.

Just as Alexius had feared, the Byzantine Empire got nothing at all: the Christian princes 'forgot' the oaths they had sworn to restore the lands to their former ruler.

For the West, these Christian principalities offered a gateway to the East. Merchants from Genoa, Venice and Pisa made huge profits from the trade in luxuries. A steady stream of pilgrims helped to fill the coffers, and Palestine was also attracting immigrants. By the end of the 12th century, 120,000 Franks had settled in the Kingdom of Jerusalem alone: the crusader states were becoming rich and strong.

The Second Crusade

In December 1144, Edessa was taken by a Turkish force under the Seljuk military leader, Imad ad-Din Zengi, and Pope Eugene III called on Christians to mount a Second Crusade. Specifically, he called on Bernard of Clairvaux, widely revered as leader of the Cistercians and a renowned orator, to stir up enthusiasm. At Easter in 1146, thousands thronged to Vézelay in Burgundy to hear Bernard preach, among them King Louis VII of France and his leading vassals. Bernard's sermon had the desired effect, then he travelled through Europe issuing the call to arms. On December 27, 1146, he addressed the Assembly at Speyer with such conviction that the Staufer King Conrad III enlisted on the spot. Christendom was on the march once more.

The following spring, the French and German contingents set out with their respective kings. But this Crusade was not as successful as the first. Conrad III's army got off to a bad start, suffering a disastrous defeat against the Seljuks in Anatolia. Louis VII's troops won a minor victory at Ephesus, but were badly beaten outside Laodicea. Numbers were severely reduced by the time the two armies linked up at Nicaea, and they were by no means a united force. Within the French camp alone there were clear differences: Raimund of Antioch wanted only the reconquest of Edessa, while Louis VII was determined to make a pilgrimage to Jerusalem. Only the Holy Places mattered, as far as he was concerned. (The French king's piety was legendary: his wife Eleanor of Aquitaine complained that she had wed a king but found herself married to a monk. She was rumoured to have had an affair with Raimund of Antioch, which may suggest a more worldly reason for the tensions between the two men.)

On arriving in the Holy City, the German and French Crusaders made the fatal decision to attack Damascus, a long-time ally of the Kingdom of Jerusalem. Politically ill-considered and militarily inept, the undertaking collapsed miserably in 1148. The Crusaders headed home, defeated.

Defeat at Damascus
The decision to attack Damascus during the Second Crusade rebounded very badly on the Christian cause. Not only did the siege of the city fail, but the undignified retreat of the Crusaders opened the way to the Muslim 'Saviour', Nur ad-Din. This illustration of the failed siege is from a book written by William of Tyre, around 1280.

Pilgrim's flask
Many pilgrims carried a small drinking flask, which became emblematic of the idea of pilgrimage. This one from the early 12th century is decorated with a siege tower motif.

A world of warriors

Heavily-armed riders with protective armour, based on cavalry of the late-Roman and Byzantine Empires, were first seen in Europe in the 9th century. As the Middle Ages progressed, armoured knights would come to dominate more than just the battlefields of Europe – the entire economic system revolved around keeping them equipped. Nobles derived their income from the feudal lands put at their disposal by the king in return for their services and support in times of war. A whole culture grew up around this essentially military caste, while the 'gentle' virtues of grace and good manners that it was held to exemplify off the battlefield inspired much of the age's music and literature.

Samurai and steppe warriors

At about the same time, a strikingly similar development was taking place in Japan's northern and eastern provinces, where warrior families were emerging as a separate class. They had honed their war skills and won political influence as fighters for the emperor, putting down rebellions among the region's natives, the Emishi. The Samurai, as they became known, lived by a strict code of honour called bushido – 'the path of the warrior'.

Mounted warriors had played an important part in the initial spread of Islam. Now, the Seljuks and Ottoman Turks found them invaluable for establishing power in the Muslim world. Originally nomadic, these peoples acquired their skills of horsemanship and mounted warfare on the Asian steppe. They maintained the tradition with troops of mercenaries and military slaves from Central Asia.

In addition to mounted cavalry, the armies of all of these civilisations had infantry, ranging from lightly to heavily armoured, often with specialised skills depending on the region they came from.

The armoured Byzanti[ne]
cavalry helped the Empire
victories over the Ara[b]
steppe peoples and Sla[v]

Armour gave
Toltec soldiers
an edge
over their
neighbours in
battle.

European knights
Islamic world
Byzantine Empire
Japanese samurai
Steppe warriors
Toltec Empire

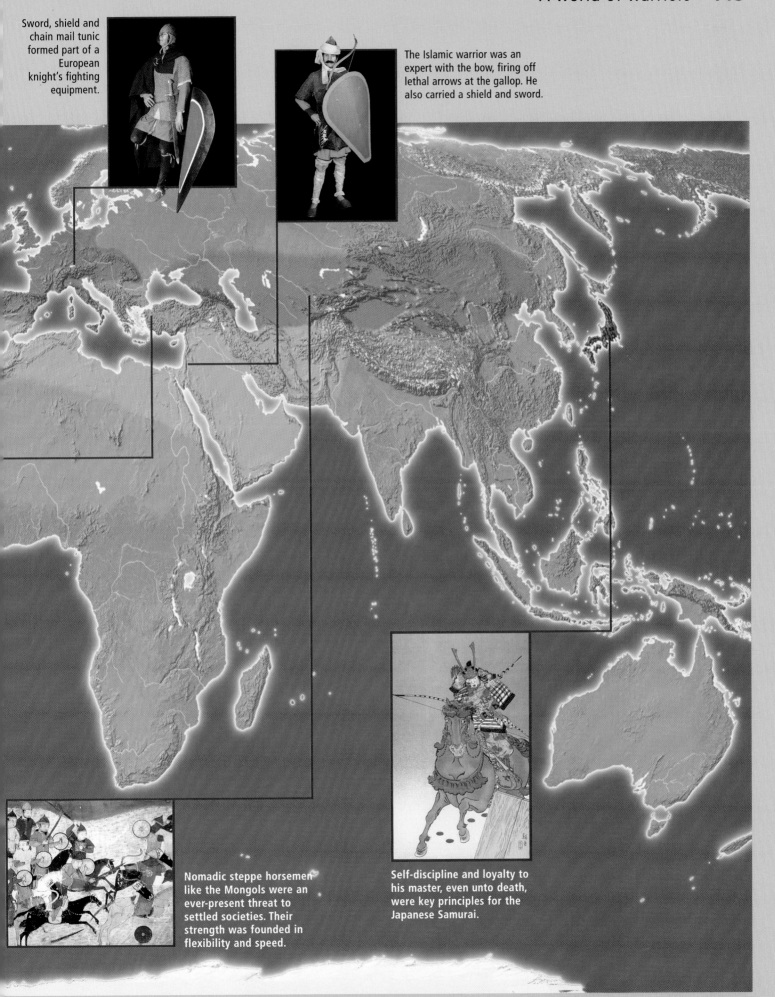

Sword, shield and chain mail tunic formed part of a European knight's fighting equipment.

The Islamic warrior was an expert with the bow, firing off lethal arrows at the gallop. He also carried a shield and sword.

Nomadic steppe horsemen like the Mongols were an ever-present threat to settled societies. Their strength was founded in flexibility and speed.

Self-discipline and loyalty to his master, even unto death, were key principles for the Japanese Samurai.

Armed and ready – a warrior's weapons

Making weapons and armour had always been the work of specialised craftsmen. The most important item of protection was the shield, in various shapes and sizes. In Europe, shields were widely made of wood, covered over with leather. Multiple layers of leather were glued together to make thick shields in the East.

Around the turn of the First Millennium, chain mail, already used much earlier by the Celts, became more widely distributed through Europe and the Islamic world. Byzantine and Middle Eastern armourers made particular use of scale-mail, sewing small metal plates on to a leather or textile lining. Lamellar armour was similar, but here rectangular sections of iron or lacquered leather were sewn not to a base beneath but to one another. This was lighter and more elastic, though still strong and durable, which made it especially suitable for cavalry. It was used extensively in the Byzantine and Islamic–Central Asian world. Round iron helmets of much the same sort were in widespread use to protect the head; these were often equipped with a nose guard, which in Europe later evolved into a visor covering the whole face.

Offensive weapons

The most important weapons for attack were swords and spears, or lances. In Europe, Byzantium and the Far East, long swords with double-edged blades were largely favoured. Scimitars, swords with slightly curved blades, were first used in Central Asia, arriving in the Near East in about AD 1000, when they were introduced by Turkish mercenaries. Bows, battle-axes and heavy clubs or maces completed the arsenal of weapons for combat.

Above: The sword of the European knight was derived from early medieval swords like this. It was not just a weapon but a crucial status symbol.

Below: The warriors of Mesoamerica wore elaborate feather headdresses into battle. Their bodies were protected by armour of padded cotton.

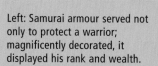

Left: Samurai armour served not only to protect a warrior; magnificently decorated, it displayed his rank and wealth.

Right: Warriors in early Mexico carried wooden shields like this one, covered with leather and dramatically decorated with feathers.

Below: A European warrior on horseback equipped with a spear, a helmet with nose guard, knee-length chain mail vest and a 'Norman shield', which provided good protection for a rider.

Charges, crossbows and catapults – techniques of warfare

Knights were equipped for fighting on horseback and would dismount in battle only if they had to. They carried long, heavy spears, but to begin with they simply lunged at the enemy with them; after the turn of the millennium, charging with a lowered lance become the favoured method. The bow and crossbow were regarded as unworthy of the dignity of the knight: they were weapons for foot-soldiers drawn from the peasantry. Noble Japanese Samurai, on the other hand, were outstanding bowmen, both on foot and on horseback. Mounted archers represented the main forces among all the Central Asian steppe peoples. They would attack in a hail of arrows, then pretend to flee. If an enemy took the bait, he would find himself charging into a trap, where more heavily armoured cavalry troops were waiting.

Siege tactics

Besieging fortified towns and castles was an important part of war. Attackers employed a variety of siege engines designed to hurl stones, burning missiles and darts through the air with great accuracy; battering rams were used against gates and walls. If a way could not be found through massive wall defences, sappers might attempt to undermine them.

Though invariably costly in lives, the attackers might seek to climb directly over the walls by mounting long scaling ladders or mighty mobile siege-towers. These had wooden frameworks and were often covered with fresh animal hides which could be dampened to give some protection against fire. In Byzantium and the Islamic world, in particular, various fire missiles were employed, including the so-called 'Greek fire'. This liquid chemical, the contents of which are still unknown, was either fired at the enemy by a pump-like siphon – an early flame-thrower – or hurled at them in grenades.

Below: Sophisticated siege engines could inflict enormous damage on masonry fortifications. The largest medieval catapults could hurl stones up to 90kg (200lb) in weight. It was therefore a priority for defenders to set these machines alight and disable them.

Right: The Samurai warrior wore lightweight armour that allowed him to operate far more flexibly than the Western knight. A Samurai could fight as comfortably on foot as in a cavalry role.

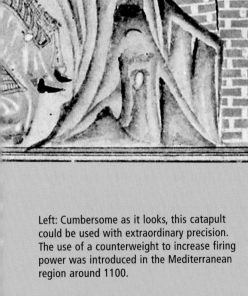

Left: Cumbersome as it looks, this catapult could be used with extraordinary precision. The use of a counterweight to increase firing power was introduced in the Mediterranean region around 1100.

Right: War among the indigenous peoples of the Americas was primarily aimed at displaying individual prowess – and seizing captives for human sacrifice.

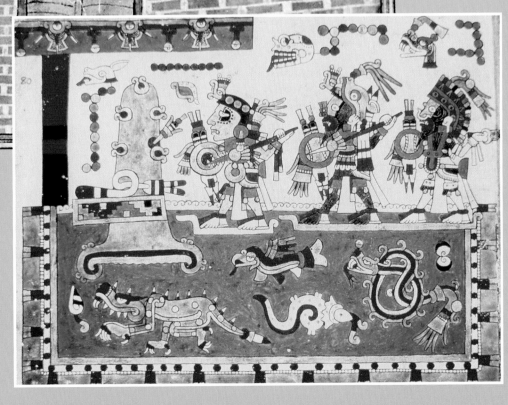

Castles, cities and encampments

Left: Harold's defeat by William the Conqueror brought a change in building style in England, as the victorious Normans consolidated their rule by constructing stone castles. These were the biggest stone buildings erected in Britain since Roman times – the most famous of them was the White Tower in London.

Below: The Middle Ages were dangerously unstable times in Europe, and the typical medieval castle was built far more for security than for physical comfort or aesthetic appeal. This one was built by the Normans in Sicily in 1076.

Right: Viking settlers in Greenland and North America lived in the simplest of homes, with walls and roof built of turf. This reconstruction is at L'Anse aux Meadows National Historic Site in Newfoundland, Canada.

The first castles of the Middle Ages were called mottes, after a medieval French word *mote*, meaning 'mound', which was just about all these early structures really were. Earth was heaped up into a hill and a simple wooden tower constructed on top. An earthen wall with a wooden palisade – and perhaps a water-filled ditch – ran round the base. Over time, wealthier lords built bigger, more sophisticated fortresses, with additional buildings and encircling 'curtain' walls of stone. Ultimately, important castles grew into well-planned fortified complexes with numerous courtyards, defensive bastions and projecting towers.

The Crusades represented a key moment in the evolution of the castle, as Byzantine and Islamic fortification techniques came to European notice at this time. There was little sign of increasing comfort inside, however. Castle interiors were gloomy, cramped and austere: defense and domination of the surrounding area were the key priorities, and the elegant château still lay a long way in the future.

The endemic instability of the times compelled cities to surround themselves with castle-like fortifications, so that they would not be at the mercy of bullying nobles. In the event of a siege, any citizen who could bear arms would help to man the walls. The autonomy of the city was fiercely guarded. In the Byzantine Empire and Far East, too, all major towns and cities were heavily fortified – Byzantium's massive walls were particularly famous.

Above: The peoples of North and Central America were gifted builders. Pueblo Indians exploited existing geological formations, like this overhanging rock shelf, to provide protection for their dwellings. The individual storeys were only accessible via ladders.

Strength in mobility

The life of the nomadic peoples of Central Asia was very different. Among the sedentary societies of Europe and the East, fine horses were expensive status symbols for a small elite. Out on the steppe, however, the horse was everyone's indispensable companion, the medium for both work and transport, and the vast grasslands provided pasture for huge herds. The mobile lifestyle traditionally included hunting on horseback with bow and arrow, and the practice stood young men in good stead when it came to war.

Below: The nomadic peoples of the steppes lived in felt gers or yurts, which could be quickly packed up when the tribe moved on. Semi-permanent 'tent cities' often grew up around the seats of powerful warlords.

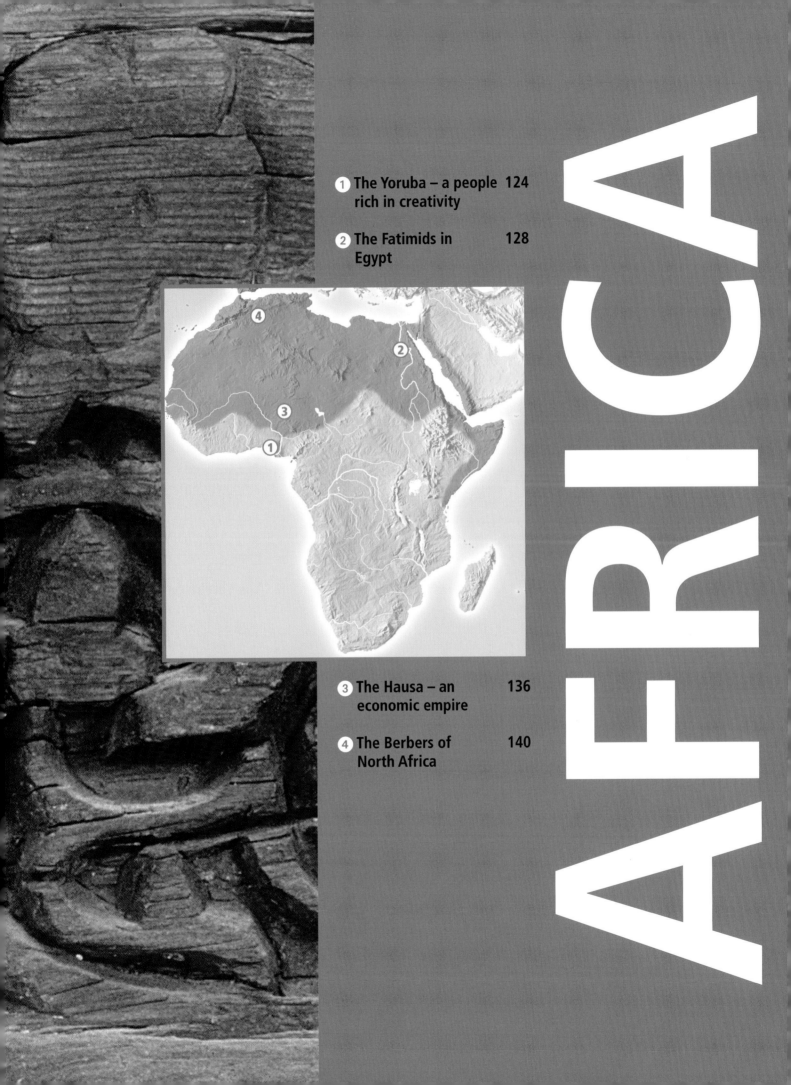

AFRICA

1 The Yoruba – a people 124
rich in creativity

2 The Fatimids in 128
Egypt

3 The Hausa – an 136
economic empire

4 The Berbers of 140
North Africa

The Yoruba – a people rich in creativity

A thousand years ago, the Yoruba civilisation flourished in the hot wetlands around the Niger delta. Despite difficult climatic and farming conditions, they created a sophisticated society that valued and excelled in craftsmanship.

Precious vessel
Bronze vessels like this were often royal gifts, to be placed with the dead as grave goods, offered to the gods, or simply given as presents at royal gatherings.

In the southwest of what is now Nigeria and the adjacent states of Benin and Togo, tough conditions confronted the population in the 10th century. An oppressively hot climate and a barren landscape made agriculture hard; pasture was scanty and cattle herds were small. And yet the Yoruba-speaking tribes built an important civilisation here, creating one of West Africa's richest-ever cultures.

The origins of the Yoruba remain obscure: they were probably immigrants from the savannahs farther to the north, but they had been well-established along the coast by at least as early as the 8th century. They were not a single nation but a number of separate clans who shared a common language and a tendency to settle into tiny urban communities. Over time, these townships came together to form loose federations, which in their turn became little kingdoms or 'mini-states'. The most important of these were Oyo and Ife.

Ife was the spiritual centre of the Yoruba for many generations. Oral traditions hold that the Ogiso kings reigned here in the 9th century, followed by the Ogiamien dynasty from about 1100; they in their turn were superseded by the Obas kings around 1200. Benin became a separate state a little later, as a dependency of Ife, though in time it would overtake its mother kingdom in power and influence.

The Yoruba creation myth

Ife quickly established itself as the cultural capital of the Yoruba, thanks largely to its mythic and symbolic significance. One of the creation myths of the Yoruba tells that, in the beginning, the world had been entirely covered with water. The King of the gods, Olorun, had sent his son Oduduwa down from Heaven, suspended from a chain, taking with him a handful of soil, a cockerel and a palm nut. Oduduwa scattered the soil over the water. Scratching about in the landmass thus created, the cockerel threw up fertile mounds of earth; here, the planted palm nut took root and grew.

When Oduduwa saw the solid Earth below him, he called the divine spirits, the 'Orishas', together and descended to Ife, where he founded his holy city and ordered the creation of humankind. His brother Obatala undertook this task, moulding men and women from the mud of the riverbank; whilst Oduduwa himself became their founding king. Oduduwa,

the story goes, gave each of his 16 divine children a crown with glass beads and sent them out to create their own kingdoms far and wide. Hence the development of the separate Yoruba states.

A cultural treasure house

The history of the Yoruba peoples may be shrouded in legend, but their artistic ability could not be more evident. Numerous treasures survive to bear testimony to the imagination and skill of Yoruba craftworkers: objects uncovered at Ife by modern archaeologists represent some of the most important examples of African art. Made with extraordinary accomplishment in terracotta and bronze, they suggest that Ife must have already been a major trading centre by the 10th century.

Advanced techniques in firing ceramics and metalworking – and the organisation of artisans into regulated groups – ensured that technical standards were easily a match for those in Europe at the time. With such technological skills and resources at its disposal, Ife became a flourishing metropolis from the 9th century. Although the city declined in economic importance after the 15th century, it still had a symbolic significance that it largely retains to the present day. Yoruba rulers derived their legitimacy from their supposed descent from the Kings of Ife.

Communicating with gods

The Yoruba left no written records, so most of what we know about their early dynasties was passed down over the centuries by word of mouth. Over time, Oduduwa's 16 spirit children multiplied into a huge number of Yoruba divinities: today, the Yoruba talk of 401 different gods (although this number is symbolic, standing for an unknowable infinity of deities). The number was swelled still

The head of a king
A bronze head found at Ife displays finely modelled features and an ornate detailed crown. Real hair was attached to the holes around the mouth to represent a beard.

further by the deification of ancestors – each family had its own important ones. The dead were seen as influencing the affairs of the living, and communication with them took place through a system of divination known as Ifa.

The divination technique involved a shaman throwing down 16 small shells into a rough circle: the shaman read their meaning according to how they landed. In this way, through the shaman, the departed ancestors could speak to their descendants, offering advice and consolation in times of difficulty. For his encounters with the ancestors, the shaman had to transcend his everyday existence through a special dance, a 'prayer made by the body'. Drummers sat in the festively decorated marketplace of a Yoruba village to create the rhythmic cacophony which facilitated this transition. The rite held for the worship of Oshun, mistress of rivers and lakes and goddess of fertility, was typical. As the drummers beat their instruments and sang, white-clothed masked figures circled around them, dancing for hours, their movements gentle and uniform but relentlessly unceasing, until they fell into a trance. This was the moment at which the gods took possession of the bodies of the dancers and shamans.

As images of the gods, masks have a very high status in Yoruba culture. They embody the connection between the living and the dead. Every extended family owns a mask commemorating some particularly illustrious ancestor, but these are only a part – albeit an important one – of a complete costume, which is firmly tied to the accompanying music, the dance, and the spatial environment in which the performance takes place. The Yoruba say that when a dancer puts on a mask, he takes on some of the power of the deity he depicts – at times, indeed, he may actually become that god. Certain masks are expressly designed to scare strangers, especially women, away from the men's secret societies.

Artistic realism
At a time when European art still followed 2-dimensional stylistic conventions, the Yoruba were creating thrillingly realistic work. This head is part of a complete figure, one of very few to have survived intact from the Yoruba heyday.

Consummate craftsmanship
A series of archaeological finds, notably the bronze and ceramic heads unearthed by German researchers in the 1930s, have underlined the variety of Yoruba culture. These caused an international sensation: such awareness and technical virtuosity had never been seen in ancient African art before. To find meaningful comparisons for these realistic images, art historians had to go to the sculptures of Greek antiquity, the 'gold standard' for artistic achievement in the western tradition. Most of these statues represent the ancestors and the gods. They include awe-inspiring images of Ogun, god of iron, fire and war, of Oko, the god of agriculture, and of the terrifying Shopona, the god of smallpox.

The skulls of these figures were often no more than a few millimetres thick. It remains a mystery how an apparently poor society – few signs have been found of personal wealth and possessions – could have developed such a rich and skilled artistic repertoire. By the 11th century, the Yoruban bonze-casters had already discovered what is known as the 'lost-wax' method of creating bronze artefacts. The technique involves making a wax impression in a mould, which is then 'lost' by being melted away to leave a perfect mould for the molten bronze.

The method is more complicated than it sounds: it makes the highest demands not just on sculptural abilities of the worker, but also on metallurgical skills. Yoruba smiths worked with alloys of copper, zinc, tin and lead to make their bronzes. How they learned these techniques remains a mystery.

Bronze and terracotta heads of this kind were presumably commissioned by the kings of the different city states. They were meant for ritual use rather than for ornament, for no animal or other subjects seem to have been reproduced: only the human and spirit antecedents of the tribe.

Women's rights

As might be expected with a culture investing such significance in its ancestral succession, Yoruba women were accorded a great deal of respect. Mothers had in their keeping the continuity of the family, assuring their status as matriarchs, despite the fact that Yoruba families were polygamous: an important man might marry many women. A household with several wives was scrupulously organised so that each had her own rooms for herself, her children and her work. They took it in turns to cook for their husband, who supplied the food. When the sons in such a family reached adulthood, they would build their own houses onto their father's. These, too, had accommodation for several wives, so that ever-growing, village-like complexes resulted.

EVERYDAY LIFE

An impoverished existence?

The richness of their artistic legacy makes it easy to forget that the Yoruba at this time seem to have lived in relative poverty, scratching a living from thin soils, supplemented by fishing. Yet the fact that an elite, at least, had the resources to invest in artworks of timeless value does suggest that the Yoruba must have had other ways of generating wealth. Kola nuts, palm kernels, beans and cotton all appear to have been grown, and these could have been traded with merchants plying the trans-Sahara caravan route. Copper may be key, however: the Yoruba were long assumed to have bought theirs from faraway trading contacts, but deposits have now been discovered in southern Nigeria.

Unusually for farmers, the Yoruba lived in towns, commuting seasonally as much as 30km (20 miles) to the outlying homesteads where they worked the land. They remained very much an urban people, though, the marketplace their focus for trade, for festivals and simply for social contact.

Sacral ceramic

Shamans came and went bearing food and drink for the women potters who worked in darkened rooms on vessels like these: they were not permitted to emerge before their work was finished.

Crucial to the Yoruba economy, making adire textiles was the exclusive concern of women. Coloured with indigo and patterned with tie-dye techniques, adire textiles combine beauty and simplicity. In the hands of Yoruba women, adire designs were often wonderfully expressive: surviving examples are as impressive in their way as the more celebrated bronze and ceramic sculptures. The indigo plant grew wild in West Africa and, according to a 10th century tradition, old women would gather its leaves, grind them up in a mortar and mix them with ash of a plant known as dyer's broom; this was rolled into balls and sold to the women dyers. Before the fabric was dyed, figures were painted on it with wax: these areas would remain white. Dyed several times, almost black fabrics could be obtained: the most industrious women were known by their deep-dyed clothing.

Although many of these ancient techniques would be lost to the Yoruba peoples in later years, they are still ranked among Africa's finest folk-artists.

The Fatimids in Egypt

The Fatimid conquest of Egypt in 969 freed the ancient land on the Nile from the domination of the Caliphs of Baghdad, and also gave rise to cultural splendour of fairytale proportions.

Caliph al-Muizz was jubilant at the news: at last his general Jawhar had liberated Egypt from the Abbasids. What, after all, gave this dynasty of Baghdad Caliphs the right to rule over so vast an Islamic kingdom? If any earthly ruler was entitled to rule so large an area, it was surely he, Ma'ad al-Muizz Li-Deenillah, the fourth Fatimid Caliph. The ruler, until now, of the North African province of Ifriqya (now Tunisia), he could trace his descent directly from the Prophet Muhammad, through the prophet's beloved daughter, Fatima, and her husband Ali. Al-Muizz was thus honour-bound to win not only religious leadership in an Islamic Egypt but the political power he saw as the Fatimids' due.

For generations the Fatimids had been trying to topple the Abbasids, plainly a dynasty in decline, and yet maddeningly slow to fall. By degrees, the Fatimids had been chipping away at Abbasid imperial power, wresting first Sicily and then what is now Algeria from their grasp. Since 967, al-Muizz had been bent on expelling them from Egypt. The time had seemed auspicious: for a number of years the vital Nile floods had failed, causing drought and dreadful famine, followed by plagues of Biblical proportions, then rats and locusts. Brought to their knees,

Pendant with sparrow
The goldsmiths and silversmiths of Fatimid Egypt created exquisite jewellery, for which an eager market existed in Europe and in Asia.

the Egyptian population had practically begged to be saved, and al-Muizz needed no second invitation. He sent a powerful army eastwards under the command of Jawhar as-Siqilli, who was both a trusted counsellor and an experienced general. The campaign could hardly have gone more easily; after a few half-hearted skirmishes the Egyptians had surrendered almost with relief. After more than 300 years, Abbasid rule was over.

A new broom

Al-Muizz told his new subjects that not only had they been ruled for centuries by a false caliph but they had been in thrall to an unacceptable version of Islam. By the Prophet's own ordination, only his direct descendants through the line of Fatima and Ali could claim to be true teachers of Muslim doctrine.

Egyptians had no alternative but to accept this ruling and submit to the authority of the Shi'ites, the Shiat Ali or 'Party of Ali'. Until then, Egyptians had followed Sunni practice, which was rooted in the *Sunna*, the written records of the Prophet's life which 'showed the way'. They followed the rule of Muhammad closely in respect of all matters of faith and conduct, but they did not need an Imam to provide religious direction. The role of the Caliph had been to lead Muslims in wisdom and justice: his lineage was not important. Now, however, the Shi'ites were to set the tone in Egypt.

Jawhar lost no time in ordering the construction of a great new mosque. Sited near the ancient settlement of al-Fustat on the lower Nile, this monument still exists: it is named Al-Azhar, which means 'most luminous', from a title conferred on Fatima herself. An institute for teaching was subsequently added, the oldest existing university in the world – the Shi'ites were no philistines, for all their reforming zeal. The first Shi'ite religious house on Egyptian soil, Al-Azhar was the nucleus of the city which would later come to be called Cairo, Egypt's shining metropolis. Eventually, it would become the capital of Shi'ite Islam.

Fatimid fighters
A paper fragment from 12th-century al-Fustat shows Fatimid troops leaving their fortress to fight Crusaders.

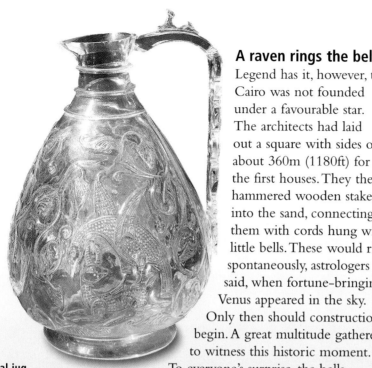

Crystal jug
Islamic craftsmen were renowned for their skill and artistry. A particular speciality was the creation of beautiful objects from rock crystal.

A home for the dead
The Egyptian name for a cemetery was *Al Qarafa*, 'city of the dead'. This Fatimid cemetery, with rounded tombs, is near the town of El-Minya on the Nile.

A raven rings the bell

Legend has it, however, that Cairo was not founded under a favourable star. The architects had laid out a square with sides of about 360m (1180ft) for the first houses. They then hammered wooden stakes into the sand, connecting them with cords hung with little bells. These would ring spontaneously, astrologers said, when fortune-bringing Venus appeared in the sky. Only then should construction begin. A great multitude gathered to witness this historic moment.

To everyone's surprise, the bells suddenly started jingling – just as the planet Mars appeared above the horizon. A cheeky raven had alighted on one of the strings at precisely the wrong time – what disasters now awaited this city?

Fortunately, someone had the presence of mind to suggest that the ill omen might be cancelled out by a good one: in a hopeful spirit, the city was named al Qahira, 'The Conqueror', 'The Victorious' – or, of course, Cairo. The new capital soon put its difficult start behind it and sprawled outwards, swallowing up al-Fustat, its venerable neighbour. Until a suitable residence could be built for him, al-Muizz remained in what is now Tunisia, and Jawhar oversaw the rapidly growing city of Cairo.

Fit for a caliph

The new city had broad streets along which the caliph could process in state on festive occasions. Its buildings were so richly adorned they seemed to have been constructed from precious jewels. Every house had its flowering garden and was protected from prying eyes by a high wall. Gigantic wheels raised water from the Nile for irrigation and domestic use. The young city almost disappeared beneath a mass of luxuriant greenery which lent it a peaceful, almost paradisiacal air. The Fatimids were fully prepared to defend their new metropolis and surrounded it with a fortified wall of sun-dried bricks.

In 972, Cairo was at last deemed fit for a caliph and al-Muizz moved to the city amidst the utmost pomp and ceremony. The fabulous palace complex had 4000 chambers and was entered via a 'Golden Gate'. Prior to his departure from Tunisia, al-Muizz had ordered all his golden treasures to be melted

The centre of life

The mosque is traditionally a place not only of collective worship and private prayer but of study. It also has a function as an administrative centre.

After the Prophet's death in 632, the Islamic kingdom had continued to expand through several centuries: military commanders had made it a priority to build a mosque as the focus for Muslim life in every region they conquered.

The mosque was the nucleus of Islamic learning. It was here that religious scholars would meet to debate theological and scriptural questions with one another. They would also pass on their knowledge to pupils and students at the mosque, informally at first, but then increasingly through the formation of official madrassas or religious academies. Islam's justly celebrated universities evolved out of these schools.

First and foremost, though, the mosque is a house of prayer. Observant Muslims must offer prayers five times a day, wherever they are, but for Friday prayer they should come together at the mosque, where men and women gather separately. The mosque is open at all times to the Muslim faithful, whenever they wish to pray, or simply want some time for quiet contemplation.

Shi'ite showpiece
With an enormous open courtyard lined with shady cloisters, the Al-Azhar Mosque in Cairo was modelled on the home of the Prophet Muhammad in Medina, which was seen as the spiritual prototype for all subsequent mosques.

down and cast into giant millstone-shaped ingots. In Cairo, these golden blocks were piled up as gateposts on either side of the main entrance to his palace. As legend has it, 70 years later, these gateposts were to come into their own.

Displays of wealth

Meanwhile, the palace was becoming a place of unsurpassable opulence. The walls of the audience hall shone with gold; the jewel-encrusted throne stood on a long dais decorated with gilded palms and artificial fruit fashioned from gemstones.

If these fairytale surroundings did not speak loudly enough, the sumptuous banquets given here left no doubt of the Caliph's wealth and power. Guests sat around a gigantic table of lacquered wood extending the whole length of the room. Exquisite delicacies were heaped on enormous gold and silver platters, or on faience plates. So immense was the wealth of the Caliph's family that al-Muizz's sister, Rashida, alone is said to have owned 12,000 precious robes.

When al-Muizz died in 975, he was succeeded by his son, al-Aziz, who was, if anything, even more ostentatious than his father. And Cairo stood to benefit from it. Many more impressive monuments were constructed during al-Aziz's 20-year reign, all of which added to the splendour of the city. The capital had him to thank for both the Golden Palace and the Pearl Pavilion – both now vanished, but still remembered with solemn awe.

This obsession with display appears to have rubbed off on the Caliphs' subjects. The rich wore headdresses of heavy fabric with gold thread. A more glamorous, self-indulgent lifestyle could hardly be imagined, and critical observers did not fail to note a certain hint of decadence. It was inevitable that change had to come.

A strict new order

Al-Aziz's son, al-Hakim, was only eleven years old when he ascended the Caliph's throne. Until now, Fatimid rule had been characterised by comparative liberalism – to the extent that al-Aziz had even married a Christian woman – but al-Hakim had very different ideas. The older he grew, the more firmly convinced he became that he had been marked out by Allah to fulfil a special destiny: the complete moral and religious renewal of the Muslim world.

Al-Hakim's sense of divine mission was not really surprising, since it was rooted in the way the Fatimids saw themselves. Even though Islamic doctrine did not have the sort of saviour figure who was central to Christianity, many Muslims believed that a direct descendant of Muhammad would appear as the Mahdi, or Messiah, to usher in a new world order of universal affluence and justice. This belief had first been proclaimed in the Fatimids' Tunisian homeland in 900 and had led to Abdallah-al-Mahdi seizing power 10 years later. A charismatic preacher, he had taught that the Prophet's descendants succeeded one

Hunting scene
Ivory carvings of astounding virtuosity could be bought at the Cairo soukh. This scene shows a Fatimid hunting party killing birds and gazelles.

advent of Abdallah-al-Mahdi, first Fatimid Caliph; al-Hakim was the seventh Imam since his reign. Small wonder, then, that he should have persuaded himself that he had been put on Earth to achieve great things. But his zeal would come as a shock to his Egyptian subjects.

Truth and renewal
Al-Hakim was hardly of an age to rule before he was informing his astonished subjects that a new era of truth and renewal had begun. The entire relationship between humanity and Allah was to be re-established, he insisted, and this was going to mean radical changes on the people's part. In order to prove themselves worthy of this relationship, the Egyptians had to reform their lives, renouncing the luxuries and conveniences they had come to take for granted. Their duty now was to purify themselves with austerity and

another in cycles of seven Imams – every seventh Imam introduced a new era and brought a new dispensation for the world. These teachers were figures of the stature of Abraham, Moses and Jesus Christ; the seventh Imam after Muhammad himself had been Ismail in the 8th century. His Ismailite age had come to an end with the

prayer. The worldly life, with all its pleasures, was officially deemed of no value; the existence of mortals must be directed at the Beyond. That this was much more than pious rhetoric became clear when al-Hakim had all secular pursuits strictly forbidden: suddenly, the life-loving Egyptians were barred from singing or making music. They were also prohibited from playing chess: boards and pieces had to be handed in to the authorities at the palace, where they were publicly assigned to the flames. Alcohol was also banned – up until now the Fatimids had taken the Prophet's strictures against it very lightly.

The new puritanism hit women particularly hard: it was not just that jewellery and fine clothing were no longer acceptable – women were not allowed to leave the house, and to ensure that this rule was followed, the Caliph forbade shoemakers to make shoes for women. Men also found their freedom drastically curtailed. Walks along the Nile were no longer permitted, and anyone caught indulging in this activity was sent home in disgrace by the guardians of public morality. A curfew made it illegal to be out after dusk.

A people divided

In the country at large the people were baffled by these changes, so the Caliph sent out emissaries to tell them about his 'New Era'. Once they had been given these briefings, they had to sign a form committing themselves to keeping all the Caliph's rules – whether they were literate or not. Most simply submitted – what else could they do, faced with the adamant insistence of the authorities?

In order to enthuse the officials involved in this thankless programme, the title *Daraz'i* was bestowed on the one who managed to collect the most signatures. The forms were popularly named after him, but thanks to a vowel shift customary in Arabic languages,

Fatimid fabric
The creature in this woven textile fragment from 9th-century Egypt is thought to be a hippopotamus.

they became known as *duruz*. This, in turn, was soon being applied to all those who had signed the form, and it has endured in the name of a special religious community, the Druse.

The Caliph's forms were only for his Shi'ite Muslim subjects. Sunni Muslims and Jews, as well as Egyptian Christians or Copts, were not merely exempt, they were prohibited from signing. This was hardly a cause for celebration on their part, however. They were also now officially excluded from all political life and marginalised from the cultural mainstream: this was to be a 'New Era' of discrimination and sectarian strife.

Relations between the 'Religions of the Book' had been peaceful until now: they had much in common in their reverence for the Bible and worship of its God. In 1003, that age of tolerance came to an end, as al-Hakim personally sanctioned attacks by Shi'ites against those of other faiths. Churches were plundered and

Al-Idrisi's world
The illustrious Arab cartographer Al-Idrisi created this map in the 12th century. He placed Fatimid Egypt at the centre of the world.

name. No less notable was his foundation of the Dar al-Hikma, the 'House of the Sciences', whose library was one of the greatest in the Islamic world. It comprised 1.6 million volumes, representing all the different branches of knowledge existing at the time. They included 2400 artistically decorated texts of the Koran.

Despite these glimmers of enlightenment, al-Hakim's 'New Era' was one of darkness and gloom for most Egyptians. Even Shi'ites chafed under the restrictions. Far from being fired with zeal, they found it oppressive, and ultimately intolerable.

It took them 25 years, but at last something snapped. The Caliph had always been in the habit of leaving his palace in the small hours to ride alone through the empty streets of his capital; one night, in 1021, he failed to return. When the guards looked for him the next day, all they could find was his bloodstained clothing, pierced with dagger cuts. No trace was ever found of al-Hakim. His diehard followers – the Druse – believed that he was still living somewhere in secret, but al-Hakim, and his 'New Era', were no more.

destroyed, and Christians were compelled to identify themselves through special clothing: they had to wear striped robes, blue headgear and a wooden cross suspended from a chain around the neck. The Jews were treated in similar fashion: although only a small minority, barely noticed before, they now had to identify themselves with yellow headgear.

Cultural restriction

The 'New Era' may have been repressive and in many ways joyless, it may have circumscribed intellectual and artistic activities, but culturally it did not close the country down altogether. Religious architecture, for example, enjoyed an impressive boom – al-Hakim completed the construction, begun in 991, of the famous Cairo mosque which still bears his

A burden lifted

The sense of relief was palpable; the religious climate relaxed immediately – mosques and churches soon co-existed peacefully once more. It did not take people long to rediscover their taste for luxury or their enjoyment of finery and frivolity. A traveller visiting the city soukh reported seeing shops, 'so filled with gold, jewels, embroidery and satin, that there was hardly any room left to sit down'.

The artworks on sale included the things which could be found nowhere else, such as intarsia work of ravishing quality – mosaics of glass and ceramic fragments, mother-of-pearl and ivory, set in wood. There were white-glazed ceramics, brilliantly painted, and breath-taking pieces – bowls, jugs, carafes – carved out of clear rock crystal. There were tortoiseshell combs and knife-handles of dazzling workmanship, and silk brocade hangings woven with gold thread – the Copts were especially adept at making these. The buyers of such treasures were drawn almost entirely from the courtier class, recently restored to a life of ostentation, who lost no time in emulating the luxurious lifestyle of their new Caliph.

For ordinary people, the impact of al-Hakim's passing was less noticeable. Their material standard of living remained substantially unchanged. As long as the Nile flood deposited its fertile mud along the river banks each year so that their crops could thrive, they could live contentedly enough. And so for many years they did, throughout the reign of al-Hakim's young son al-Zazir, who ruled under the regency of his elder sister. Al-Zazir died of plague in 1036, after which his own seven-year-old son al-Mustansir succeeded, his reign directed by his mother and viziers.

Al-Mustansir reigned for almost six decades, until his death in 1094, weathering a period of unrest during the 1060s. An expansionist foreign policy had virtually bankrupted the state, so when the Nile flood failed several years in a row, no funds were available for relief supplies of grain. Cairo's people faced death by famine. Taking pity on them, the Caliph is said to have announced that they could remove small pieces of the Golden Gate with files, to buy bread for themselves and for their families. What the philanthropic ruler had not foreseen was that his starving subjects would descend on the gates in droves: in no time at all, most of the precious gold was gone. The Caliph had what little gold remained brought back inside the palace to safety.

Political unrest flared throughout the country; angry mobs roamed the streets of Cairo, burning and looting – not even the 'House of Sciences' was spared. Outright anarchy was at last averted and order restored, but there was no mistaking the fact that the high-point of Fatimid rule had passed.

Mythical beast
With a lion's body and falcon's head, the griffin had a pedigree stretching back to pharaonic times, when it was seen as a symbol of a victorious ruler. This bronze sculpture, created in the Fatimid period, can now be seen in Pisa.

The Hausa – an economic empire

Some time towards the 11th century, a number of scattered village communities in northern Nigeria, Ghana and Togo came together in a loose federation that became the inter-dependent and increasingly prosperous Hausa trading states.

Weight in gold
Ghanaian gold was one of the most important commodities to be traded by the Hausa. Values were calculated with ornamental weights, such as this lovely gold fish.

According to legend, Bayajidda, Prince of Baghdad, had a falling-out with his angry father: he took flight on his horse and rode for many days. Crossing the vast desert, he headed on through the territory of Borno, beside Lake Chad, until at last he came to the town of Daura, where the Hausa lived.

As darkness fell, Bayajidda started to look for a place where he could sleep in safety: the night was dark and he feared his father's men were still pursuing him. He searched for shelter in vain, until finally an old woman took pity on him and offered to hide him. Bayajidda begged her for water, since he was dying of thirst, but the old woman had none to give him. The people of Daura, she explained, were allowed to extract water from their well only once every seven days. A giant snake guarded it jealously at other times. Driven by his thirst, and displaying great courage, the Prince killed the snake and drank deeply from the well.

Now the Hausa could have as much water as they wanted, whenever they needed. News of Bayajidda's deed spread like wildfire through the region. In her gratitude, the Queen of Daura took Bayajidda as her husband and made him King alongside her. His heroism has been celebrated ever since.

Riding to prosperity

Like foundation myths the world over, the story of Bayajidda contains the odd grain of historical truth. The connection with the Arab world was crucial to the Hausa, who built their prosperity on the trans-Sahara trade and eventually adopted Islam. And the Prince's ride acknowledges the importance of the horse in Hausa history: it was on this animal that the fortunes of the Hausa were largely founded.

Long before the Arabian camel or dromedary was introduced to the deserts of Africa, small but extremely tough little horses were widespread in the southern Sahara. They were neither beautiful nor elegant to look at, but their hardiness and endurance made them invaluable as mounts and as beasts of burden.

These horses enabled the Hausa to establish a network of trading links extending all the way to Egypt and beyond, bringing them into close and constant commerce with the wider world. Buoyed up by the prosperity this created, the Hausa became one of sub-Saharan Africa's most important civilisations between 1050 and 1150.

The Hausa capital of Kano was built of mud bricks, like this house there today.

A hazy history

The real origins of this resourceful people, whose descendants can be found in northern Nigeria and adjacent countries to this day, are only very vaguely understood by modern scholars. Almost all the written sources – in Arabic records – were destroyed at the beginning of the 19th century on the orders of the Islamic firebrand, Muhammad Bello. (The Sokoto caliphate to which he was heir took a scorched-earth attitude to the earlier history of the region, seeing its own

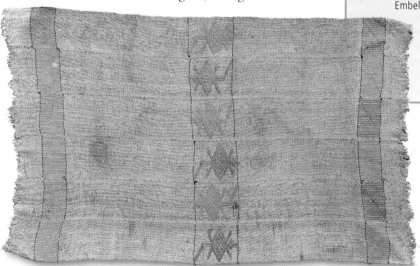

foundation as marking a sort of 'Year Zero'.) As a result, we must rely on the Hausa's rich but not necessarily reliable oral tradition and on such scanty data as can be gleaned from archaeology and from later Arabic sources.

Through the middle centuries of the First Millennium, it appears that the Hausa lived as nomadic pastoralists, ranging over a wide area. Their territories at this time extended northward across present-day Nigeria and Niger as far as the Aïr Mountains, and eastward to the

---

Much-travelled traders

The cities of the Hausa grew as their wealth did, and the greater their prosperity the higher their expectations. Raw materials, slaves and craftwork were exported in return for luxuries from faraway places and trading increased in volume through the 11th century. The traders made gruelling and dangerous journeys across vast expanses of forbidding desert to reach the markets of Egypt and Arabia. But the rewards were great: their products fetched good prices, and Hausa traders were among the wealthiest inhabitants of the towns.

Crocodile cloth
Embellished with a crocodile motif, this Hausa fabric shows the skill of their textile weavers.

---

shores of Lake Chad in Central Africa. From the 7th century, however, Arab expansion into North Africa began to have a knock-on effect in the regions south of the Sahara. Tuareg nomads pushed into the northern fringes of the Hausa homeland, whilst rival herders from Borno began encroaching from the east. Meanwhile, powerful peoples to the west prevented the Hausa from responding by expanding their own territories in that direction.

This seems to have been the point at which the Hausa gave up their nomadic lifestyle. Legend has it that Bagauda, grandson of Bayajidda, leading a tribal group from the north founded the first important Hausa city of Kano (although archaeological evidence suggests that settlement and iron-smelting were here long before the Hausa heyday). Kano remains the region's metropolis: the imposing mud-brick walls to be seen today were probably built in the 14th and 15th centuries, but almost certainly give a sense of the earlier city.

Seven states – one goal

The Hausa state appears to have evolved as a federation of smaller communities: the smallest unit was the village or *gari* (plural *garuwa*). Over time, some developed into towns or *birane* (singular *birni*), each of which would have been surrounded by protective walls, like Kano's.

Politically speaking, the Hausa's was a very loose-knit confederation: they shared a common language and cultural traditions, but never really formed a single state. Every town had its own leader, and there appears to have been a degree of democracy in the succession, as the ruler in many of these towns was elected by local peers. Certain dynasties held greater influence, however: Bayajidda is said to have been succeeded by his seven sons who, in time, became founders of the first seven Hausa states.

The chronicles describe these as the 'legitimate' states, the *Hausa Bokoi*: they included Daura, Katsina, Zaria, Biram, Gobir, Rano and Kano. In addition, there were the 'illegitimate' communities, the *Banza Bokwai*. The Hausa lived here too, but were only a minority. Among these were Gwari, Kebbi, Kororofa, Ilorin, Nupe, Yelwa and Samfara – so the Hausa influence extended far beyond their own seven states. A striking aspect of the 'legitimate' states was that they had a high degree of economic specialisation. Depending on geographical position and available resources, each took on its own distinct role in a mutually complementary economic scheme.

Kano, for example, exploited its rich deposits of iron ore, though its people also grew and processed indigo and cotton, a specialisation shared with the state of Rano. Zaria specialised in obtaining slaves and supplied the other Hausa states with labour. Katsina and Daura were situated near the start of the main caravan routes to the north and east. They took charge of external trade on behalf of the federation as a whole. Textiles were exported, as well as gold from reserves in Ghana, along with slaves from Zaria.

In return, the Hausa's neighbours supplied them with salt brought from the Taghaza mines in the western Sahara, and the highly coveted cowrie shells from the Atlantic coast that were sometimes used as currency. Other indispensable import items from the north included weapons, which were, for the most part, delivered to Gobir in the extreme west. This was a militarised state and it took primary responsibility for defending the federation's borders. All in all, the system worked well. The Hausa were considered one of the wealthiest peoples in Africa in the 11th and 12th centuries, and their influence extended far beyond their areas of settlement. That influence can still be seen today: Hausa is spoken by almost 25 million people in western and northern Africa and remains the language of choice for regional trade.

The coming of Islam

The Arab influence on Hausa culture is unmistakeable, and it cannot be attributed to trading contacts alone. Its presence becomes detectable in the early 11th century, at a time when the Hausa still worshipped animist gods, such as the Dala, the sacred hill at the heart of Kano. The Arabs do not appear to have proselytised with any seriousness among the Hausa; still less was there an attempt to enforce conversion. But there are clear signs that Islam appealed to the elite, perhaps because of its apparent modernity and glamour – it represented the allure of a wider world. Yet there was no mass movement among the people at large, and no sudden conversion. The first Muslim missionary, Muhammad al-Maghili, did not arrive in the region until the 15th century, and the large-scale adoption of Islam did not come until even later. Even so, we must thank Arabic literature for the few written reports we have on the early history of the Hausa. It was the Arab cartographer Al-Idrisi who first, literally, put the Hausa on the map in 1145.

Tablet inscription
Arriving as early as the 11th century, Islam slowly spread among the Hausa. This wooden Hausa tablet is inscribed with texts from the Koran. In the background is a gold weight in the form of a fish.

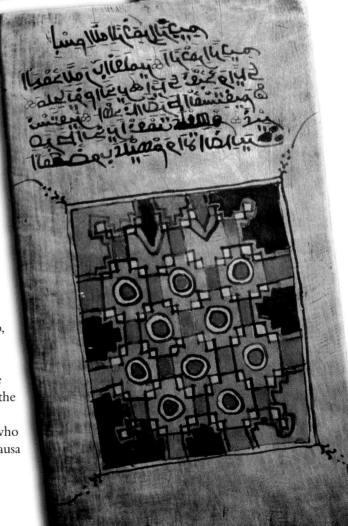

The Berbers of North Africa

With their conquest of North Africa, the Arabs took over political and religious leadership in the region. In time, though, the indigenous Berbers became powerful enough to build their own empire, centred on Morocco.

City of mud
The city of Timbuktu began life as a Tuareg encampment. The Berber Almoravids took it in about 1100 and before long it had solid mud-brick walls and buildings. The Great Mosque seen here was actually constructed in the 14th century, after the Almoravid era, but is in traditional mud-brick style. One thing about the city has not changed to this day: it still has no road or railway connection.

It was to Abdallah Ibn Yasin that Allah revealed the vital truth one day, in 1050, when he was praying: only unity could make the Berbers strong. Though formidable fighters, until now they had inflicted wounds only on each other in never-ending internecine struggles; united they could be the most powerful force in the Maghreb. Abdallah Ibn Yasin realised that mutual solidarity and Muslim zeal could carry his people forward to a glorious future.

There were few signs of either in his Berber brothers. Swaggering warriors, they were wedded to ideas of individual honour and blood-feud; though nominally Muslims, they paid only lip-service to Muhammad's creed. This was going to have to change. And Abdallah Ibn Yasin was the man to change it. At first, he confided his thoughts only to close friends, but it

was not long before tribal leaders came to hear his message. He was a persuasive speaker who got his ideas across to the tough and unpretentious Berber chieftains: all were inspired by his view of Islam and his vision for the Berbers. Ibn Yasin described Allah as a man much like themselves: a demanding patriarch who required unquestioning loyalty and courage of his people.

Holy war

It was an idea that made a lot of sense to a brave and honourable but essentially unreflective people: the Berbers were to be the instrument of God. It was Allah's will that all unbelievers be converted to the true faith – including Muslims who failed to follow the Koran. Whenever Abdallah Ibn Yasin spoke of spiritual Jihad in terms of 'Holy War' he knew he was speaking in a language that the Berbers understood:

fighting had always been part of their life. His new dispensation endorsed existing interests of the Berber tribes and sanctified their customary campaigns of plunder as Holy War.

A serious, passionate and eloquent man, Abdallah Ibn Yasin was no ordinary Berber. He was one of a group of Muslim warriors of the faith. He had lived for years in a *ribat*, a fortified border castle, serving to protect against enemy incursions and secure the caravan routes. In the 11th century, the ribats had become politico-religious communities, manned by highly motivated warriors sworn to the defence of Islam. Asceticism on the one hand and military training on the other were the twin disciplines to which they dedicated themselves. These ideals were foreign to the Koran, but they struck a chord with desert nomads, schooled from birth in courage, toughness and endurance.

The message of Muhammad
A miniature from a history of Muhammad and the first caliphs shows the Prophet preaching. He is swathed in veils, since it was forbidden to re-create his image.

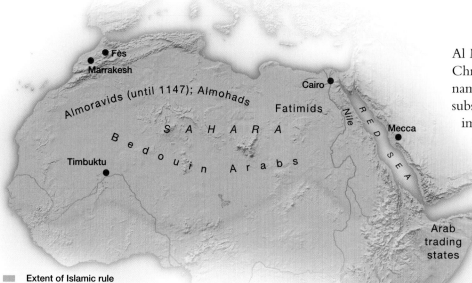

Extent of Islamic rule

● Main towns

Al Murabitun, 'Men of the Ribat'. The Christian Spaniards would corrupt this name into the 'Almoravids' when it subsequently became the name of the first important Berber dynasty, and it is under this name that the Al Murabitun have passed into western history. They rode camels and wore voluminous capes, large, tightly wound cloth turbans – and black face veils in the Lamtuna style.

Black veils

The ribats south of the Sahara had been largely self-sufficient and gone unnoticed, until Abdallah Ibn Yasin began preaching the new Islam in around 1050. His message was the ribat way re-interpreted for a mass audience, and it happened that he delivered it just as the Sanhadja Berbers were on the rise. This large and warlike tribe originated south of the Sahara in an area along the Niger, at what was then the outer limit of the Muslim world.

In the early 1060s, the Sanhadja were united under the leadership of Yusuf Ibn Tashufin, a pupil of Abdallah Ibn Yasin and chief of the Lamtuna, or 'veiled ones', a Sanhadja clan. They took their name from the black veils they wore across their faces. A sinister sight as they rode into battle, they were every bit as ferocious as they looked, and happy to follow Yusuf Ibn Tashufin to death or glory. Yusuf Ibn Tashufin's army, small to begin with, grew rapidly with the addition of new warriors for Islam. Battle-hardened nomads from the Saharan heartland, they called themselves

Founding Marrakesh

In 1061, Yusuf Ibn Tashufin succeeded in subjugating the Berber tribes of southern Morocco and bringing all the Sanhadja Berbers under his leadership. But the Almoravids did not stop there. Within two years, Ibn Tashufin had established a residence in the region which, in the Berber dialect, was called simply Mraksh or 'town'. The founding of Marrakesh was a clear indication that Ibn Tashufin was a leader for the long haul, rather than the type of opportunist warlord the Berbers had seen so many times before. It showed that he intended to remain in this conquered land.

Where there had been only camel-hide tents, a city now sprang up with a mosque, a market, mud-brick houses and even subterranean canals for the water supply. Soon traders, craftsmen, artists and scholars were streaming in to take up residence. The Almoravids, meanwhile, were carving out a country for their capital. Within two decades they had subdued tribes in the surrounding area as well as conquering all of Morocco and most of Algeria.

From across the Strait of Gibraltar, meanwhile, events in the Maghreb were being watched with mixed emotions.

The Mosque of Marrakesh
Built by the Almohads in the early 12th century, the Koutoubia Mosque in Marrakesh is one of modern Morocco's best-known landmarks.

Much had happened on the Iberian Peninsula since the glorious year of 711, when an army of Arabs and Berbers had succeeded in spreading Islamic rule across large parts of Spain. In al-Andalus, they had created a flourishing, forward-looking kingdom: culturally speaking, the most advanced state in Europe at the time.

A difficult decision

By 1086, however, Spain's Moors had started to feel the strain: al-Andalus had disintegrated into squabbling princedoms. Emboldened by this, the Christian kings were redoubling their efforts to bring about the Reconquista or 'reconquest' of the Muslim south, sensing that they might be able to expel the Moors from Iberia altogether.

Andalusia with his troops even as Yusuf Ibn Tashufin was mustering his Berber army on the African coast. A few days later, they set sail across the Strait of Gibraltar for southern Spain. Sophisticated Spanish Moors may have looked askance at these black-veiled Berber warriors, but they were obviously the right men for the task: their appearance alone was calculated to strike terror into Christian hearts. And a more powerful, more highly motivated troop could hardly have been found. They brushed the Christians aside with contemptuous ease. Ibn Tashufin's army inflicted a devastating defeat on Alfonso's forces at the Battle of Badajoz, at which a hundred thousand men are said to have lost their lives.

Silver jewellery
Unlike the Arabs, the Berbers favoured silver over gold for their jewellery – despite the fact that the trans-Saharan gold trade passed through their territory.

The Moorish princelings were in a quandary: should they plead with these uncouth desert nomads for military assistance? What were the Almoravids likely to want in return? Should they capitulate to the Christians or cooperate with these ferocious fanatics, who accepted no other law than the Koran? In the end, they decided to entrust their fates to the 'Men of the Ribat', uncivilised and uncongenial as they might be, because most agreed with the Emir of Seville, who said he would rather herd the Almoravids' camels than the Christians' swine.

The Almoravids did not come a moment too soon. Alfonso VI of Castile was driving inexorably southward into

Among infidels

Grateful as they were, the Moors must have breathed a sigh of relief when they realised that the victorious Ibn Tashufin had no intention of remaining in their country. Instead, he was content to take his men back to North Africa and receive payments of tribute from a distance. The suspicion and unease were mutual: Ibn Tashufin was not disposed to linger, and his Berber troops were happy to be returning to the more familiar conditions of the Magrheb. Al-Andalus was too refined, too rarefied, too rich for their tastes. Indeed, Ibn Tashufin and his men despised the decadence they saw at the princes' courts. Fine silk cushions, lavish banquets, alcohol and all manner of licentiousness and luxury: this was not the way in which true Muslims should live. Neither were they impressed by the much-vaunted scholarship and learning of al-Andalus: what did any believer need but the Word of the Koran? They were men of straightforward and rigid beliefs, from which any hint of deviation was a betrayal of the truth. No right-thinking Muslim had any business devoting his mind to philosophy or science: such things were nothing more than lies and devilry.

A few years later, their sense of Islamic mission overcame their feelings of revulsion: in 1090 they returned to clean up al-Andalus. These false Muslims, Ibn Tashufin felt, were as much infidels as any Christian or Jew, and it was the Almoravids' duty to mount a Holy War against them. As Ibn Tashufin made his way through the kingdom, bringing 'true Islam' with 'fire and the sword', his Moorish subjects may have wished that they had, after all, contented themselves with tending the Christians' swine.

There was great political significance in a conquest that incorporated Andalusia into an enormous Berber kingdom with dominions extending deep into the Sahara. For the first time, the entire territory of western Islam was combined under a single supreme ruler, with its political and spiritual centre in Morocco.

Of Islam and amulets

Meanwhile, back in North Africa, the Berber tribes had been enjoying so quiet a time that it was easy to forget their warlike traditions. Along the fertile coastal strip, settled communities grew their cereals, fruit and vegetables as normal, and in the arid, mountainous interior, nomad groups wandered with their flocks from one grazing ground to the next. They shared some of the religious zeal of the Almoravids, thanks to the tireless efforts of wandering Koranic scholars, who brought the teachings of Islam to the most far-flung communities. Yet such teachers did not have things all their own way: many people clung to much earlier pre-Muslim traditions, which could not be readily reconciled with Islamic orthodoxy.

Particularly difficult to dispel was the popular belief in imps and demons, and in the 'evil eye' which brought bad luck, illness or even death. Ironically, it was the happiest people who were most at risk from these dark forces – small children, brides and young mothers.

Some protection was afforded by magic charms or amulets. These might be items of silver jewellery, worn only by women, or amulets in the form of eyes to ward off

Pilgrim water
For the medieval pilgrim, the journey to Mecca was long, hard and potentially dangerous. A full water bottle was an essential part of every pilgrim's equipment. Background: A piece of Berber silver jewellery

the evil eye. Other defences that some resorted to included mystic drawings and verses on the walls of houses. Henna was used to paint magical patterns on to the faces, hands and feet of women and children in the hope that they would provide protection against evil influences.

Then there was disguise: a young bride might be so swathed in veils as to be unrecognisable, so no jealous rival's curse could find her out and strike her barren. The Berbers saw envy as an ever-present and powerful force for evil. It was therefore customary to work deliberate mistakes into especially beautiful objects of craftwork, such as carpets, so as not to provoke the envy of anyone who saw them. Even close friends and relatives were to be feared: you never knew who might give you the evil eye. The scholars could preach all they liked: they were not going to prevail against superstitions that sprang from such ancient tribal traditions, and spoke to the deepest reaches of the psyche. However, the Berbers still saw themselves as pious Muslims; Islam and folk beliefs comfortably co-existed.

The Almoravids might be tolerant of Berber folk beliefs, but their indulgence did not extend to Shi'ite Islam. Sunni Islam was rigorously enforced as the official creed. The differences were admittedly profound: the factual question of Muhammad's true succession entailed untold doctrinal implications and spiritual nuances. In general terms, it could be said that Shi'ism was the more mystical, while Sunnism was more disposed to trust in good practice and in human reasoning. Either branch could lend itself to extremism: in Almoravid Spain, books not conforming to Sunni teaching were publicly burned.

Full circle

When Ibn Tashufin died in 1106, his son and successor, Ali Ibn Yusuf, made Seville his second residence. He was a very different person from his father. Not for him the Spartan lifestyle, the straw pallet and bread and water: under Ibn Yusuf and his successors the Almoravid regime grew increasingly relaxed.

The new emirs enjoyed silk cushions and opulent meals; they took wine served by pretty slave girls – and this was happening not just in Spain, where the ways of the court recalled those of the Moorish princes so despised by Ibn Tashufin, but actually in the Almoravids' Moroccan home. Inevitably, there was a reaction. History repeated itself, with a new teacher taking on the role so fatefully assumed by Abdullah Ibn Yasin half a century before.

His name was Ibn Tumert. He had been banished from Marrakesh for his outspoken criticisms, and now lived in isolation in Tinmal, high up among the rugged peaks of the Atlas Mountains. Years earlier, he had made a long and eventful journey, both physically and ideologically, through the Islamic world, carefully watching and pondering all he saw. He had made the *Hajj*, the pilgrimage to Mecca, of course, but also visited Cairo and Damascus, speaking to scholars and teachers wherever he went. It is probable, too, that he visited the Abbasid capital, Baghdad, which would have had an important influence on his thought.

Islam reinterpreted

When Ibn Tumert returned to Morocco in 1107, he was full of uncompromising ideas which he was soon sharing with the Berbers of his own Masmuda tribe. He was outraged by the moral waywardness and love of luxury that he saw around him, and he attacked what he felt was the poverty of the Almoravids' Islamic understanding. They had never learned to read the Koran, he said; their spirituality was hopelessly banal, and Abdallah Ibn Yasin's Allah was an anthropomorphic caricature. The Almoravids saw God as the pagans saw their idols, he claimed bitterly: their Islamisation might just as well never have happened. Allah had to be understood as a single, all-encompassing entity. Accordingly, Ibn Tumert's followers called themselves Al Muhawidun, the 'Confessors of Divine Unity', a name eventually simplified to the 'Almohads'.

The Masmuda may not have found Ibn Tumert's theology easy, but his passion and conviction were compelling. And besides,

the new thinking tapped into ancient rivalries: the Sanhadja Berbers had been enemies of the Masmuda for generations.

Threat from the mountains

The Almoravids were slow to wake up to the trouble that was brewing in the Atlas Mountains. Not until 1127 did Ali Ibn Yusuf attempt to take the rebel stronghold at Tinmal, and by that time the Almohads were well on the way to organising themselves into a formidable fighting force, one which might smash the Sanhadja ascendancy once and for all. Three years later Ibn Tumert died, and though the Almohad movement might easily have imploded at this point, his protégé Abd al-Mumin was ready to take over.

Al-Mumin was to prove a more than capable successor – and he came to power at a crucial moment. Patience was required, but he was ready to wait, sensing that Almoravid power was on the wane. Based as it was on an alliance of Berber tribes, the Almoravid state was intrinsically unstable: such traditionally quarrelsome groups could only be successfully unified against an external enemy. Times of peace were more perilous politically than those of war for Berber leaders – and for almost four decades there had been no major campaign of conquest. When Ali Ibn Yusuf died, in 1143, Abd al-Mumin recognised that the Almoravids had lost an outstanding ruler. He was ideally placed to exploit the power vacuum that resulted. Expanding steadily from his mountain fastness, al-Mumin took Fez in 1145, which gave the Almohads control over the entire north of the Maghreb.

Abd al-Mumin was not tempted to sit back and enjoy his triumph – his forces, too, might fall apart without a common cause to bond them. Having demolished palaces and mosques to wipe away the stain of Almoravidism from Fez, he next turned his attentions to Andalusia. There Almoravid rule was unravelling. The troops were in open mutiny because they were not being paid enough; the tribal chiefs were squabbling; and the Moorish intelligentsia were kicking against the Koranic scholars' repressive hold over the arts and culture. The time was clearly ripe for another Holy War for al-Andalus: this one would set Berber against Berber.

Berber fights Berber

In 1147, Abd al-Mumin and his Masmuda Berbers invaded al-Andalus and occupied it with little opposition. Then he went back to North Africa where, pressing his military advantage, al-Mumin pushed southward and laid siege to Marrakesh, the Almoravid capital. He took it after nine months. As he had before in Fez, he had all monuments to his predecessors' rule torn down, to erase their blasphemous existence from Muslim memory. Pulling down the Almoravid Mosque, he had a new and even more splendid house of worship erected: the Koutoubia Mosque which, it was claimed, could hold 25,000 believers.

Not only in Marrakesh, but throughout their realms, the Almohads built monuments to their reign: imposing mosques and other public buildings. In 1150, Abd al-Mumin had a border castle, strategically sited on the Atlantic coast, extended into a fortified palace complex – the nucleus of Rabat, the present-day capital of Morocco.

Ultimately, the Almohad founder was to become more powerful than any Berber prince before him: he called himself Caliph and endowed himself with the honorific 'Ruler of the Faithful'. Under Abd al-Mumin and his successors, through the late 12th century, the Almohad dynasty was destined to grow in influence, first equalling and then surpassing the achievements of the Almoravids.

Muslim pulpit
Every mosque has a *minbar*, a stepped pulpit beside the mihrab or prayer niche. Muhammad himself spoke from a raised platform, so all could see and hear him. This *minbar* was in the Koutoubia Mosque, Marrakesh.

1 The Toltec kingdom   150
  of Quetzalcoatl

2 Sailing westwards –   157
  the Vikings in America

3 Cahokia – a   162
  Mississippian
  metropolis

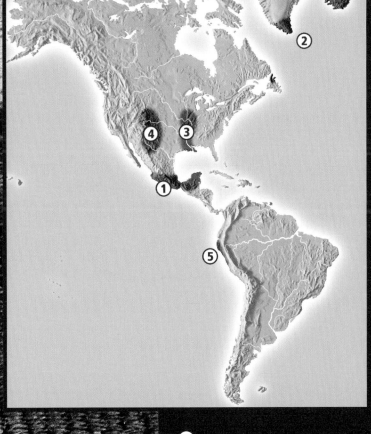

4 The early Pueblo   166
  farmers and
  architects

5 The Chimú of   173
  coastal Peru

AMERICA

The Toltec kingdom of Quetzalcoatl

Myths and legends surround the history of the Toltec civilisation, but later cultures looked back to its heyday as a Mesoamerican 'golden age'.

The birth of Quetzalcoatl
A relief carving represents the birth of Topiltzin, a mighty Toltec ruler who, it was claimed, was the incarnation of the feathered serpent, Quetzalcoatl.

When the first Europeans arrived in Mexico in the early 16th century they were awestruck by the richness of the Aztec civilisation. But the Aztecs themselves spoke of an age of even greater splendour. 'There at Tula they were indeed rich,' reported one, speaking to the Spanish priest Fray Bernardino de Sahagún. 'Of no value was food; the multicoloured cotton grew … And all the green stones, the gold, they were not costly.'

Yet the auguries 600 years earlier had not been particularly promising. Mexican civilisation appeared to be at an end. Teotihuacán, one of the largest cities in the world, had been sacked by unknown invaders in the 8th century. They had left the great Mesoamerican metropolis a smoking ruin, its demoralised people dispersed into village communities to live as subsistence farmers, making whatever living they could from the soil.

They might have found it easier had it not been for the warlike peoples drifting down from the north through the 9th century, barbaric raiders who preyed on the defenceless farmers. Among the worst were the Toltecs, a subgroup of the Nahua. In fairness, the Toltecs had themselves been uprooted, dislodged by drought from their homeland, where they had previously lived peaceably as hunters and agriculturalists.

Climatic changes were sweeping through North America at this time, producing chaos across the continent. Forced by circumstances to become warriors, the Toltecs pushed steadily southward: under the legendary leader Mixcoatl ('Cloud Servant'), they occupied much of the Valley of Mexico.

As far as can be gleaned from the archaeological evidence and mythology, by about 900 things were beginning to settle down – including the Toltecs, who intermarried with the farming people of the region. For what followed, however, we are completely dependent on the mythic record.

Topiltzin – king and god

Mixcoatl's successor and the second Toltec ruler was Topiltzin ('Our Lord One Reed'). He is said to have been a king of such stupendous wealth that his houses were built of green jade, silver and precious shells. It was also said that he gave his subjects the skills of agriculture, medicine and writing, as well as the calendar on which all their chronicles were based. In his reign maize was available in such abundance that the smaller cobs were not eaten at all, but burned for heating the ritual sweat-baths.

Amongst the exaggerations, however, are tantalising glimpses of what might actually have been. Certain aspects of Topiltzin's myth ring true. Legend has it, for example, that as a young man he was compelled to go into exile, because a nobleman had had his father murdered. There may indeed have been violent power struggles early on in the history of the Toltec state. The story goes that, like any good legendary hero, he came back to kill his father's murderer and claim his rightful inheritance: there is good evidence that he may indeed have had to fight hard for his position of power.

It may have been to bolster that position and provide a religious base for his rule that Topiltzin identified himself with the god Quetzalcoatl – the 'Plumed Serpent'. A rattlesnake-deity adorned with the spectacular green tail-feathers of the quetzal bird, he was a blatant symbol of fertility and creativity. Worshipped in the time of the Olmecs, a thousand years before, he would be revered, too, by the Aztecs. But Topiltzin took things further. Not only did he make himself the high priest of the serpent god, but he identified with him so closely that he adopted his name, calling himself Ce Acatl Topiltzin Quetzalcoatl.

A fitting capital

By the second half of the 10th century, the divinity of the Toltec ruler was taken for granted. At about this time, a new capital city was

Chac Mool
A stone warrior from Chichén Itzá holds a small bowl in his lap: this would have been used to hold the hearts of human sacrificial victims.

established. The centre of the Toltec kingdom, it was given the name Tula, a Nahua word which means 'capital and centre of the world'. With a population of up to 50,000, Tula was far smaller than Teotihuacán had been at its height, but the city was impressive by the standards of its time. Lying some 60km (40 miles) north of modern Mexico City, Tula is today a vast archaeological dig extending over an area of 9km² (4sq miles). Modern researchers are not, however, the first excavators of this metropolis: the Aztecs ransacked the ruins several centuries before. Yet while

they looted Tula's material heritage, they transfigured its memory into one of an earthly paradise. The city, they said, was a place 'where the blue water stretches and the white bulrushes grow, where the white reeds spread out and where the

TIME WITNESS

The Toltec calendar

The Toltec calendar system was underpinned by precise astronomical observation, but in reality, it was two systems combined. One of these was a basic calculation of 260 days, which was based on the length of the standard pregnancy. The second system, known as the 'long count', stood for the solar year of 365 days.

Every 52 years, these two calendar systems would coincide to produce a time of the most fearful portent for the Toltecs.

Calendar dates
Combined here with dot and line numbers, these four hieroglyphs represent different dates in the Toltec calendar.

white pastures are, where white sand is found and the coloured balls of cotton hang, where colourful water-lilies float and one can find the site of the magic ball court'. The Aztecs liked to think that they themselves were the true successors to the Toltecatl, a Nahua word which means 'master builders' or 'artists'.

The more systematic excavations of modern times have cast doubt on the Aztec idealisations. Though they have confirmed the monumental scale on which the city was built, in large parts the architectural vision seems to have been uninspired and the quality of workmanship indifferent. The atmosphere seems gloomy, even threatening to the modern visitor: symbols of death and of military power are everywhere.

The most impressive building of all is the five-step Pyramid of the Morning Star. This has reliefs of feathered serpents with skulls in their mouths around its base; other decorations depict jaguars with ferocious teeth and eagles eating human hearts. At the summit of the pyramid is a group of fearsome-looking warriors, carved in solid stone, each standing some 4.6m (15ft) tall. It is thought that they once supported the roof of a temple. There is certainly nothing welcoming in their aspect. With their tall feather headdresses, breastplates and arms held tightly against the sides of their bodies, they present a stern picture, threatening woe to any enemy who dared to approach the Toltec capital.

Together with another large temple pyramid, the Pyramid of the Morning Star flanked a huge plaza on which stood a rectangular sacrificial platform and a stone skull ledge. Here, too, are the macabre, but apparently once brightly painted, Chac Mools – reclining warriors of stone in whose laps were hollow bowls designed to hold the hearts of sacrificial victims.

The general population lived in flat-roofed houses arranged in threes and fours around inner courtyards. In the centres of these living units were altars and shrines to domestic deities. The dead were buried in pits directly underneath the houses.

Feathered Serpent versus Smoking Mirror

Quetzalcoatl was not the only deity worshipped by the Toltecs; he had a rival in the terrifying Tezcatlipoca, a sorceror and god of war. His name meant 'Smoking Mirror', and he would later be described in the writings of the Aztecs as a cruel, capricious god, who acted 'according to his own will and whim'. When offended – as he was, all too easily – he inflicted dangerous diseases as punishment: 'If someone did not fulfil a vow or promise, or broke his fast, the god would throw at him leprosy, syphilis, swollen knee-joints, cancer or boils … and other diseases.' Perhaps Tezcatlipoca was angered by the moves of

Ce Acatl Topiltzin Quetzalcoatl to replace the sacrifice of human victims with that of snakes, birds, butterflies, even offerings of flowers, and to assuage any thirst for human blood by 'auto-sacrifice'. In what seems a bizarre practice to the modern mind, worshippers drew their own blood by threading thorn-tipped leather thongs through their tongues or ears.

'Smoking Mirror' was a jealous god. To his followers he was unique and all-powerful: he had created heaven and earth and knew all the thoughts and deeds of humans. He was depicted with yellow and black stripes across his face; he carried a mirror on his forehead, and in his hands he held a throwing spear, lance and shield. Since his priests would acknowledge no other god, violent conflict was inevitable:

Dedicated to the Morning Star
The most important monument in Tula, the Toltec capital, this five-step pyramid was dedicated to Quetzalcoatl. In the foreground are the remains of columned halls.

Stone guardians
These awesome monoliths shaped like stone warriors once supported the wooden temple roof of the Pyramid of the Morning Star.

Gulf of Mexico, climbed onto a raft made of the bodies of snakes and sailed away. Hardly had he disappeared over the horizon, however, than his return began to be prophesied: one day he would come back to lead the Toltecs once again.

The legend was to endure into the time of the Aztec ruler Montezuma II. The Aztec calendar had confidently predicted that in the year '1 reed', the white-skinned, bearded Quetzalcoatl would come back to resume his reign (in the European calendar, that year was 1519). So when, in 1519, the Spanish Conquistadors led by the white-skinned, bearded Hernán Cortés appeared, Montezuma was understandably perturbed.

In other versions of the legend, Quetzalcoatl's raft made landfall on the Yucatan peninsula: there he was greeted hospitably by the Maya and worshipped as a god. One day, however, he put on his robe of quetzal feathers and his mask of turquoise and immolated himself: his ashes rose heavenward and his heart became the Morning Star. Strangely enough, Mayan sources report the arrival of foreigners in 987. They speak of a conqueror called Kukulkán, or 'Feathered Serpent'. He conquered the whole peninsula and built his capital in Chichén Itzá. Excavations confirm close Mayan–Toltec contacts at this time.

The old city made new

In Chichén Itzá (the Maya's 'Old City'), the invaders built a new administrative centre, blending Mayan and Toltec styles. With its Temple of the Warriors on a step-pyramid and the Court of a Thousand Columns at its base, the complex recalls the Pyramid of the Morning Star in Tula. There are Chac Mool sculptures and serried rows of skulls as well.

The indigenous traditions of the Maya themselves were not suppressed, however: the mask of the rain-god was still prominently displayed in some of the

Man and coyote
Covered with mother-of-pearl mosaic, this intriguing clay sculpture from Tula depicts the head of a bearded man – presumably Quetzalcoatl – peering out from the jaws of a coyote. Background: The fire serpent, Xiuhcoatl, in stylised form on a mosaic shield from Chichén Itzá.

ultimately it led to a palace coup. Tezcatlipoca's priests, the story goes, plied Quetzalcoatl with pulque, an intoxicating drink made from the juice of the maguey plant, then seduced him into performing shameful sexual acts. So remorseful was he that he abdicated his position and went away, leaving the field to his rival.

Quetzalcoatl's flight – and return

It was in 987, according to the chronicles, that Quetzalcoatl went into exile with his followers. He went to the coast of the main temples. A large fresco in the Temple of the Warriors demonstrated how Maya farmers in their villages lived side by side with the Toltecs after their arrival from the sea. Further south, amidst a hilly landscape, was the old cultural centre of Uxmal. Here, too, Toltec influence is apparent. The buildings – pyramids, palaces and holy buildings – are among the high points of Mayan architecture.

The Serpent dynasty

Back in Tula at the end of the 10th century, after Quetzalcoatl's departure, the so-called Serpent dynasty began to establish itself. Through a combination of armed strength and skilful marriage alliances, its kings tried to create favourable conditions with the Mixtecs, their neighbours to the south. The Nuttall Codex, a beautifully illuminated 'book' created on a continuous strip of tanned stag leather, tells of the wedding of the great Mixtec chief 'Smoking Eye' with the lady 'Three Stone Knife' from Tula.

Flourishing trades

As the city continued to thrive, so too did the rural area surrounding it, whose population was actually double that of the urban centre. The Toltec farmers grew mainly maize, beans, cocoa plants and cotton. Their vegetables may not have grown quite as tall as palm trees (as the Aztecs would later claim) but agricultural yields do appear to have been high. The cotton crop gave rise to a thriving 'cottage industry' in weaving: the Toltec women attained great mastery in this art. Despite the more exaggerated Aztec claims, multicoloured cotton did not grow spontaneously in the Toltec kingdom, but the weaver who tired of the natural colour spectrum (white through to brown) could call on a variety of natural dyes. Crushed cochineal insects supplied carmine red, for example, whilst the body juices of a certain snail provided purple. Paintings and reliefs may still be seen, showing the superlative textile products of the Toltecs: wrap-around skirts and embroidered ponchos for the women; loincloths, kilts and cloaks for the men.

Many craftsmen in Tula earned their living from working obsidian, as there were important deposits of this substance in the vicinity. A hard, black volcanic 'glass', it could be splintered into shards, which made excellent blades – a crucial resource in the absence of iron or bronze-working technology. Tools and utensils made of obsidian were traded by the Toltecs across long distances. Travertine, a stone used to make milky, translucent vessels, also played an important role.

Royal piercing
A scene from the Nuttall Codex shows the King of Tula inserting a jewel into the nose of a Mixtec prince, 'Eight Stag Jaguar Claw', an act conferring royal dignity.

Artwork of gold and feathers

The New World lagged far behind the Old when it came to metalworking. The Toltecs, like their neighbours the Mixtecs, would be pioneers. They extracted gold by panning the river sand: they called the resulting nuggets *teocuitatl*, 'heavenly drops'. Along with gold and silver, smiths used tumbaga, an alloy of gold and copper, in making jewellery. Tumbaga had a reddish sheen and was harder than either of the two pure metals.

Workers in feathers enjoyed very high status in the Toltec kingdom, since the finest plumes were prized more highly than silver or gold. Beside cocoa beans and cotton, feathers were the most important form of currency; worked into jewellery or clothing, they signalled the wearer's wealth and dignity. As decoration in a warrior's hair, they announced his courage and bravery. The most prized feathers came from the quetzal bird, a fabulously beautiful creature with a blood-red breast; its emerald green tail feathers could form a train of up to 1m (3ft) long. No one was allowed to kill this divine bird; instead, it was captured and solemn prayers were offered as its tail feathers were pulled out, then the bird was released. Other birds' feathers were valued too – toucan and parrot feathers in particular – to be worked into dramatic ceremonial robes.

A three-legged vase
This unusual Toltec vessel was found in a tomb in Chichén Itza. Designs have been etched into the black decorative panels.

Disease, famine and war

The reign of the Serpent dynasty was dogged by the same sort of power struggles that had been seen in Tula during the time of Ce Acatl Topiltzin Quetzalcoatl. This was hardly surprising, given the number of different peoples to which the metropolis was home. Immigrants from the north, from the Mexican highlands, from the Gulf coast and probably from elsewhere, too, were all to be found living in and around what was clearly a very cosmopolitan capital. It seems likely that several languages were spoken in Tula. The mix of peoples would not always have been harmonious: no doubt there would have been competition between different groups, and incidence of plague or famine would have exacerbated any enmities between them.

By the late 12th century such afflictions were coming thick and fast. In 1558 Fray Bernardino de Sahagún's Aztec sources told him: 'Then came the drought and lack of water, and a large number of people died … Worms ate up the grain in the stores, and there were many other catastrophes. One could almost believe there had been a rain of fire, and for 24 long years there was such a terrible drought that rivers and springs dried up.'

The Toltec fall and Aztec rise

In these apocalyptic conditions, King Huemac was utterly helpless. In desperation he sought to reintroduce human sacrifice to appease the gods. The move did nothing to placate his people, though: they rose up in fury and he fled – to no avail, as he was caught and savagely murdered.

Nor was he the only casualty. Frantic, the people even destroyed statues of the gods and sacked the sacred temples – so utterly betrayed did they feel by their divine powers. It was an act of symbolic self-destruction, however, as Tula now lay unprotected and there were enemies only too ready to take advantage.

The Chichimeca or 'Dog People' had been drifting southward from the deserts of the north, just as the Toltecs themselves had once migrated. As Tula burned, they moved in on the stricken city. Over the years, further waves of immigrants followed. The last of these, in the early 13th century, were the Aztecs, who would interpret the Toltec civilisation as a template for their own.

Sailing westwards – the Vikings in America

The intrepid spirit of the Vikings took them farther west than anyone was known to have gone before: across the wide Atlantic to Iceland, Greenland and finally America – 500 years before Columbus.

It was the year 985, and a fleet of 25 longships tossed and heaved as they laboured through the surging, storm-whipped waves of the north Atlantic. For most it was a voyage into the unknown – though danger could be counted on in waters where heavy seas, thick fogs, enormous icebergs and even schools of whales posed lethal risks. Yet this did not deter the would-be colonists. Awaiting them was a country so fertile it had been called 'Green Land'. For the increasing numbers in Scandinavia who found themselves landless, the thought of a

homestead of their own in the new territory was a great incitement, but there were other things to spur the adventurous spirit. Back in Norway, Harald Finehair's centralising rule had succeeded in uniting the country – but at the cost of upsetting a great many noble families. The Vikings had set sail and taken possession of the Faeroes, Shetlands and Orkneys as early as about 860; settlement had also taken place round the coasts of Ireland.

It may have been from Irish monks that the Vikings learned of the existence of Iceland: a few ascetic souls had established

A new life
Viking settlers in northern Newfoundland built homesteads like those that they knew in Greenland – and like this one in a modern reconstruction at L'Anse aux Meadows. With little wood for construction, thick sod walls were built up on stone foundations. Grass sods were also the main roofing material.

The discoverer of Greenland
No contemporary portrait exists of Eirik the Red, fearless Viking and the first European to walk on the soil of Greenland. This highly improbable 17th-century depiction shows how people in the Baroque period imagined him.

religious communities there. If they could make the perilous voyage in their coracles of willow and hide (surprisingly seaworthy as these traditional vessels were) the longships of the Vikings could surely follow. And follow they did: by the mid-10th century, about 20,000 people had settled round the Icelandic coast, whose fertile soil was eminently suitable for agriculture. There were few trees – those that were there were predominantly birch – and no land mammals apart from the Arctic fox. The ocean around, however, offered rich fishing; there were seals and walrus to be hunted; and huge seabird colonies provided a source of meat and eggs. The entire stock of domestic animals – cattle, pigs, sheep, horses and poultry – had to be imported. These were the conditions under which Eirik the Red and his father settled in Iceland in 970. Both had got themselves into trouble

in Norway and had to leave rather suddenly. But the land allotted to them turned out not to be particularly fertile.

Exploration in exile

Eirik the Red got his nickname from his flaming hair, but he had the temper to match. It was not long before he was embroiled in further quarrels. Several men lost their lives and in 982 Iceland's common executive and legislative assembly, the Althing, sentenced him to three years' banishment. Unwelcome as he was in Norway, he resolved to set sail in the opposite direction, to find the land which had been spoken of in rumours for some time. A man known as Gunnbjörn, blown off course by storms on a journey from Norway to Iceland, reported seeing snow-topped mountains far to the west.

It was not much to base so hazardous an undertaking on. There were no real points of reference for navigation: the only means of orientation were the position of the sun over the horizon by day, and at night the light of the Pole Star. Data about distances, wind directions and ocean currents was accumulated over time, by trial and error (all too often fatal). Such information was transmitted by word of mouth, though would eventually be written down, as in the 13th-century *Landnámabók* ('Book of Settlements'). This was worth its weight in gold, offering navigators the tried-and-tested knowledge of generations, such as: 'Experienced men say that it takes seven days to sail from Stad in Norway west to the Horn on the eastern coast of Iceland…'.

Eirik the Red could call upon no such assistance as he set sail westward, but presumably felt he had little to lose. After just a few days at sea, a rocky coast rose up before him. There was no safe haven to be seen there, so he followed the coastline southward until he had rounded the island's southern tip. He used the three years of his banishment to explore this new-found territory as thoroughly as he could. Many of its fjords reached far inland where, to his surprise, he found green valleys, sheltered by hills, in which cattle could be herded and the soil could be tilled. Here, too, the ocean was full of fish, and whales and seals abounded: a good life could be had here for the hardy. When the term of his exile came to its end, Eirik returned to Iceland and set about persuading colonists to come back with him and start settling what he called 'Greenland'.

Eirik had a proven record as a ne'er-do-well, and later historians claimed that he had cynically given Greenland an inappropriate name with the intent of 'talking up' his new colony for his own ends. In fact, climatic conditions in the Viking period were much warmer than they are today, turning harsher only towards the end of the 12th century. And even in modern times, while the interior may have remained icy, along the southern fjords, at least, this has been a genuinely 'green land'.

Colonists in Greenland

This was how, in 985, 25 ships came to be battling through the waves towards southern Greenland. On board were men, women, children and their livestock. They had with them everything they might require to create a new life for themselves in virgin, unpeopled territory, from timber and tools to fishing nets and cooking utensils. The land they were heading for may have been benign, but the waters they had to cross to get there were anything but, fully living up to their fearsome reputation. Only 14 of the ships eventually reached their destination. The others sank or were blown hopelessly off course. Even so, some 700 colonists did attain their goal, making landfall near the southern tip of Greenland.

There, Eirik built his farmstead, Brattahlid, on a steep rise above the fjord which was named after him, Eiriksfjord. His home became the centre of the so-called East Settlement, which expanded quickly to comprise 450 farms grouped around this and adjacent fjords. Brattahlid has been identified through modern excavations; the remains of a church, built by Eirik's wife, Thjodhild, were also found. She had been converted to Christianity by her son, Leif, who had been baptised during a sojourn in Norway. After his return to Greenland, the settlers had followed his example and by shortly after 1000 the population were all Christians.

Meanwhile, some of the first colonists had made their way more than 600km (400 miles) farther north along the coast, where they had founded a 'West Settlement' in present-day Godthabsfjord. Between these two centres, a slightly smaller Middle Settlement was established. Despite the milder conditions compared to the climate today, life in such high latitudes was hard. Growing cereals had to be abandoned and agriculture was effectively reduced to the cultivation

Farmstead on Eiriksfjord
Little remains today of the home Eirik built at Brattahlid, Greenland. Apart from the stone foundations, all the construction materials were perishable.

In memorium
Pictorial stones were carved to commemorate those Vikings who could have no burial. Though many remembered in this way died in battle, far more were lost at sea.

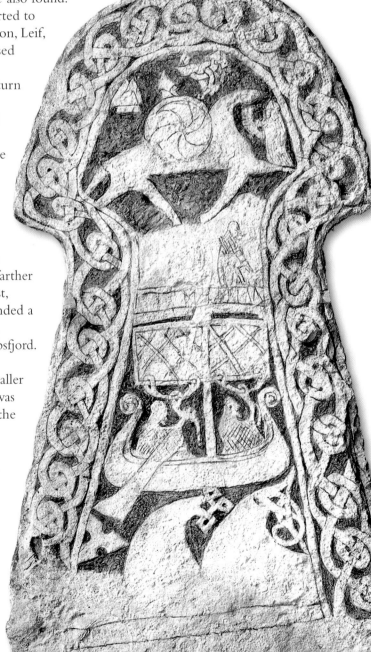

Precious iron
A 12th-century wood panel shows a smith testing a sword on an anvil. Always valuable in the Middle Ages, iron was doubly prized in Greenland where there was little wood. Iron tools made by Viking smiths can be seen in the background. The remains of a Viking forge were found at L'Anse-aux-Meadows, Newfoundland.

misadventures of another mariner. In 985 Bjarni Herjolfsson sailed from Iceland for Greenland, following his parents who had joined Eirik the Red. His ship was blown far to the south, but he pressed on westwards until finally he sighted a coast; inland, vast forests extended as far as the eye could see. Hence the name he gave it: Markland, or 'Forest Land', which was probably present-day Labrador. Bjarni and his crew were probably the first Europeans to set eyes on the American continent. It was clearly not Greenland, though, and so Herjolfsson turned north. At last he reached Greenland, where his reports caused a considerable stir. Leif Eiriksson determined to find this unknown country.

In about 1001, Leif set sail with a ship and 35 men, retracing in reverse the route taken by Bjarni Herjolfsson. Having begun by crossing the Davis Strait west of Greenland, he sailed south past a mountainous coast which he called Helluland, or 'Land of Stone Slabs' – almost certainly modern Baffin Island. Bjarni's account had promised less rugged realms, and so Leif Eiriksson continued on his way: at last he was able to land in Labrador. He and his shipmates were not to know it, of course, but when they stepped ashore they stepped into history, reaching the New World half a millennium before Columbus.

Their preoccupations were altogether more mundane, but they were ecstatic at their discovery: after the harsh conditions of Greenland, this was paradise. Salmon teemed in the streams, and they thought

of feed plants for cattle which the settlers reared alongside goats and sheep. Cattle could graze outside only during the summer and had to be brought into byres for the long winters. Fortunately, the colonists had the wealth of the ocean at their disposal and they hunted in the frozen north.

The discovery of America

Like his father, Leif Eiriksson had a restless, reckless streak and was not content to linger long at home. And he, too, found himself in a position to profit from the

the land so fertile, the climate so benign, that their cattle would be able to graze all year. They decided to over-winter here and established a semi-permanent camp. One day, a man disappeared while out exploring. When he reappeared, he excitedly told his companions about wild grapes he had discovered – whether they were really grapes or some kind of berry hardly matters. Leif decided to call the new country Vinland, or 'Wine Land'. He returned to Greenland to tell the astonished settlers what he had found.

War with the Skrälinge

Just how far south Leif's expedition had actually taken him is unclear – he may even have ventured as far as present-day Boston. Either Leif or a successor would certainly make it as far as the northern tip of Newfoundland. Here, at L'Anse-aux-Meadows, an archaeological excavation in the 1950s uncovered the first irrefutable evidence of the Viking presence in North America. We cannot know, of course, whether this was actually Leif's outpost, but the groundplans of the grass-sod houses, a blacksmith's forge, as well as a range of metal objects confirm the link between this settlement and the Viking culture of Greenland and Iceland.

A year after Leif's return, his brother Thorvald took 30 men on another voyage to Vinland. They arrived safely, but soon after their arrival they encountered unknown people: Native Americans, though the Viking sagas referred to them disparagingly as Skrälinge – 'Weaklings'. They used the same name for Greenland's Inuit, with whom they appear to have had endless spats over hunting territories. The Skrälinge, the sources said, were 'dark-skinned, with tangled hair, large eyes and broad cheekbones' and they fought with bows and arrows and stone-tipped spears. Early encounters usually turned out badly for the Skrälinge, but then reinforcements seem to have been summoned from further inland. Soon numerous canoes approached, and the Vikings were assailed

by a hail of arrows. Thorvald was killed, and his surviving companions deemed it safer to withdraw. They returned to Greenland, but the dream of a life of abundance in Vinland refused to die and further attempts to establish permanent settlements were made.

In about 1005, Thorfinn Karlsefni set sail with three ships, 160 men and a few women, as well as cattle and essential tools and weapons. After their first landing, they overwintered – probably a little too far to the north, as finding food proved difficult. When spring came they sailed farther south, where all the fish and game they could possibly want awaited them. Their arrival did not go unnoticed by the Skrälinge, however. Canoes appeared, but their occupants did not dare come close. The next winter passed without incident, and over the next year the two communities even began tentatively to trade. It was a doomed relationship, however, and misunderstandings soon led to renewed hostilities between settlers and natives. It was a conflict which the colonists had to lose. The Skrälinge were hugely superior in numbers to the Vikings, who were a long way from possible reinforcements back in Greenland.

'Although the land is rich,' wrote Karlsefni, 'we would never be able to live in safety and without fear here, because of the people already living here.' There may have been other attempts at colonisation, but if so, they were fated to founder on the same imbalance. The voyage to Vinland had proved a historical cul-de-sac as far as Europe was concerned: the existence of this new world, with its Skrälinge, sank back into oblivion.

A pocket god
Even after the Vikings' conversion to Christianity, elements of their old religion persisted as superstitions. Many seafarers carried figures like this one; the status of the old gods subtly shifted, and idols became talismen.

Cahokia – a Mississippian metropolis

The construction of cities and temple pyramids was not restricted to Central and South America. In the Mississippi Valley, the remains of the city and culture of Cahokia include more than a hundred earthen pyramids.

Not far from what is now St Louis in Mississippi, there was once another city, Cahokia. In its 11th-century heyday it was the largest centre of Native North American culture and was so important and influential that this era of the entire continent's pre-Columbian history is now referred to as the Mississippian period. Mississippian culture stretched far beyond the Mississippi Valley, extending from present-day Oklahoma in the west to Georgia in the east, and from Wisconsin in the north to the Gulf of Mexico. It seems to have evolved out of the preceding Hopewell culture of around AD 700 – although this date is somewhat arbitrary. Like their Hopewell predecessors, the Mississippians threw up monumental mounds of soil at the heart of their settlements, but the purpose of some of these earthworks appears to have been completely different. They were not primarily burial mounds, they were the foundations for temples – more like the pyramids of Mesoamerica.

Like the Hopewell, Mississippians grew maize, beans, gourds and sunflowers in the fertile alluvial plains of the great river and its tributaries. They also gathered wild plants and caught fish, water birds, turkeys and deer to supplement their diet. Farmed produce – especially maize – made up their staple food, however, and since maize is poor in minerals, they set great store by the availability of salt. Trade in this 'white gold' was crucial to the Mississippian economy.

Population centres

With the food supply assured, the population began to rise significantly. New settlements appeared up and down the Mississippi. Some grew larger than others and clearly had a regional importance as tribal centres. An aristocratic caste of chiefs and priests emerged. It was in these local capitals that the Mississippians built their flat-topped, rectangular mounds of earth, with steps leading up to platforms on the top, where log-framed temples were constructed.

Mound of the monks
Little remains of the one-time splendour of Cahokia's largest earthen pyramid, but its great size reflects the power and importance it must once have held. It is named not for Mississippian priests but for the Trappist monks who settled here much later.

These mounds and their surrounds were further enclosed by log palisades, intended to protect not just the sacred shrines but also the lodges of the community's leading members. Their homes would have had reed walls sealed with lime, and may well have been brightly painted, inside and out, perhaps with mythological scenes.

Class distinctions

With more than a hundred earth pyramids, large and small, and covering some 1600 hectares (4000 acres) Cahokia left all other regional centres in the shade. Around AD 800, it had been a small village but it seems to have grown rapidly. It reached its metropolitan height in the 11th century. Many homes there were rectangular in shape, with stout timber-post frames supporting reed walls, weatherproofed with lime, and sloping reed-thatched roofs.

Each lodge had room to house an extended family – perhaps up to 30 people. At the centre was a hearth, with a smoke vent above. In some cases lodges appear to have been grouped around open plazas in distinct quarters; often they were clustered around the earth mounds – perhaps arranged hierarchically. So each tribe may have had its own mound in its own part of the city – the chief and his family would have lived on top, with the homes of his dependants lower down.

The entire northern flank of Cahokia was protected by a fortification of wooden palisades.

Weeping warrior
The motif of the 'weeping eye' – shown here on a warrior's portrait – features widely in Mississippian art. It is thought to have symbolised tears of the gods, which fell to Earth as rain.

Soul guardian
An engraved shell plaque shows four woodpecker heads protecting a central sun. Birds were guardians of the dead, while the sun was the guarantor of life.

residences for the city's ruling families. All of these were overshadowed, however, by the main pyramid. Constructed in four terraces or steps and rising to a height of 33m (108ft), in area and total volume it was bigger than the Great Pyramid of Khufu at Giza, in Egypt. In front of it was the main assembly area, where cult rites were carried out by the chiefs and priests, in the presence of the entire population.

Gifts for the chief

It was only natural that the nobility should live alongside the gods; their pre-eminence was based on their close connections with the deities. The leadership of the chiefs was both ritual and administrative: they pleaded with the gods at religious ceremonies and presided over the collection and distribution of the harvest. They deducted a proportion as a form of 'tax'.

In the 18th century, a French explorer travelled among the Natchez of the lower Mississippi, who maintained many rites of the earlier Mississippian people. He recorded that, every month, tribute in the form of food was delivered to the chief. The handover was conducted with solemn ceremony. 'Festivals usually take place when the Great Chief requests food …', he wrote. 'On the last day of the festival the gifts are heaped up in front of the door of his hut.' The celebrations also served to 'give thanks to the chieftain for the good he had done for his people'. The status of the ruler was underscored by the insignia he wore. These were generally made of precious materials. He might, for example, have carried a symbolic axe, with a blade and handle fashioned from a single piece of polished stone.

Attendants in death

The power of these rulers is also clearly reflected in the scale of their tombs. Some pyramids excavated by archaeologists contained burial chambers in which great hoards of precious grave goods had been

A ring of many larger and smaller villages spread out around the city. Each of these had its own pyramid, as well as varying numbers of homes. Adding the estimated population of these outlying settlements to that of the city itself – about 20,000 – the total for this 'greater Cahokia' may have been as many as 50,000 people.

The heart of Cahokia city was a sacred precinct, surrounded by a second fortified wall with gateways. This was not just a secondary line of defence but a crucial sacred and social boundary. It separated the areas inhabited by the lower chiefs and common people from the almost 90-hectare (220-acre) precinct in which the gods' temples were sited and where the very highest of Cahokia's nobility lived.

Within this inner zone further huge platform pyramids rose, with temples and left. One such tomb from Cahokia provides insight into the sort of rites that might have formed part of the burial ceremony of the highest-ranking personages. The deceased was laid out on a bed made up of some 20,000 shell beads, with 800 stone arrowheads piled in heaps alongside, together with copper and decorated mica plates. This particular priest-chieftain was also accompanied by an impressive retinue of attendants, including 50 young women aged from 18 to 24 years, all apparently strangled.

Here, too, Mississippian custom was echoed in that of the 18th-century Natchez, for whom the high chief was seen as the incarnation of the sun. Only he and a very few special priests were allowed to enter the temple, in which a sacred fire was kept burning, day and night. When the 'Great Sun' died, his wives, close relatives and servants were all strangled so that they could keep the patriarch company in death.

The Sun cult and human sacrifice

To judge by the number of circular sun symbols in the craftworks of the time, worship of the Sun must have been very important in Mississippian culture. Tall wooden totem poles uncovered at Cahokia also appear to have been associated with a Sun-cult and the calendrical division of the solar year – understandably a concern of what was a fundamentally agrarian civilisation. A circle of wooden posts with a centre post, also at Cahokia, is believed to have been used in similar rituals. An understanding of the astronomical cycles would have been exclusive to the upper class, which would have drawn much of its power from

this privileged knowledge. Little else is known about the Mississippians. Only artistic remains bear witness to their spiritual world. Varied motifs such as birds, snakes and jaguars were carved into shells or mica wafers, or engraved on thin copper sheets. Mythological creatures were represented, too, and other artworks show religious dances and human sacrifices. These last seem to have been bound up with a fertility cult relating to the growth of maize. One image shows a priest killing his victims with a ceremonial club shaped like a maize plant. Human blood, symbolic of the life force and to the rain, is thought to have ensured the fertility of the fields. Like so many other agrarian cultures, the Mississippians invested great spiritual significance in the cycle of the seasons, of death and rebirth.

The Mississippian earth-mounds are so like those of ancient Mexico it may be that travelling traders from far to the south contributed to the development of this North American culture. Though the possibility of influential contacts with Mesoamerica cannot be ruled out, it is not so hard to imagine the Mississippian versions simply evolving out of the burial mounds of earlier indigenous cultures like the Hopewell.

Whatever doubt there may be over Cahokia's beginnings, there is no doubt that by the end of the 12th century it was a civilisation in decline. The city first stopped growing, then stagnated, then it dwindled into insignificance, though elsewhere – at Moundville in Alabama, for instance – the Mississippian culture would continue to endure for a few centuries more.

Mesoamerican influence?
Mississippian ceramics are varied both in shape and decoration. This tripod vase (left) found in Arkansas clearly shows close similarities with Central American models. In the background is a black ceramic pot from Moundville, Alabama.

The early Pueblo – farmers and architects

The industrious Pueblo made North America's southwestern desert bloom. They invented irrigation systems, and in their ingenious high-rise communities – known as pueblos – erected the first multistorey buildings in America.

The conquistadors would call these people Pueblo, because they lived in villages – *pueblos* in Spanish. Other indigenous communities lived in villages too, of course, but these were particularly striking because their adobe apartment blocks were like nothing any European had ever seen. More correctly, they belonged to the Anasazi people, whose ancestors had been farming in the American Southwest for over a thousand years. Yet this name had been thrust upon them, too. Given to them by their Navajo rivals, it means 'Ancient Strangers': what the early Anasazi might have called themselves is not known.

Pueblo petroglyphs
The Anasazi left behind many rock drawings which collectively represent an impressive picture gallery of men and the animals they hunted, including stags, bison and bighorn sheep. There are also foot prints and a wheel.

Making the most of a hostile land

The Anasazi settlement area lies where the present-day states of Arizona, New Mexico, Utah and Colorado meet. The region had not been treated generously by Nature. Deep ravines and barren plateaux created a rugged, fissured terrain that received very little rainfall. Summer temperatures soared above 40°C, while winter brought falls of snow. These were not the most favourable conditions for farming. And yet, through a combination of sheer hard work and the development of a marvellously efficient irrigation system, the Anasazi had thrived.

They grew maize, gourds and beans – the nutritionally complementary 'Holy Trinity' of New World crops – and became more secure economically as the generations passed. By the end of the First Millennium they had been able to move out of their traditional circular pit-huts, roofed over with reeds, into above-ground square-shaped dwellings built of stone or adobe. At first the simplest of structures, these were added to and elaborated over time until they became the stylish pueblos which would so impress the Spanish.

At the beginning of the 11th century, Chaco Canyon saw a building boom: large complexes were constructed in the Pueblo style. Many were built from large sandstone blocks, carefully arranged on

The people of Mesa Verde chose the most inaccessible sites they could find to build their pueblos.

EVERYDAY LIFE

Irrigation technology

The Anasazi of North America's arid southwest were highly imaginative and enterprising in their employment of irrigation – and in making the most of the region's meagre natural water supply. Since the Chaco Wash River was not much more than a trickle, they collected the rainwater running down the canyon walls, too. Rain falling on the uplands above had always found its way down the valley's sandstone sides: the Anasazi carved out special gutters to capture this water and to channel it into reservoir basins at the bottom. From here it was conducted and directed, via a system of ditches and dams, to whichever part of the field-system where it was needed most. There was generally enough water available for domestic use, too.

A comparable system at Mesa Verde was even more impressive. One reservoir basin here contained two million litres of water. 'Lake Mummy', as it is known, was artificially constructed and reinforced. Water was distributed from here via a canal some 800m (2600ft) in length into a network of smaller irrigation channels. These circulated not just the rainwater but the vital minerals it carried, which were laid down in the fields as a nourishing deposit.

Mesa Verde also had rock springs, but these were high up in the steep sides of the canyons, some 270m (880ft) above the valley floor. Water was life, however, and so intrepid climbers set off daily, with clay jars strapped to their backs, to fetch water from these precious sources.

Geometric design
The Anasazi of Chaco Canyon made ceramics with their own distinctive decorative style. Patterns were passed from mother to daughter. Pots from Chaco Canyon are noticeably paler than pots found at Mesa Verde, which have a striking black-and-white colour scheme.

top of one another to form the core of the walls, then covered with an outer skin of dressed stones. The masonry is so well constructed, it did not require mortar, which would not stand the rigours of the climate for long. The buildings rose in storeys, each roofed with wooden beams and woven willow wattles sealed with clay. In its turn, each roof served as the floor of the next living unit above creating, in effect, an apartment block. The canyon's largest settlement, the Pueblo Bonito

('Pretty Village'), had approximately 800 rooms on five storeys and extended in a huge D-shape around a semi-circular open area. About 1000 people could have lived here, mainly on the upper floors – the lowest levels seem to have been used for storage. Beneath the central arena were the subterranean ceremonial rooms, the kivas – these retained the circular form of the old pit-dwellings.

Ceremonial centres

The construction of Pueblo Bonito alone represents an extraordinary achievement for a people with such scanty resources at their disposal. Still more astonishing is the fact that no less than 14 complexes of similar size were built in and around the Chaco Canyon, as well as a multitude of smaller villages and hamlets. To build all this, the Anasazi would have had to acquire and transport into their remote valley an estimated 200,000 tree trunks and more than 10 million sandstone blocks. They did this without draught animals, reliant only on manpower.

The 'Pueblo' label is probably fixed now, but modern researchers doubt whether these complexes were ever really villages as such. They suspect that no more than 5000 people ever lived permanently in the canyon as a whole. The large Pueblo Bonito, it is thought, would have had about 200 full-time residents. Of the 85 rooms of the Pueblo Alto, the 'High Village', probably only five were permanently occupied by people. The rest would apparently have served religious and economic purposes.

If this interpretation is correct, then Chaco Canyon was a spiritual centre, inhabited year-round by a small elite. At festival times, pilgrims would have flocked here in thousands from the surrounding communities, bringing tributes of produce and sacrificial gifts. Such gatherings would also have provided an opportunity for trading and social contacts, including making marriage alliances outside the immediate family group.

The turquoise lords

This theory would also account for the astonishing quantity of fine jewellery found here, especially work in turquoise, which had great significance among America's native peoples. At some point, the people of the pueblos had gained control over the important turquoise mines near Santa Fe, about 160km (100 miles) east of Chaco Canyon. Archaeologists have found more than 60,000 turquoise fragments and jewellery pieces in the canyon's settlements. Those of the highest quality were found in the larger pueblos.

Agriculture may have sustained the Chaco culture, but its affluence and power were founded on its trade in jewellery and ceremonial items. Just how wealthy the Anasazi were by this time is confirmed by the discovery in the pueblos of prestigious articles brought all the way from Mesoamerica.

Colourful parrot feathers, bones of tropical birds, bells of copper, and rare seashells must have come from the Pacific coast of Mexico.

The power of the turquoise lords extended far beyond the confines of Chaco Canyon. At least 70 separate communities, distributed over an area of almost 65,000km² (25,000sq miles), came under their rule. These villages were connected to the centre by a network of roads, most of which were arrow-straight and very wide – around 9m (30ft) wide, although some lesser roads were nearer 4m (13ft). The marked-out routes were cleared of bush and rubble and lined with low stones at intervals. The longest stretches of road were more than 80km (50 miles) long, and in some cases were surfaced with ceramic shards. Steps were

Pueblo Bonito
Pueblo Bonito looked something like an amphitheatre, as in this reconstruction. It was almost certainly built according to detailed astronomical calculations, and orientated so as to make the most of the Sun at every time of year.

Approximately 32 kivas, round subterranean chambers, were for religious ceremonies.

Apartment buildings were tiered, rather like theatre-seats, with five storeys at the back, reducing towards the front.

Access to apartments and kivas was via ladders through the roofs or walls.

cut to help wayfarers over the more rugged stretches of terrain and there were roadside shelters for those caught out at nightfall. Beside the roads were signal stations, which allowed the transmission of news – whether by beacon fires, smoke signals or light reflection.

United in religion

Just what sorts of travel took place along this network, and what kind of goods were transported along it, remains something of a puzzle to researchers. Some of the most carefully constructed roads appear to end abruptly in the middle of nowhere – perhaps they led to sacred sites. The Sun cult was the spiritual framework that bound the Pueblo peoples together. The passage of the Sun through the sky was observed with the utmost interest by the priests, who determined the times for sowing and harvesting.

Intriguing light was cast on this cult by the discovery, in 1977, of a spiral petroglyph (a rock drawing) on a mountain slope above the Chaco Canyon. At the time of the summer solstice, a narrow shaft of sunlight formed by a cleft in the top of an adjacent boulder shines down to bisect the spiral form exactly. Similar petroglyphs have since been discovered marking the spring and autumn equinoxes, but their significance is obscure. Prosperity for any agrarian people is precariously

Art for art's sake?
The Anasazi were skilled ceramic artists. Along with pots for everyday use, they created decorative sculptures like this human figure. Background: The Pueblo Bonito complex in Chaco Canyon, New Mexico.

poised: bad weather, crop disease or pests can destroy a harvest. Out here in the desert, for all their sophisticated irrigation systems and determined toil, the Anasazi were effectively pitting themselves against Nature, year after year. Their economic miracle could therefore have come crashing down at any moment – which may account for all their efforts, marked by a near-obsessive adherence, ritual routines to stay on the right side of the gods and of Nature.

The creation and the kiva

The Anasazi had a creation myth that told how, once upon a time, the Maize Mother had come out of a hole in the Earth to lead humanity to light and life. The soil was thus the source of life and growth, as well as the place of death and burial.

This is the sacred paradox summed up in the construction of the Pueblo's subterranean cult-rooms, the symbolic meeting-points between this world and the next. At the centre of each circular kiva was a hole called a *sipapu*: this represented the entry to the underworld. Beside this was a hearth with a ventilation shaft above. Around the walls was a bench, in front of which was a stone-lined depression – this may have had hides stretched across it to form a foot-drum. There were niches in the walls, perhaps to receive sacrificial offerings; the floors offered plenty of space for dancing.

Every clan had its own kiva, it seems – over 30 have been identified at Pueblo Bonito alone – but some were particularly large, up to 20m (65ft) in diameter, and it is assumed these were for use by the elders of the community as a whole. It seems likely that ritual dances would have been accompanied by rhythmic drumming, while priests made offerings of maize flour or other items. At the end of a ceremony, the participants would have climbed up ladders again, out into the blinding sunlight – just as the life-giving Maize Mother Goddess had first emerged out of the Earth.

The go-betweens

The Pueblo tended to appeal not directly to the gods themselves, but to Kachinas who mediated between this world and the next. The word kachina was ambiguous, reflecting an ambivalence inherent in Pueblo religion, being used both for an ancestral spirit and for the elder in the sacred dance. When he donned the kachina's mask, he assumed the spirit's identity and called down the deities' protection upon the clan.

Dances to appease the Earth took place under the cover of the kivas, but other rites were conducted in the open air. In long rows of 20 to 30, the kachina-priests would dance in the central arenas of their pueblos, pleading for rain and for the general well-being of the community. At the winter ceremonies there were also animal dances, with men masked to represent stags, wild sheep or pronghorn antelope; other routines re-enacted the creation myth and the cycle of life.

These dances, so important for community life, were organised by secret societies: every young man was inducted into one of these societies after appropriate initiation rites. Each dancer was elaborately attired, his skin brightly painted with pigments, his body adorned with silver and turquoise jewellery. A fox's tail hung down from every belt. A tortoise rattle was attached below each man's left knee so that every dancer added to the rhythmic sound as the chanting rose to its climactic cacophony.

Environmental catastrophe

The Anasazi of Chaco Canyon could not, in the end, secure their survival. Around 1130, a clear decline began. The reasons are not certain, but a 50-year drought that occurred about this time appears to have made what was always a challenging environment completely impossible. The cultivable areas contracted as streams and underground aquifers dried up, while the Anasazi themselves may unwittingly have contributed to their plight.

The canyon slopes had never been thickly timbered, but by cutting down what trees there were for the construction of their pueblos, they had exposed the delicate topsoils to erosion. With no grazing to keep it there, the game moved on; agricultural productivity plummeted, and with it the morale of the Anasazi. Desperation bred social conflict and, in time, the collapse of a discredited Sun-cult; the flow of pilgrims dried up and with it the trade in turquoise.

From around 1130, no more houses were built or renewed in Chaco Canyon. Once-flourishing sites were increasingly abandoned. More and more people were

Lizard dish
Ceramic dishes with images of animals were in daily use among the Anasazi and were also left as offerings with the dead.

leaving to settle in the valleys of the Rio Grande and Zuni River or on the uplands of the Colorado Plateau. This dispersal destroyed the cohesion of the Anasazi people, and the scattered groups diverged both culturally and linguistically.

In the north, the refugees made contact with Anasazi blood relatives, who had also settled in deep canyons and with whom they had long been in contact through trade. At Colorado's Mesa Verde, there were complexes very similar to those at Chaco Canyon. Mesa Verde is a huge plateau, which the indigenous farmers had managed to coax into productive life, hence the name given to it by the Spanish – *mesa verde* means, literally, 'green table'.

Though communities in the Mesa Verde started out living in pit-dwellings on the flat table-top itself, by the 9th century they were building pueblos in the surrounding canyons. The Mesa Verde societies reached their zenith some time towards the 12th century. As at Chaco Canyon, sophisticated irrigation technology ensured their harvests and raised standards of living, but culturally this community was distinct. Kivas here were not round but rectangular in plan, and the people of Mesa Verde also had their own striking black-and-white ceramic style.

Retreat to the hills

It remains unclear whether the Chaco Canyon people came to Mesa Verde as helpless refugees or as invaders looking for a fight. Either way, their plight appears to have had a dramatic impact on the lives of their new hosts. The Mesa Verde people started to abandon their unprotected

Patterned prey
The Anasazi were hunters as well as farmers, and meat made a welcome addition to their diet. This striking black-and-white ceramic represents an antelope, and is typical of the Mesa Verde style.

settlement centres and withdraw into sites in remote and inaccessible canyons. Here, they built multi-storey blocks of dwellings, closely packed onto narrow rocky ledges, perched above deep chasms and often shielded by overhangs, hence almost invisible from above. Only small communities could live in such units – some only accommodated a single extended family.

The people living in these communities would have had to perform great feats of daring just to go about their daily lives. Every basket of maize, every item of game, every piece of firewood had to be raised – or lowered – to the pueblo, which must have presented a serious logistical challenge. Old people were effectively pueblo-bound, while small children were at constant risk of falling: to accept such conditions, the people must have feared some even greater danger.

Conflict and cannibalism

While there is no archaeological evidence for warfare, grisly discoveries do support the theory that there were violent conflicts – and worse. In a valley west of Mesa Verde, archaeologists found the skeletal remains of three children, three men and one woman, all of whom had been killed, dismembered and then eaten by the aggressors. This was evident from the cuts the attackers had made on their victims' bones as they hacked the flesh away, as well as the lack of marrow in bones that had been broken open. This murder occurred around 1147, at just about the time when a great drought was driving people from their settlement sites. A further 38 cannibalistic finds support the theory that the fall of the Chaco Culture must have given rise to great political volatility and social turmoil.

The Anasazi Culture as a whole was not quite finished yet: in its rocky hideaways around the Mesa Verde, it would survive for another century and a half until here, too, it was overtaken by environmental catastrophe.

The Chimú of coastal Peru

In the shadow of the Andes, a people of kings and craftsmen created an impressive empire and culture. They left behind the ruins of fabulous cities and treasures of gold and jewels.

The Chimú people of coastal Peru seem to have been particularly fond of jewellery and beautiful objects. Towards the end of the First Millennium their craftsmen began creating, in enormous quantities, jewellery of quite astonishing quality using gold, silver, copper, bronze, spondylus shells, turquoise and emeralds, among other gems and semi-precious stones. Discoveries seem to indicate that much of this was for personal adornment and expressed individual tastes:

Decorated for death
The shape of the eyes and the conspicuous jewels in the nose and ears of this death mask are typical of those made by the Chimú.

there was more demand for necklaces, masks, pectoral ornaments and ear and nose-discs than for ritual objects such as knives, bowls and stone or ceramic figures.

Like other peoples of the Andean region, the Chimú wove glorious fabrics, including finely spun and colourfully dyed cotton for their clothing. Rugs and wall hangings were made from the wool of alpaca and vicuña, its wild relative. Many fabrics were embroidered with beads, shells, feathers or finely worked gold and silver appliqué. Chimú ceramics, though not as impressive as those of the earlier Moche, are still quite outstanding. And as well as being unusually creative in their crafts, the Chimu were intrepid architects and engineers.

The Chimú state had risen slowly over the course of six centuries. It started out as a little principality in the Moche Valley, about 500km (300 miles) north of modern Lima. By the 12th century, it was the dominant power of the region, and it would endure until it was swept away by the Incas in the mid-15th century. When the Incas conquered Chimú, they acquired a ready-made empire that extended for 1000km (600 miles) along the coast, from the Chancay Valley 50km (30 miles) north of Lima to the Valley of Piura, just south of the present-day border with Ecuador.

Fashion footwear
Chimú sandals have been found with geometric patterns stamped into the leather straps. Wealthy individuals had shoes decorated with gold and turquoise appliqué.

Legendary origins

Like the later Inca Empire, the Chimú incorporated many tribal groups and cultural differences, so there were many versions of their origin myths. These boil down to two main narratives, each of which helps to shed light on how the Chimú culture may have come about. One legend tells of a king called Naymlap who came from far out in the Pacific in a flotilla of reed rafts and landed on the northern coast of Peru in about the middle of the 9th century. He brought with him his wife, Ceterni, as well as a harem of subordinate wives, 40 attendants and a green stone idol, Yampallec, in his own likeness. Naymlap founded a place called Chot where he had a palace built. Today it is presumed that this refers to the ruins of Chotuna and Chornancap in the Lambayeque Valley, 150km (95 miles) north of the Moche Valley.

The kingdom prospered under Naymlap's legendary 12 successors until the last king, Fempellec, decided to move Yampallec, not realising that this risked the safety of his realm. A sorceress appeared before him; she was so beautiful he allowed her to seduce him. It began to pour with rain, and did not cease for 30 days. In a normally dry land, such a deluge was an unprecedented calamity. When a year's drought and famine followed, the people deposed Fempellec and threw him into the ocean. Such environmental disasters can now be explained by El Niño, but the Chimú had only mythological explanations for such cataclysms.

Taycanamu

The second legend has similarities with the first: it too involves a king, Taycanamu, arriving from the ocean. Making his home in the Moche Valley, he founded the city of Chan-Chan, and under his descendants, this became the capital of an empire. By the time of Taycanamu's grandson, it stretched from the Jequetepeque Valley in the north to the Santa Valley in the south.

Tradition has it that at the end of the 12th century, one of the Chimú rulers in the Jequetepeque Valley placed the newly founded administrative centre of Farfan under the control of a provincial governor called Pacatnamu. No further expansion took place under the following five or six rulers, called caciques, but the last king,

Minchancaman, conquered vast areas to the north and south. At this point, he was forced to capitulate to the Incas – a new and irresistible force in Andean geopolitics. Such legends no doubt contain an element of truth, although they were intended mainly to boost the image of the king and his ancestors in the eyes of his subjects.

Channels of prosperity

Coastal Peru is extremely arid: indeed, rainfall is almost non-existent. Some water was to be found in streams that ran down the mountainsides from the high Andes, but much of that evaporated long before it reached the sea. Capturing and managing this scarce resource was a challenge that the Chimú rose to with flying colours. Rulers made the constant extension and control of the irrigation network their number one priority, and in so doing they dramatically increased the

EVERYDAY LIFE

Road network

Infrastructure was extremely important to the Chimú rulers, and the road network came second in importance only to the irrigation system. The capital, Chan-Chan, was connected by well-maintained roads to provincial centres not only in the Moche Valley but right across the empire. Roads were wider and better constructed nearer the main towns and were typically edged with low walls; desert tracks were simply marked with posts.

land area available for agriculture. They linked the Moche Valley with the neighbouring Chicama Valley by means of a canal over 80km (50 miles) long, for example, and similar canal-connections were built between important valleys in the north. In all, some 20,000ha (50,000 acres) were under irrigation – a figure not matched by modern Peru until 1960. Water management was vital to the economy, so it was organised centrally, and the inhabitants of three towns in the upper Moche valley appear to have been engaged solely in the maintenance of the irrigation system.

City of specialisations

Chimú cities, among them the imperial capital, Chan-Chan, were also centrally organised. Chan-Chan stood beside the Pacific. From small beginnings in the late

Lost in sand
Half a millennium of high winds covered the larger part of the old Chimú capital with sand, but excavations are revealing Chan-Chan's streets and buildings.

9th century, it expanded inexorably until it eventually covered some 20km² (about 8sq miles), making it the largest city in pre-Columbian South America. More than 30,000 people lived here, in three separate areas, strictly regimented by state bureaucracy and divided along lines of economic function and social class.

Craftsmen lived in the city's western barrio, where thousands of reed huts on pebble foundations were crammed together in a network of narrow lanes, with just enough space for access to the houses and to the barrio's 125 wells. These were large, stone-built rectangular basins; the water level was regulated via the canal system in the valley. Many thousands of craftspeople lived here with their families,

The Lambayeque Valley had been famed for its arts and crafts, especially the work of its goldsmiths in the north. The craft-worker class was well-respected, a position reflected in the closeness of their barrio to the city centre, but also in the evidence of better living standards. Meat – from llamas or guinea pigs – featured far more in their diet than in that of the farming folk. They were even allowed to wear ear-pegs, but only ones made of wood.

Lower orders of workers lived farther from the centre, in outlying districts or in the Moche Valley. There was specialisation out here, too; one village to the west of Chan-Chan is known to have specialised exclusively in growing cotton. All round the city the farmers worked in fields, called *pukios*, in which the soil had been scraped away to allow the roots of the plants to reach low-lying groundwater. Fishermen also lived outside the city, beside the shore; their work carried no prestige, despite being invaluable.

Dress material
The Chimú were fond of patterned fabrics, like the fragment below, as well as jewellery (background). The women sewed loincloths and tunic-like shirts for their menfolk, while they themselves wore lengths of cloth wound around their bodies and secured them with pins.

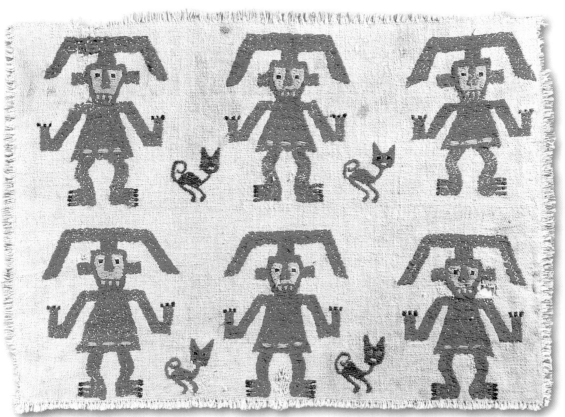

making sacrificial objects and luxuries out of wood, textiles, precious metals and ceramics. Different specialisations had separate sections of their own. After the conquest of the Lambayeque Valley, the population of craft barrio in the city suddenly grew.

Ruling classes

A second main district was set aside for the administrative class and for members of the lower nobility. Their dwellings were small palaces, scaled-down versions of the homes of the ruling caste. They were built of sun-dried adobe bricks, or from the larger tapial blocks which were made by packing earth, pebbles and chopped reeds into large wooden moulds and allowing them to set. Interior walls were rendered with finely washed clay to produce a smooth finish. Houses were roofed with woven mats stretched over wooden beams – if roofed at all. Rain was so scarce here that the need to keep dry did not figure in a builder's calculations.

The real palaces were to be found in the very centre of the cities – ten in all seem to have been built by successive rulers. Surrounded by walls up to 12m (40ft) high and 600m (2000ft) long, they are known by the Spanish name, *ciudadelas* ('citadels'), but they may not have been primarily defensive in function.

The palaces were rectangular in plan and subdivided into three – like the city itself. A single narrow entrance on the north side gave access to a labyrinth of corridors, living quarters, wells and countless storage rooms, interspersed with courtyards and larger open spaces. The corridors often seem to end in cul-de-sacs, and the routes to storage rooms led past unusual U-shaped chambers, the so-called *audiencias*. These were raised up on platforms and each of their three walls had two niches let into it – they may have been control-rooms for clerks checking stores and deliveries. The Chimú rulers received their tax in tribute, and saw their wealth as their god-given right. The punishment for stealing from them was death. The special significance of the *audiencias* is confirmed by evidence of ritual sacrifices of llamas and even humans, which seem to have taken place beneath some of these platforms.

The *ciudadelas* were decorated with clay reliefs that were cast in moulds then attached to the still-moist plaster of the walls. A rich artistic source, these reliefs show animals such as serpents, pumas, fish, squid, seals and pelicans. Some are straightforward portrayals and almost miraculously life-like. Others represent moments of dynamic action – seabirds plunging to catch fish, or fish surging forward in swimming shoals. There are also anthropomorphic beings, human forms and geometric patterns: the subject repertoire as a whole recalls that of Chimú's potters, goldsmiths and weavers.

The last structure to appear in any *ciudadela* was a burial mound, where the mummy of the ancestral ruler was placed in a T-shaped main chamber. Bodies mummify naturally in the aridity of Peruvian coastal plain, so the dead could be present at the shamanistic ceremonies of the living. Like other Andean cultures, the Chimú kept their dead ancestors in state, surrounded by rich treasures, and brought them outside to appear in person at important ceremonies. Smaller T-shaped chambers were the resting places of family members and descendants. In several cases, human sacrifices were offered and left with the family dead; in one tomb chamber alone, the remains of more than 90 young women were found.

A tale of two kings?

It was long assumed that each successive ruler mentioned by name in the Taycanamu legend had built one of the *ciudadelas*, to be first his palace and then later his mausoleum. More recently, however, it has been established that these complexes were built two at a time. This suggests that two kings may have reigned simultaneously – which would chime with Andean tradition. Sources from several cultures – including the Inca – suggest two kings reigned at once, their reigns apparently complementing one another in some mystic way. But as the Chimú left no written records, and their oral traditions were only recorded by the Spaniards a century after their Empire's end, there is no way of really knowing.

Ritual knife
The figure on this gold ceremonial tumi knife wears the pectoral decorations and large ear-ornaments of a Chimú dignitary. Three bunches of feathers adorn his headgear.

1 The peopling of   180
  Polynesia

2 The Maori – in search 184
  of new land

OCEANIA

The peopling of Polynesia

Over thousands of years, adventurous seafarers sailed from island to island across the Pacific until, from the 10th century onwards, they opened up Polynesia as habitable territory.

By the 10th century, when the last islands of the South Pacific had been colonised, the Polynesians had long forgotten their origins and early history. A vague mythological record had taken the place of any actual recollection: they traced their origins back to the legendary land of Hawai-ki, which means, roughly, 'the place from which our ancestors came'. This might have been somewhere on the Asiatic mainland or in Melanesia, but could have been as comparatively close at hand as the Marquesas.

Archaeological evidence suggests that the settlement of Polynesia started some 5000 years ago along the coasts and offshore islands of southeastern Asia. Entire family groups had set out in those days, loading their outrigger canoes not only with food and water, but also seeds and herbs to plant in their new homes. They took domestic animals, like pigs and chickens, to complement whatever natural foods they might encounter in the unknown lands in which they hoped to find a future. And they carried with them distinctive pottery – now known as 'Lapita' from the site in New Caledonia where investigators first discovered it – of a sort which would eventually be found across the whole of Polynesia.

Eastward adventure

As each island group was colonised and population pressures grew, exploratory forays were made, pushing farther and farther eastward. By about 1300 BC, Melanesia had already been settled, followed not long after by Fiji, Tonga and Samoa. Soon a scattered society extended right across the western Pacific region.

Towards 150 BC, settlers landed on the main islands of eastern Polynesia: Tahiti, the Society Islands, the Cook Islands and the Marquesas. From the last two, a succession of new voyages of discovery may have been made, with groups striking out in different directions through the following centuries. By about AD 500, colonists had probably reached Hawaii, as well as Easter Island in the eastern Pacific.

Despite the vast distances involved and the varying climatic conditions, the Polynesians evolved a surprisingly

Out of an egg
The Easter Islanders believed that they had hatched out of a bird's egg. The volcanic rock sculpture below appears to show a figure emerging from an egg. Each year, when the islanders held a competition to choose their leader, they gave the winner the title 'Bird Man', which he would hold for the next 12 months.

homogeneous culture across their whole range of settlement. Differences developed over time, but all showed clear kinship. As groups had dispersed to their new island homes, they took with them an established culture which encompassed not only traditional skills such as boat-building and navigation, but also language, mythology, art and a religion centred on tribal ancestors. Throughout the Pacific, this is reflected in the huge monuments they erected: temple complexes, burial mounds and awe-inspiring statues.

Nowhere is this extraordinary heritage more evident that on one of the remotest outposts of Polynesian culture – Easter Island. Starting a settlement on this small

volcanic island must have been incredibly difficult. The island, which the seafarers called Rapa Nui, or 'great paddle', was still covered with forest when they arrived. The newcomers must have taken several generations to adapt to a comparatively cooler climate. Simply establishing a reliable food supply would have posed significant problems. Though all the

Legacy in stone
Unique to Easter Island, these gigantic statues weigh up to 70 tonnes each. Erected between about AD 1000 and 1600, it is assumed that they represent powerful ancestors.

indications are that pigs were reared in the Marquesas, where we think the settlers came from, this extremely useful domestic animal appears to have been completely absent from Easter Island. Why that should be is not known; perhaps the first explorers took animals with them that did not survive the long and arduous ocean journey.

Whatever the reason, there was no pork on Easter Island, and according to legend, it became a haunting focus for nostalgia: the chieftain Hotu Matua was said to have yearned for the 'land of good food and greasy lips'. This became the name by which the Easter Islanders referred to the Marquesas, as they struggled to make do with poultry, or the meat of wild water rails and pigeons. Such was the islanders' hunger for meat that the numbers of these native species slumped dramatically as the human population rose.

Despite their complaints, the supply of food in general must have been adequate to fuel the population rise. By the 10th century, approximately 10,000 people lived on this small island, which was separated from its nearest neighbours by some 2400km (1500 miles) of open sea.

The people certainly had the energy to undertake some extraordinarily strenuous building activities.

In about AD 1000, the islanders began to build enormous stone temples, which played a part in their cult of ancestor-worship. The ghosts of the dead were regarded as a real presence in the ritual lives of the Easter Islanders, just as they were in other societies across Polynesia. Communities consisted of different family groups who derived their origins from a small number of shared ancestors whom the islanders all worshipped.

This is the background to the monumental stone figures, called *maoi*, unique to Easter Island. One theory is that these colossal statues may depict the ancestors and function as mediums, to whom the dead spirits could return after being invoked at religious ceremonies.

Competitive construction

Despite individual differences between the stone heads, the *maoi* possess some shared characteristics. They all consist exclusively of a head, an upper torso and long arms, and the slender fingers always end at the navel: the Polynesians firmly believed that knowledge bequeathed by their ancestors resided in the stomach.

Experts have wondered how a people apparently so technologically ill-equipped could succeed in creating, transporting and erecting such giant statues, each one of which weighs many tonnes. Easter Island was still densely wooded at the time, with huge stands of a particular species of giant palm. The trunk of this palm could have made rollers suitable for helping to transport a stone figure of just about any size. Once the islanders had chiselled a big enough stone block out of the volcanic rock – easy enough with stone hammers and wedges – they probably employed a system of ropes and rollers to move their colossal burden. Then, with the help of strategically placed ramps, wooden levers could be used to heave the boulder on to its waiting plinth.

Venice of the Pacific
Perhaps the most mysterious of the constructions in the Pacific is Nan Madol, once an important ceremonial centre, just off the island of Temwen in Micronesia. Set in a shallow lagoon and accessible only by boat, the complex is built on an artificial archipelago of 92 man-made islets. Shell necklaces and plant fibres (background) were among items used as currency in the South Seas.

VIEWPOINT

Polynesian roots – in Asia or America?

On April 28, 1947, Norwegian explorer Thor Heyerdahl set sail from the coast of Peru aboard the *Kon-Tiki*, a boat he had constructed himself from balsa wood and reeds. He was headed for the South Seas, his objective being to demonstrate that the wave of settlement which had populated Polynesia could have originated in South America just as easily as in Asia.

Heyerdahl's boat was modelled exactly on vessels known to have been used by the early Polynesian seafarers at the time of their voyages of exploration. Even so, his undertaking was dismissed as quixotic nonsense by the experts. Quite simply, nobody believed his flimsy-looking craft was capable of crossing of some 7000km (4500 miles) of open Pacific water. But, amazingly, he confounded his critics: after 101 days he made landfall in the Tuamoto archipelago east of Tahiti.

Proving that such a voyage could have been made, however, was not the same thing as proving that it had been. Soon archaeological evidence was piling up to support the Asian origin theory for the islanders. First, the 'Lapita' ceramic style so popular with the Polynesians was traced back to Indonesian roots. This was backed up by supporting linguistic evidence. Finally, the matter was clinched by irrefutable DNA tests.

Mystical figures
Small sculptures like these carved out of wood, stone or, as in this case, human bone, are thought to have represented divinities. They were often used to guard a clan's sacred sites.

Once the rock was in place, it was then carved into shape; facial features included eyes of white coral and dark stone pupils. In time, a competition arose between the island's different clans, as to who could erect the largest *maoi* figure – the winner measured an astonishing 10m (30ft).

This contest went on until the island was stripped bare of trees and ecological catastrophe ensued. Soil was eroded, birds stayed away and all the most important sources of food dried up. What had hitherto been peaceful competition between the island's clans became a desperate struggle for survival.

Hawaiian paradise

Their kinsfolk on other islands were a great deal more fortunate. As experienced navigators and fishermen, the Polynesians everywhere were able to supplement their diet with a varied supply of fish and other seafood. But a good balance of livestock and varied agriculture certainly helped an island community to thrive. The plants they took with them on their journeys, including yam and taro tubers, were cultivated wherever they went, but it appears that some of the most successful farmers in the whole of Polynesia were those who established themselves in the Hawaiian island group.

Using the simplest tools, the Hawaiians created an extensive system of terraces in order to make the island's steep volcanic hillsides cultivable, and they irrigated their terraced fields with a clever system of canals. This enterprise was richly rewarded with a bountiful harvest of root vegetables and tubers. Yams, sugar cane, bananas and coconut palms also flourished in the tropical climate. In such paradisiacal conditions, a contented people thrived, their numbers – and affluence – mounting steadily. By the year 1200, Hawaii alone had a population of more than 20,000 people – arguably the luckiest on Earth.

The Maori – in search of new land

The colonisation of New Zealand, the last large land area on Earth to be settled, brought to an end the Polynesian expansion in the Pacific. The date of their arrival is uncertain, but was probably early in the Second Millennium.

Fearsome impressions
The Maori decorated the prows of their boats with artistic carvings. These represented the spirits of their ancestors and were intended to strike fear into any opponents they encountered.

Maori legend has it that Kupe, the chief of Hawai-ki, once had a dream in which he was told to sail southwest until he reached a large island. So he put to sea with his friend Ngahue, his wife and others in two *waka* (sea-going canoes) and they sailed for weeks across the empty ocean. At last, on the horizon, they saw a huge cloud – a sure sign of land – and Kupe's wife called out 'He ao' ('a cloud'). In time, this became Aotearoa, 'Land of the Long White Cloud'. The legend surely contains elements of truth. Hawai-ki, the half-mythical homeland, may represent the Marquesas, thought to be the departure-point for the last Polynesian voyages of exploration.

Led by the birds and stars

Every year, at the beginning of summer, great flocks of birds set out from the northern Pacific. Flying southwestward, they disappear over the horizon, and the significance of their flight was not lost on the Polynesians of a thousand years ago – birds in such numbers had to be heading somewhere. Out beyond the horizon, there had to be a large expanse of land, towards which all these birds were flying instinctively.

The Polynesians' instincts involved a restless desire to set out into the unknown, to cross unfamiliar waters and to colonise new lands. Perhaps the discoverers of New Zealand set sail at the same time as the migrating birds took flight. The months of October and November were always considered the ideal time for voyaging, as there tended to be fewer severe storms at that season.

As so often before, the brightly shining constellation of the Southern Cross showed the way to explorers leaving behind the limits of their known world: Polynesians had been successfully navigating by the stars for thousands of years. This time, however, it was to bring them to much the largest landmass they had ever settled. North to south of New Zealand's two islands measured 1600km (1000 miles). In addition, the new land presented the Polynesians with a completely new environment, very different from the far-flung coral islands on which their societies had evolved. Aotearoa was almost completely forested, and though the far north was warm, the climate overall was much cooler than they were used to. Undaunted, the newcomers – around 100 people, researchers estimate – set out to survey their new home. They travelled all round the coasts in their canoes, founding villages near the sea, usually in the sheltered, warmer areas on the east side of both islands. They built rectangular gabled huts, grouped around a village square. Within 200 years, the Polynesian discoverers and their descendants had completely opened up New Zealand's two islands.

Aotearoa's lower temperatures and changing seasons were totally unsuitable for many of the plants the Polynesians had brought with them. Coconut palms, breadfruit trees, banana plants and sugar cane needed tropical conditions, and all fared badly in the southern winter. Yams and taro tubers also struggled, growing to much smaller size than they would have in the tropics. Only the sweet potato really thrived. This plant originated in the Andes and had reached eastern Polynesia by an unknown route. It did well in these cooler temperatures, but even so it had to be protected from

Handy talisman
Tiki, the first human, carved from whalebone. Such carvings were passed down from generation to generation as good luck charms. It was said that Tiki fashioned a wife for himself out of wet clay.

The big moa hunt

For centuries, the Maori's main source of food seems to have been the moa, a large flightless bird which inhabited New Zealand's forests. Several dozen different species existed, from smaller types, not much bigger than turkeys, to great giants standing 2.5m (over 8ft) tall. These huge birds would have weighed in at an astonishing 200kg (440lb) – perhaps more.

Large flightless birds developed on New Zealand because of the lack of large predators, and the moa were bound to be vulnerable if one ever found a way to the islands. Once the Maori had arrived they were doomed. By around 1500 the moa was extinct,

and the Maori were left looking for another food supply. However, the downward spiral of the moa had actually begun long before the coming of the Maori. Originally, the islands appear to have supported a population of several million birds, but by the time the Polynesians arrived there were only an estimated 160,000.

Quite how a moa was caught has never been explained in detail. The Maori may have used dogs and spears, but traps were also effective. Moa bones made good spear points, fishing hooks, awls, needles and more. The thick shells of their eggs served as durable water containers.

winter frosts. The Maori soon learned to make roofed storage pits so that they could store their seasonal harvest safely in the ground.

A monster chicken

The traditional domestic animals of the Polynesians do not seem to have settled in easily either. Neither pigs nor chickens appear to have been a feature in New Zealand. Perhaps the domestic animals did not make it through the long voyage, or perhaps the new settlers felt they were unnecessary – the islands were home to several species of flightless birds that provided dinner without too much trouble. These were the moa, which means 'chicken' in Polynesia, and just one of the larger birds would feed a family for many days.

Moas lived in the temperate forests of the southern part of North Island and on the eastern side of South Island. In addition, there was the smaller kiwi – another flightless, though unrelated

Lethal weapon
Along with the spear, the club was the most important weapon of the Maori warrior. In peacetime it was carried as a symbol of rank.

bird – as well as a variety of birds such as parrots, water rails and pigeons which could be easily caught.

A lifestyle change

The difficulties of farming and keeping livestock – and the easy availability of wild game – prompted a radical change in the Maori lifestyle. Like all Polynesians, they were good fishermen and farmers, but they stopped farming here at an early stage. More and more, they became hunter-gatherers, living on what the land (and surrounding seas) provided naturally.

As time went by, the techniques of agriculture and animal husbandry were forgotten. In the far north of the northern island, where flightless birds no longer lived, the newcomers hunted seals, dolphins and sea birds instead. Rats were considered a special delicacy among the Maori; they could be roasted or preserved in their own fat in gourd halves. Gourds were grown less for food than for their tough shells, which made excellent containers of all kinds. The art of making ceramics was not developed here, even though New Zealand was well endowed with a range of suitable clays. Given the strength of the Polynesian pottery tradition, this is surprising: perhaps the first incomers originated from islands in which the secrets of Lapita ceramics had been forgotten. Or perhaps they were content with their serviceable gourd containers.

Hard times

The Maori supplemented their diet of mainly meat and fish with fruit and a variety of roots, notably those of the bracken-fern, which could grow up to 60cm (2ft) tall. Known as aruhe, this was soaked in water before being roasted in hot ashes: though less nutritious than the traditional types of vegetables, it was a filling substitute.

As long as there was enough food for everyone, the Maori tribes lived peacefully enough. But life became more difficult as time went on. The moa population simply could not survive the relentless assault it was sustaining. Numbers fell until there were no birds left. Without them, the existence of the Maori themselves was suddenly threatened: the battle for survival had become very hard indeed. There is evidence that very few Maoris lived beyond their 40th year and many died a great deal earlier (although one theory puts some of the blame for this on eating bracken-fern, which was poisonous).

Underworld art

There were many kinship connections between New Zealand's first communities, and over time, a network of trading links developed. Raw materials were unevenly distributed: the highly prized green stone called nephrite, for example, was only found on South Island. The Maori there mined the rich deposits systematically and shipped them by canoe to the coastal villages of North Island. A type of jade, nephrite was known to the Maori craftsmen as *pounamu*, and much sought after for making their austerely beautiful pendants and other jewellery, as well as precious axeheads for use in religious ceremonies. This mineral was so important to the Maori they named the entire South Island after it, calling it Te Wai Pounamu, or 'Place of the green stone'.

Wood was plentiful and craftsmen fashioned it into works of rare quality. The skill of woodcarving was greatly revered by the Maori. Their mythology makes it clear that the craftsman's inspiration is divine: the story goes that the secret of woodworking was stolen from the gods by a man named Rua. The sea god had

Fish amulet
The Maori had come from the ocean, and this fact was central to most of their myths. Fish motifs occur again and again in their jewellery, as in this stone pendant worn as a pectoral ornament.

snatched Rua's son and taken him down into his kingdom, so the desperate father dived into the deep to try to get him back. He found the boy a prisoner in a house that was adorned from roof-ridge to foundation with amazing carvings: no human being had ever seen the like. Rua rescued his son – but he also took some carvings with him, and ever since the Maori have crafted similar decorations for their homes and the prows of their canoes. As in Polynesian art, Maori carvings appear to symbolise the spirits of the ancestors, from whom the community hoped to have protection and assistance.

Those ancestors were assumed to be omnipresent and their spiritual power could be felt everywhere. Countless myths associated with them were transmitted orally from one generation to the next: the Maori never developed a written script, but their stories were not forgotten.

Page numbers in *italic* refer to the illustrations and captions.

A

Aachen 8, 109
Abbasid caliphate 72, 128
Abd Ar Rahman I 20, 21
Abd Ar Rahman II 20
Abd Ar Rahman III 20, 22–3
Abdallah-al-Mahdi 132
Abu Said *98*
Adelheid of Burgundy 9, 10
Adud ud-Daula 73, 74, 75
Aethelred II, king of England 31
Aggersborg 30
agriculture
    Anasazi 166
    Burma 100
    Chimú 176
    Chinese 83, 85
    European 11, 22
    Islamic Spain 22
    Mississippian 162
    Polynesian 183, 185–6
    Toltec 155
    Yoruba 127
Ala ad-Din Muhammad 99
Alamut *96*, 97
Alaungsithu, king of Burma 104, 105
Albertus Magnus 49
Aleppo 36, *95*, 97, 99
Alexius I, Emperor of Byzantium
    108, 109, 110, 112
Alfonso I, king of Aragon and
    Navarra 26–7
Alfonso I, king of Portugal 27, *27*
Alfonso VI, king of Castile 24, 25, 26,
    143
Algeria 128
Almohads 146-7
Almoravids 26, 27, 142, 143-4, 145,
    146, 147
Alp Arslan 41, 97, 98
Ananda Temple 104, *104*
Anasazi people 166-72, *166*
Anawratha, king of Burma 100-3, 104
ancestor worship 126, 177, 182, 187
al-Andalus 20-7, 143-4, 147
Angkor 100
Anglo-Saxons 32, 56, 57, 58
Anno, Archbishop of Cologne 12
Antioch 111, 112
Aquinas, Thomas 49
Arabs *see* Islam and Muslims
Aristotle *73*
armies
    Byzantine 38
    Chinese 77-8, 83-4
    Islamic 24
    Seljuk 96
    see also warfare
armour 114, 115, 116, *119*
Arpad 33

art and crafts
    Anasazi *166, 168,* 169, *170, 171,*
      172, *172*
    Berber *143, 144*
    Burmese *101, 104, 105*
    Buwayhid *75*
    Byzantine *34*
    Chimú 173-4, *173, 174,* 176, *176,*
      177, *177*
    Chinese 76-7, 79, 80, *80,* 81, *81,* 82
    Fatimid *128, 130, 132, 133,* 134-5,
      135
    Hausa *136,* 138
    Islamic *22*
    Japanese *88,* 90, *92*
    Korean *66-7, 68-9*
    Mississippian *163, 164, 165*
    monastic *47*
    Moorish Spain *22*
    Polynesian *180, 180, 181,* 182-3,
      183, 184, 185, 187, *187*
    Toltec *150, 151, 154,* 155-6, *156*
    Yoruba *124,* 125, *125,* 126-7, *126*
asceticism 48, 141
Assassins *96,* 97, 98
astronomical clock *79*
astronomy *71,* 75, 98, 152, 165
Avicenna (Ibn Sina) *74,* 75
Ayyubid dynasty 99
al-Aziz, Caliph 131-2
Aztecs 150, 151, 152, 154, 156

B

Badajoz, Battle of 143
Baffin Island 160
Bagan 100-5
Baghdad 71-5, 94, 96, 98, 99, 146
Baldwin of Boulogne 110, 111, 112
Bamberg 11
banknotes 82
baptism 16, *29,* 34, *43*
Bari 52
Basil II, Emperor of Byzantium 37,
    38, *38,* 40, *43,* 44
Bavarians 6, 33
Bayajidda, Prince of Baghdad 136,
    139
Bayeux tapestry *54-5,* 57, *57*
Benedict of Nursia, St 46, *46*
Benedict IX, Pope 12
Benedictine order 46-9
Benin 124
Berbers 26, 140-7
Bernard of Clairvaux, St 14, 15, 49,
    113
bills of exchange 82
bishops 60, *60,* 63, *63*
Bjarni Herjolfsson 160
bodhisattvas *68, 83, 101*
Bohemians 33
Bohemund of Tarent 110, 111, 112
bows and crossbows 118
Brandenburg 10

Brattahlid 159, *159*
bread stamps 27
Britain
    Anglo-Saxons 32, 56, 57, 58
    English language 58
    Normans 54-9
    Vikings 31, 32
bronze *24,* 30, *30, 124,* 125, *125,* 127,
    135
Brun, Prince of Lorraine 8
Budapest 35
Buddhism
    Burma 100, *100,* 101-3, *101, 104,*
      105
    Japan *91,* 92
    Korea 68, 69, 70
    Mahayana Buddhism 101
    Theravada Buddhism 101
Bulgaria 36, 37, 38
Burgundy 9, 12, 15
burials
    Chimú 177
    grave goods *124, 156,* 164-5
    Mississippian 164-5
Burma 100-5
Buwayhids 71-5, 94, 96
Buyeh (Buwayh) 72
Byodoin Temple *90-1*
Byzantine Empire 9, 36-41, 44, *114,*
    121
    and the Crusades 108, 109, 110,
      112
    wars with Seljuks 41, 97-8, 108

C

Caesarea Cappadocia 41
Cahokia 162-5
Cairo 129-31, 146
calendars
    Aztec 154
    Mississippian 165
    Toltec 151, 152, *152*
caliphates 73
    see also individual caliphs
calligraphy *85*
canals 79-80, *175*
cannibalism 172
Canossa 62, *63*
Capet, Hugo 13, 14, *14,* 16, 19
Capetians 13-19
Carolingian Empire 6, 13, 46
castles and fortresses *120-1,* 121
    Crusader castles *110-11,* 121
    Norman *120*
    ribats 141
    Seljuk *95*
    Viking 30, 31, *31*
cathedral schools 16
Catholic Church *see* Church
cavalry *114,* 114, 116
Cefalú cathedral *50-1*
celadon *66, 67, 68, 69, 80*
cemetery, Fatimid *130*

ceramics
    Anasazi *168, 170, 171, 172, 172*
    Buwayhid 75
    Chimú 174
    Chinese 80, *80*
    Korean *66-7, 68-9*
    Mississippian *165*
    Polynesian 180, 186
    Toltec *156*
    Yoruba 125, 127
Chaco Canyon 166, 168, *168,* 170
Chagri 94
Chai Rong, Emperor of China 76
chainmail 57, *96, 115,* 116
chalice *36*
Chan-Chan 175-6, *175*
Charlemagne 6, 8, 9, 13
Charles III, king of France 6, 13, 14,
    54
Chartres 14, 16
chess *16,* 18, 26, *26,* 133
Chichén Itzá 154
Chichimeca 156
Chimú 173-7
China 69, 100
    Song dynasty 76-85
chivalry 17
Chornancap 174
Chotuna 174
Christianity
    Copts 133, 134
    Denmark 28, *28*
    Holy Roman Empire 6, 8, 9, 10-11
    Hungary 34-5
    medieval spirituality 15-16
    Orthodox Christianity *43,* 44
    pilgrimage 24, *113, 144*
    Vikings 159
    see also Church
Church 8, 10-11, 12, 18
    bishops 60, *60,* 63, *63*
    Church-state relations 8, 9, 10, 11,
      14, 15, 50-3, 60
    Investiture Contest 60-3
    papacy 8, 9, 10-11, 12, 60
    Western Schism 40-1, 108
    see also Crusades
Cistercian order 15, 49
citizenship 18
civil service
    Burmese 105
    Chinese 78, 82, 85
    German 12
    Iranian 96
    Islamic 74, 75
    Korean 69, 70
Clairvaux 49
Clement II, Pope 12
Clement III, Pope 62, 63
Cluny 46-9, *48-9*
Cnut, king of England, Denmark and
    Norway 32, 56
coinage
    Byzantine *39*

Chinese 82
Korean 69
Seljuk *98*
Sicilian *51*
Cologne 109
Confucianism 78
Conrad I, king of Germany 6
Conrad II, Holy Roman Emperor 11, 12
Conrad III, king of Germany 113
Constantine VII Porphyrogenetus, Emperor of Byzantium 39, *39*, 41
Constantine IX Monomachos, Emperor of Byzantium *37*, 41
Constantinople 9, 38-40, *41*, 44, 108
convents 19, *19*
copper 79, 127
Córdoba 21, 24, 25
Cortés, Hernán 154
courtly love 17
creation myths 124-5, 170
Croatia 35
crown regalia *8*, *33*, *34*, *76*
Crusader castles *110-11*, 121
Crusades 17, 27, 97, 99, 106-13, *129*
First Crusade 106-12
People's Crusade 109
Second Crusade 15, 49, 113
Cyprus 36
Cyrillic script 44, *45*

D,E

Dalmatia 35
Damascus 99, 113, *113*, 146
Danegeld 31
Denmark 28-32
Desiderius, Peter 112
divination 126
Domesday Book 57-8
Dominican order 49
Druse 133, 134
Dublin 32
Easter Island 180, *180*, 181-3, *181*
Edessa 111, 112, 113
Editha of Wessex 7, 9
Edmund II, 'Ironside', king of England 32, 56
education 16, 98
Edward the Confessor, king of England 32, *32*, 55, 57
Egypt 97, 99, 128-35
Eirik the Red 158-9, *158*
El Cid *21*, 25, 26, 27
El Niño 174
Eleanor of Aquitaine 113
Eugene III, Pope 113

F,G

famines 11, 109
farming *see* agriculture
Fatima (daughter of Muhammad) 128, 129

Fatimids 97, 111, 128-35
featherwork 116, 156
fertility cult 165
feudalism 18, 58
feuding 18
Fez 146
Finns 43
Forchheim 6
France, Franks 6, 13, 14, 23, 33, 109, 113
Capetian dynasty 13-19
see also Normans
Franciscan order 49
Fujiwara dynasty 86-93
Fulcher of Chartres 106, 108
furnishings *19*
Fyrkat 30
gaming 18
Geoffrey of Anjou 59
Germany 6-12, 14, 60
Geza, Archduke 34
Glaber, Raoul 11
Gnesen 11
Gnezdovo, treasure of *42*
Go-Ichijo, Emperor of Japan 90
Gobir 139
Godfrey of Bouillon 110, 112
Godthabsfjord 159
Godwin, Earl of Essex 32, 56
gold *47*, 104, *136*, 139, 156, *177*
Golden Gospel *10*
Gorm the Elder, king of Denmark 28, *28*
grave goods *124*, *156*, 164-5
Great Silla Kingdom 67, 68, 80
Greek fire 118
Greenland 159-60, 161
Gregory V, Pope 11
Gregory VI, Pope 12
Gregory VII, Pope 48, 60, 62, *63*
Guido of Arezzo 17
guilds 79, 81, 85
Guiscard, Robert 52, 63
Gunnbjörn 158

H

Hagia Sophia, Constantinople *37*, 39, 40, *41*
Haithabu 30-1, *30*
al-Hakam II, Caliph 23
al-Hakim, Caliph 131, 132, 133, 134
Hamburg 10
Hamdanids 75
Harald Bluetooth, king of Denmark 28, *28*
Harald Hardrada, king of Norway 55, 56
Harald Harefoot, king of England 32
Harald II, king of Denmark 32
Harold II, king of England 32, 55-7, *120*
Harthacanute, king of Denmark 32
Hasan as-Sabbah 97

hashish 97
Hastings, Battle of 32, *54-5*, 56-7
Hausa 136-9
Havelberg 10
Hawai-ki 180, 184
Hawaii 180, 183
Heaven and Hell, beliefs in *14*, 16
Helgaud *14*, *15*
Henry I, king of England 59
Henry I, king of France 55
Henry I, king of Germany 6, 8, *35*
Henry II, Holy Roman Emperor 11
Henry II, king of England 59
Henry II, king of Germany 34
Henry III, Holy Roman Emperor *10*, 12, 47, 60
Henry IV, Holy Roman Emperor 12, *12*, 60, *60*, 62-3, 110
Henry V, Holy Roman Emperor 12, 59, 63
Heyerdahl, Thor 183
Hisham II, Caliph *23*, 24
Hohenstaufen dynasty 53
Holy Lance 9, 34
Holy Roman Empire 6, 8, 9, 10-11
see also individual emperors
Hopewell culture 162, 165
horses 121, 136
houses
Chimú 176-7
Hausa *137*
Korean 68
Mississippian 163
pueblos *121*, 166-8, *167*, *169*, 172
Russian 45
Viking 30, *120*, *157*
Huemac, King 156
Hugo of Franconia 9
Huizong, Emperor of China 85
human sacrifice *119*, *151*, 153, 156, 165, 177
Hungary 11, 33-5
Huns 33, 94
Hyunjung, king of Korea 70

I

Ibn Al Athir 26-7
Ibn Tashufin, Yusuf 142, 143, 144, 145
Ibn Tumert 145-6
Ibn Yasin, Abdallah 140-1, 142, 146
Ibn Yusuf, Ali 145, 146
Iceland 157-8
Ichijo, Emperor of Japan 89
al-Idrisi 53, *134*, 139
Ife 124, 125
Imad ad-Din Zengi 99, 113
Imad ud-Daula 73
Incas 174, 175
incense *69*
indigo 127, 139
Inuit 161
Investiture Contest 60-3

Iran 72, 73, 96, 99
iron 79, 139, *160*
Iron Pagoda 78
irrigation 75, 100, 168, 172, 175, 183
Isfahan 72, 73, 94, 98
Isidor of Seville 17
Islam and Muslims
Berbers 140-7
Buwayhids 71-5, 94, 96
and the Crusades 106-13
Fatimids 97, 111, 128-35
Hausa 136, 139, *139*
Seljuks 41, 75, 94-9, 108, 109, 110, 111, 113, 114
Shi'ite Islam 72, 73, 94, 97, 98, 128, 129, 133, 134, 145
in Sicily 51-2
in Spain 20-7, 143-4, 147
Sufism 98
Sunni Islam 94, 98, 128, 133, 145
Ismailites 97, 98
Italy 9, 10, 12
Norman Italy 50-3
ivory *16*, *34*, *52*, *132*

J,K

Japan 69, 114
Fujiwara dynasty 86-93
literature 90-1
Jaroslav the Wise, Grand Duke 45
Jawhar as-Siqilli 128, 130
Jelling 28
Jerusalem 97, 108-9, *109*, 111-12, 113
jewellery
Anasazi 169
Berber *143*, *144*
Chimú 173-4, *173*
crown regalia *8*, *33*, *34*, *76*
Fatimid *128*
Maori 187, *187*
Russian *42*
Jews 18, 21, 52, 109, 133, 134
jihad 111, 141
John I Tzimiskes, Emperor of Byzantium 36-7
John XII, Pope 9
junks 80
Jurchen 70
kachinas 171
Kaesong 67, 68, 70
Kaifeng 76, 77, 81, 85
Kano *136*, 138, 139
Kerman 73
Kerullarios, Patriarch 40
Kherson 44
Khitan Tartars 70, 84
Khuzistan 73
Khwarezmia 99
Kiev 42-5, *44*
kivas 170, 172
knights *16*, 17, 18, *107*, 109, 114, 118
military orders *107*, *110*
weapons and armour *115*, *116*

Koguryo 67
Korea 66-70
Kubyaukgi Temple 103
Kyanzittha, king of Burma 104
Kyongju 67
Kyoto 90

L

Labrador 160
lacquerware 69
Ladislav I, king of Hungary 35
Ladoga 43
Lambayeque Valley 176
Landnámabók (Book of Settlements)
    158
L'Anse aux Meadows *120, 157, 160,*
    161
Last Judgment 16, 58, 108
Laughing Buddha *84*
laws
    France 17, 18, *18*
    Russian 44
Lechfeld, Battle of *6,* 9, 33-4
Lehel 34, *34*
Leif Eiriksson 159, 160, 161
León 24
Liao 84, 85
libraries
    Baghdad 75
    Cairo 134
    Córdoba 25
    Kiev 45
Lisbon 27
literacy 16
literature 17, 90-1
Lombardy, Lombards 9, 23
longships 30, 158
Lothar II, king of Italy 9
Louis 'the Child', king of France 6, 13
Louis I, 'the Pious', Emperor 46
Louis IV, king of France 9
Louis VI, 'the Fat', king of France 15,
    17, 18
Louis VII, king of France 113

M

madrassahs 98
Magdeburg 7, 9-10
magic and charms 144-5
Magnus the Noble, king of Norway
    32
Magyars 6, *6,* 9, 33-5
Mahabodi Temple 104
Mahdi (Messiah) 132
main de Justice 14, 18
maize 151, 162, 165
Malik Shah *94,* 98
Maniakis, George 52
al-Mansur 24
Manuha, king of Thaton 102
manuscripts *11, 17, 43, 49, 56, 58,*
    62, 71, 73, 94, 107, 109, 110

Manzikert, Battle of 41, 97
Maori 184-7
map of the known world
    11th century *15*
    12th century *134*
Marrakesh 142, 1*42,* 147
masks
    Anasazi 171
    Chimú *173*
    Korean *70*
    Yoruba 126
Mathilda, Empress *58,* 59
Maya 154-5
Mecca 97
medicine *74, 75*
Medina 97
Medinat al Zahra 22-3, 24
Memleben 6
mercenaries 37-8, 43, 44
Mesa Verde 168, *168,* 172
Mesopotamia 96, 111
metalwork
    Chinese 79
    Moorish 22, *23,* 24
    Toltec 156
    Yoruba 127
    see also bronze; gold; iron; silver
Mexico 150, 152-3, 155, 156, 165
Michinaga 86, 89-90
Minamoto clan 88, 93, *93*
minstrels 17
Mississippians 162-5
Mixcoatl 150
Mixtecs 155
moa 186, 187
Moche Valley 174, 175, 176
Molesme 49
Mon 100, 104
Mongols 99, 105, *115*
monks and monasteries 15, 16-17
    Buddhist 70
    Cluny 46-9, *48-9*
    Mont St Michel 13
    Saint-Denis 16-17
    Viking raids 30, 31
monopolies 82, 85
Mont St Michel *13*
Monte Cassino 46
Montezuma II 154
Montoku, Emperor of Japan 86, 88
Morocco 144, 146, 147
mosaics *36-7, 154*
mosques 131
    al-Aqsa mosque, Jerusalem 112
    al-Azhar Mosque, Cairo 129, *131*
    Great Mosque, Cordóba *2-3, 20-1,*
        21, 25
    Great Mosque, Isfahan 98, *99*
    Koutoubia Mosque, Marrakesh
        142, 147, *147*
    Tinmal Mosque *146*
mottes 121
mound builders 162-3, *162,* 165
Mozarabs 21, 26

Muhammad 94, 112, 128, 132, *141, 147*
al-Muizz, Caliph 128, 130, 131
Mu'izz ud-Daula 73, 74
al-Mumin, Abd 146-7
Mumnu 67, 69
Murasaki Shikibu 87, 88, 91
music
    Islamic 25
    Japanese 91
    musical notation 17
    Viking 31
al-Mustakfi, Caliph 73
al-Mustansir, Caliph 135

N,O

Nan Madol *182*
Natchez 165
Native Americans 161, 162-72
navigation 80, 158
nephrite 187
New Zealand 184-7
Nicholas II, Pope 52
Nigeria 124, 127, 138
Nikephoros II, Emperor of
    Byzantium 36
Nizam al-Mulk 98
nomadic peoples 33, 41, 70, 76, 94,
    121, *121,* 138
Nonnebakken 30
Normandy 31, 54-5, 59
Normans 6, 46
    castles *120*
    in England 54-9, *120*
    in Italy 50-3
Norway 28, 31, 32
Novgorod 43
Nur ad-Din 99, 111
Nuttall Codex 155, *166*
obsidian 155
Odo, Bishop of Bayeux 57
Oghuz Federation 94
Olaf Tryggvasson, king of Norway 31
Oleg, Prince of Kiev 43
Olga, Duchess 44
Omar Khayyám 98
Orthodox Christianity *43,* 44
Otto I, 'the Great', Holy Roman
    Emperor 6, *6,* 7, 8-10, 23, 33, 34,
    36
Otto II, Holy Roman Emperor 10
Otto III, Holy Roman Emperor
    10-11, 34, 35
Ottonian dynasty 6-11, 14
Ourique 27
Oyo 124

P,Q

Paekche 67
palaces
    Baghdad 74
    Cairo 130-1
    Chimú 177

Kaesong 68
Palermo 51, 53
Palestine 37, 111, 112, 113
    see also Jerusalem
papacy 8, 9, 10-11, 12, 60
Paris 14, 16, 17, 19
Parthians 94
Paschal II, Pope 63
patrician class 19
peasants
    Chinese 82-3, *82*
    European 11
Peru 173-7
Petchenegs 41, 43
Peter the Hermit 109
petroglyphs *166,* 170
philosophy 73, 78
pictorial stones *159*
pilgrimage 24, *113, 144*
Plantagenets 59
Poland 11
Polo, Marco 103
polygamy 127
Polynesia 180-7
Portugal 27
printing technology 78-9, *85*
Pueblo Bonita 168, *169,* 170
Pueblo Indians *121,* 166-72
pyramids 152, *153,* 164
Pyu 100
al-Qahir, Caliph 72
al-Quaim, Caliph 96
quetzal bird 156
Quetzalcoatl *150,* 151, 154, *154*

R

Rabat 147
Radziwill Chronicle 43
Raimund of Toulouse 110, 112, 113
Reconquista 25-7, 143
Reichskirchensystem (State-Church
    system) 8, 9, 10, 11, 60
Reims 16
relics *40*
religion
    Anasazi 168, 170-1
    Hausa 139
    Mississippian 162-3, 164, 165
    Polynesian 182, 187
    Toltec 151, 153-4
    Viking *161*
    Yoruba 125-6
    see also Buddhism; Christianity
Rheims 14
ribats 141, 142
rice cultivation 83, 100
road systems
    Anasazi 169-70
    Chimú 175
Robert I, king of France 14
Robert II, 'the Pious', king of France
    14-15
Robert, Abbot 49

rock crystal *130*, 135
rock drawings *166*, 170
Roger I, king of Sicily *51*, 52
Roger II, king of Sicily *50*, 52-3
Rollo, Duke 54
Romanos II, Emperor of Byzantium 36
Romanos IV, Emperor of Byzantium 41, 97
Rome 9
Rudolf of Rheinfelden 62
Rukn ud-Daula 73
Rum-Seljuks 98, 99
rune stones 28, *28*
Rurik, Prince 43
Rus 43, 44
Russia 42-5

S

Saint-Denis, monastery of 16-17
Saladin 99, 111
Salerno 50
Salian dynasty *9*, 11-12, 14
Samanids 72, *72*
Samsam ud-Daula 75
Samuil, Tsar 38
Samurai *93*, 114, *115*, *116*, 118, *119*
Sancho II, king of Castile 25
sandals, Chimú *174*
Sanhadja 142, 146
Santiago de Compostela 24
Saracens 6, 10, 46
Saw-lu, king of Burma 104
Saxony, Saxons 6, 8, 9, 12, 33
sculpture
    Anasazi *170*
    Burmese *104*
    Crusader *112*
    Fatimid *135*
    Korean *68*
    Polynesian *180*, *181*, 182-3
    Toltec *151*, *154*
    Yoruba *126*
Scythians 94
Sei Shonagon 91
Seiwa, Emperor of Japan 88
Seljuks 75, 94-9, 114
    acquisition of Iran and
        Mesopotamia 94, 96
    and the Crusades 109, 110, 111, 113
    Rum-Seljuks 98, 99
    wars with Byzantium 41, 97-8, 108
Serpent dynasty 155, 156
Seville 20
sewerage systems 19
shamans *126*, 127
Shandshar 99
Sharaf ud-Daula 75
Shenzong, Emperor of China 84-5
shields 116, *117*
Shi'ite Islam 72, 73, 94, 97, 98, 128, 129, 133, 134, 145
ships
    Chinese junks 80

Maori *184*
Polynesian 183
Viking longships 30, 158
Shoguns 93
Shwezigon Pagoda *100*, 103, 104
Sicily 51-2, 53, *120*, 128
sieges 118, *118-19*
silk 22, 80, 81
Silk Road 80
silver *23*, *36*, *76*, *143*
Sima Guang 82
Skrälinge 161
slavery *23*, 30, 39, 72, 139
Slavonia 35
Slavs 6, 8, 9, 10, 23, 43, 44
Soissons, Battle of 14
Somani Mausoleum *72*
Song dynasty 76-85
Song of Roland 18
Spain
    Moorish Spain 20-7, 143-4, 147
    Reconquista 25-7, 143
    Taifa period 24-5
spears 116, 118
Speyer 9
sport and games 18
Sri Lanka 104, 105
Stamford Bridge, Battle of 56
steles *146*
Stephan I, St, king of Hungary *33*, 34-5
Stephen, king of England *58*, 59
stocks *18*
stupas *102-3*
Sufism *98*
Suger, Abbot 14, 17
Sun cult *164*, 165, 170
Sunni Islam 94, 98, 128, 133, 145
Sutri, Synod of 12
Sven Forkbeard, king of England and Denmark 31, 32
Sven II Estridsen, king of Denmark 32
Svyatoslav I, Duke 43
Swabians 6, 33
swords 116, *116*
Sylvester II, Pope 35
Sylvester III, Pope 12
Syr Basin 94
Syria 97, 99, 111

T

Taira clan 88, *89*, 93
Taizu, Emperor of China 76-8
Tancred of Lecce 110
Tang dynasty 76
Tanguts 84, 85
al-Tartushi 31
taxation
    Byzantine 40
    Chimú 177
    Chinese 82-3
    Church 18
    Islamic 21, 26

Korean 69
Taycanamu 174
tent cities 121
Teotihuacán 150
textiles
    Bayeux tapestry *54-5*, 57, *57*
    Chimú 174, *176*
    Chinese 79, 81
    Fatimid *133*, 135
    Hausa *138*, 139
    Norman *53*, *54-5*, 57, *57*
    silk 22, 80, 81
    Toltec 155
    Yoruba 127
Tezcatlipoca 153
Thaton 100, 102
Theophanu, Empress 10
Thorfinn Karlsefni 161
Timbuktu *140-1*, 145
Toledo 25
Toltecs *114*, 150-6
Topiltzin 150-1, *150*
totem poles 165
tournaments *16*, 17
trade
    Berber 145
    Burmese 104
    Byzantine 39-40
    Chinese 79, 80-1
    Hausa 136, 138, 139
    Korean 69
    Moorish Spain 22
    Russian 43, 44
    Seljuk 98
    Viking 30-1, 32
    Yoruba 127
travertine 155
Trelleborg 30, 31, *31*
troubadours 17
Tuareg 138
Tudela 26
Tugril Beg 41, 75, 94, 96
Tula 150, 152-3, 155, 156
Tunisia 128, 130, 132
turquoise 169

U, V

Ummayad caliphate 20
Urban II, Pope 63, 106, *106*, 108
urban life
    Byzantine 39-40
    Chimú 176-7
    China 81-2
    France 18-19
    Russia 44-5
    Spain 25
    Viking 30-1
Uxmal 155
Valencia 26
Varangians 37-8, 43, 44
Verdun, Treaty of 14
Victor III, Pope 63
Vikings 20, 28-32, 37, 43, 54, *120*

raids 28, 30, 31
voyages of exploration 157-61
Vinland 161
Vladimir the Holy, Prince of Kiev 37, *43*, 44, 45

W

Wang Anshi 85
Wang Kon 67, 69, 70
warfare 118-19, *118-19*
    see also armies; warriors; weapons
warriors 114-15
    cavalry 114, *114*, 116
    Islamic *115*, 142
    Japanese Samurai *93*, 114, *115*, *116*, 118, *119*
    mercenaries 37-8, 43, 44
    Mongols 115
    Seljuk *96*, 114
    Toltecs *114*
    see also knights
weapons 84, *97*, 116-17, *116-17*, 118, *186*
Western Schism 40-1, 108
Westminster Abbey 32, 57
White Tower, Tower of London 58-9, 59
Widukind of Corvey 8
William I, 'the Conqueror', king of England 32, 54-5, *55*, 56-8, *120*
William I, 'the Pious', Duke of Aquitaine 46, 48
William II, 'Rufus', king of England 58, 59
women
    aristocratic 19, 91
    Chinese 77
    education 16
    French 19
    Islamic 133
    Japanese *87*, 88, 91
    Yoruba 127
woodcarving
    Chinese 77, *83*
    Japanese *92*
    Maori *184*, 187
Worms, Concordat of 12, 63
writing case *145*
writing systems
    Cyrillic script 44, *45*
    Japanese 91

X, Y, Z

Xia 84
Yidshong, king of Korea 70
Yorimichi 86, 90
Yoruba 124-7
Yoshifusa 86, 88
Zaragoza 26
al-Zazir, Caliph 135
Zhou Gong Di, Emperor of China 76
Ziryab of Baghdad 25

Abbeviations: t = top, c = centre, b = below, l = left, r = right, T = Timeline, B = background.

akg = akg-images
BAL = Bridgeman Art Library
TAA = The Art Archive

Front cover: Emperor Constantine IX Monomachos of Byzantium – akg/Erich Lessing
Back cover (top to bottom): Archiv Friedrich/Interfoto; Adam Woolfitt/CORBIS; Photo12/Interfoto; TAA/Archaeological Museum Lima/Dagli Orti; akg/Werner Forman.

1: Hermann Historica OHG/Interfoto; 2/3: Axiom/Doug McKinlay; 4/5: Archiv Friedrich/Interfoto; 6: picture-alliance/akg; 6/7: Bildarchiv Monheim; 7: Bildarchiv Monheim; 8: Kunsthistorisches Museum, Wien/BAL; 9 t: Aisa/ Interfoto; 9 b: Kunsthistorisches Museum, Wien; 10: akg; 11: RMN/Bilbliothek National Paris/Martine Beck-Coppola/BPK; 12 and T: Aachener Domschatz, Aachen, Giraudon/BAL; 13: Aisa/Interfoto; 14 t and T: Interfoto/Karger-Decker; 14 b: akg; 15: Aisa/Interfoto; 16: Interfoto/Photos12; 17: Bibliotheque Municipale, Laon, France, Lauros/Giraudon/BAL; 18: akg/Visioars; 19: akg; 20/21: Interfoto/Weltbild; 21 and T: Aisa/Interfoto; 22: TAA/Real Collegiata San Isidoro Leon/Dagli Orti; 23: Interfoto/AAA; 24: Louvre, Paris, France, Peter Willi/BAL; 24/25 B: Aisa/Interfoto; 25 and T: Interfoto/Anthony; 26: bpk Berlin; 27 t, b and T: akg; 28, 29: Aisa/Interfoto; 30 l: akg; 30 r: picture-alliance/akg; 30/31: Interfoto; 31: age fotostock/mauritius images; 32: akg/British Library; 33: Foto Marburg; 34: László Faragó/Jász Múzeum; 35: bpk Berlin/Leiden, Bibliotheek van de Rijksuniversiteit/Lutz Braun; 36, 36/37: Aisa/Interfoto; 38 and T: Ullstein Bilderdienst; 39: akg/Werner Forman; 40: akg/Erich Lessing; 41: Aisa/Interfoto; 42/43: Christer Åhlin/The Museum of National Antiquities, Stockholm Schweden; 43: akg/Erich Lessing; 44: Alamy Images; 45: Aisa/Interfoto; 46/47 B: Interfoto/Zill; 46, 47: Interfoto/Alinari; 48/49: Interfoto/Photos 12; 49: Bibliotheque Municipale, Dijon, France, Giraudon/BAL; 50/51: Interfoto/Anthony; 51: Interfoto/AAA; 52: bpk Berlin/Kunstgewerbemuseum, Staatliche Museen zu Berlin/Arne Psille; 52/53: picture-alliance/akg/Erich Lessing; 54/55, 55 and T: Interfoto/Alinari; 56: akg; 56/57, 57: Interfoto/AAA; 58: akg/British Library; 59: Alamy Images/Jack Sullivan; 60: akg/Rabatti-Domingie; 61: Interfoto/Archiv Friedrich; 62: Interfoto/Karger-Decker; 63 B: Archiv Friedrich/Interfoto; 63: Interfoto/Alinari; 64/65: Adam Woolfitt/CORBIS; 66/67: The Detroit Institute of Arts, USA/BAL; 67: V&A Images/Interfoto; 68 and T: National Museum, Seoul, Korea/BAL; 69: British Museum; 69 B: RMN/Musee Guimet/Jean-Yves et Nicolas Dubios/Bpk; 70: David Sanger Photography/Alamy; 71: Interfoto/Bildarchiv Hansmann; 72: Aisa/Interfoto; 73: TAA/Topkapi Museum Istanbul/Dagli Orti; 74: Aisa/Interfoto; 74/75 B: Bischöflisches Dom und Diözesanmuseum, Mainz; 75: RMN/Musee national de Ceramique/Martine Beck-Coppola/Bpk; 76: Asian Art & Archaeology, Inc./CORBIS; 77 and T: Interfoto/Bildarchiv Hansmann; 78: Aisa/Interfoto; 79: Science Museum/SSPL; 80, 80/81 B: V&A Images/Interfoto; 81: Interfoto/Bildarchiv Hansmann; 82: NW China/BAL; 83: Heritage Images/The British Museum; 84: AAA/Interfoto; 85 B: RMN/ Musee Guimet/Thierry Ollivier/Bpk; 85: RMN/ Musee Guimet/Ravaux/Bpk; 86: Jon Arnold Images/Alamy; 87: TAA; 88: Heritage Images/The British Museum; 88/89 B, 89, 90, 91: Aisa/ Interfoto; 92: picture-alliance/obs; 93 l, 93 r and T: TAA; 94 and T: British Library; 95: Michael Nicholson/CORBIS; 96 and T: Bischöflisches Dom und Diözesanmuseum,Mainz;

96/97: Archiv Friedrich/Interfoto; 97: Bischöflisches Dom und Diözesanmuseum, Mainz; 98 l: Interfoto/Bildarchiv Hansmann; 98 r: Scala/HIP; 99: TAA/Dagli Orti; 100: Bildagentur Huber/Grafenhain; 101 and T: V&A Images/Interfoto; 102/103: Aisa/Interfoto; 104: AAA/Interfoto; 105: AAA/Interfoto; 106, 107: Aisa/Interfoto; 109 and T: Bibliotheque Nationale, Paris, France/BAL; 110 t: akg; 110/111: Dr. Daniel Burger; 112: akg/Erich Lessing; 113 t: Bibliotheque Municipale de Lyon, Frankreich/BAL; 113 b: Bischöflisches Dom und Diözesanmuseum, Mainz; 114 b: Aisa/Interfoto; 114 t: akg/Werner Forman; 115 bl: Photo12/Interfoto; 115 tl and tr: Bischöflisches Dom und Diözesanmuseum; 115 br: TAA; 116 t: akg; 116 tr: picture-alliance/akg; 116 br: Mireille Vautier/Alamy; 117 b: Photo12/ Interfoto; 117 t: akg; 118 and T, 118/119: Bischöflisches Dom und Diözesanmuseum; 119 t: British Museum, Ancient Art and Architecture Collection Ltd./BAL; 119 b: akg/Werner Forman; 120 t: picture-alliance/akg; 120/121: Friedrich Rauch/Interfoto; 120 b: Tim Thompson/Corbis; 121 t: Günther Rauh/Interfoto; 121 b: akg/Visioars; 122/123: Photo 12/Interfoto; 124: AAA/Interfoto; 125 and T: Aisa/Interfoto; 126: akg/Werner Forman; 127: Private Collection, Heini Schneebeli/ BAL; 128: picture-alliance/akg/Erich Lessing; 129: TAA/ British Museum; 130 t: V&A Images/Interfoto; 130 b, 131: picture-alliance/akg/Erich Lessing; 132: RMN/Musee du Louvre/Hervé Lewandowski/Bpk; 133, 134, 135: Aisa/Interfoto; 136: Bildarchiv Hausmann/Interfoto; 137: Scala/Werner Forman; 138: RMN/Musée du quai Branly/Jean-Gilles Berizzi/Bpk; 139: akg; 140/141: Aisa/Interfoto; 141: Aisa/interfoto; 142: Mattes/Mauritius Images; 143: Corbis/Francesco; 145: TAA/Museum of Islamic Art Cairo/Dagli Orti; 146/147 B: Robert Harding/Digital Vision; 146: RMN/Musée du quai Branly/Jean-Gilles Berizzi/Thierry Le Mage/Bpk; 147 and T: akg/Erich Lessing; 148/149: TAA/Archaeological Museum Lima/Dagli Orti; 150: TAA/National Anthropological Museum Mexico/Dagli Orti; 151: Aisa/Interfoto; 152: Museo Nacional de Antropologia, Mexico City, Mexico, Giraudon/BAL; 153 t: TAA/Dagli Orti; 153 b: Interfoto/Hans W. Mohm; 154, 154/155 B: TAA/National Anthropological Museum Mexico/Dagli Orti; 155: British Museum, London, UK, Ancient Art and Architecture Collection Ltd./BAL; 156: TAA/Mireille Vautier; 157 and T: akg; 158: Arnamagnaen Collection, Dänemark/BAL; 159 t: akg/Werner Forman; 159 b: Interfoto/Bildarchiv Hansmann; 160/161 B: Interfoto/AAA; 160: TAA/Oldsaksammlung Oslo/Dagli Orti; 161 and T: TAA/Historiska Museet Stockholm/Dagli Orti; 162 and T: avenue images; 163: akg/Werner Forman; 164: akg/Werner Forman; 165 B: Richard A. Cooke/ Corbis; 165: Logan Museum of Antropology/Beloit College; 166: Chris Howes/ Wild Places Photography/ Alamy; 167 and T: Aisa/Interfoto; 168: George H. H. Huey/CORBIS; 169: Dorling Kindersley; 170/171 B: Robert Harding/Walter Rawlings; 170: The Newark museum/Art Resource/Scala; 171: akg; 172: Mauritius/Superstock; 173 and T: Interfoto/AAA; 174: TAA/Museo del Oro Lima/Dagli Orti; 175: Aisa/Interfoto; 176/177 B: Interfoto/Photo 12; 176: TAA/Archaeological Museum Lima/Dagli Orti; 177 and T: Aisa/Interfoto; 178/179: akg-images/Werner Forman; 180: akg/Nimatallah; 181 and T: Interfoto/Silvia; 182: Douglas Peebles Photography/Alamy; 182/183 B: akg/François Guenet; 183: akg/François Guenet; 184: Bonhams, London, UK/BAL; 185 and T: TAA/Lucien Biton Collection Paris/Dagli Orti; 186, 186/187 B, 187: akg/Werner Forman.

Maps originated by Müller & Richert GBR, Gotha, Germany, and translated into English by Alison Ewington

The Illustrated History of the World:
THE EARLY MIDDLE AGES was published by The Reader's Digest Association Ltd, London.

First English edition copyright © 2006
The Reader's Digest Association Ltd
11 Westferry Circus, Canary Wharf, London E14 4HE
www.readersdigest.co.uk

Reader's Digest English Edition
Series editor: Christine Noble
Volume editor/writer: Michael Kerrigan
Translated from German by: JMS Books
Design: Jane McKenna
Copy editor: Jill Steed
Proofreader: Ron Pankhurst
Index: Marie Lorimer
Colour proofing: Colour Systems Ltd, London
Printed and bound by: Arvato Iberia, Europe
Production controller: Katherine Bunn

Reader's Digest, General Books
Editorial director: Julian Browne
Art director: Nick Clark
Prepress account manager: Penelope Grose

We are committed to the quality of our products and the service we provide to our customers. We value your comments, so please feel free to contact us on 08705 113366, or via our website at: www.readersdigest.co.uk

If you have any comments or suggestions about the content of our books, you can email us at: gbeditorial@readersdigest.co.uk

First published as *Reader's Digest Illustrierte Weltgeschichte: GLANZVOLLES MITTELALTER*
© 2006 Reader's Digest – Deutschland, Schweiz, Österreich
Verlag Das Beste GmbH – Stuttgart, Zürich, Vienna

Reader's Digest, German Edition
Writers: Karin Feuerstein-Praßer, Andrea Groß-Schulte, Marion Jung, Dr. Cornelia Lawrenz, Karin Prager, Otto Schertler, Karin Schneider-Ferber, Dr. Holger Sonnabend
Editing and design: Media Compact Service
Colour separations: Meyle + Müller GmbH + Co., Pforzheim.

ISBN: 0 276 44120 6
CONCEPT CODE: GR 0081/G/S
BOOK CODE: 632-004-1
ORACLE CODE: 351600021H.00.24